The Heroines of
SOE

F Section Britain's Secret
Women in France

Squadron Leader Beryl E. Escott

The
History
Press

First published in 2010
Reprinted in 2010
This paperback edition first published in 2011

The History Press
The Mill, Brimscombe Port
Stroud, Gloucestershire, GL5 2QG
www.thehistorypress.co.uk

British Library Cataloguing in Publication Data.
A catalogue record for this book is available from the British Library.

ISBN 978 0 7524 6313 1

Typesetting and origination by The History Press
Printed in the EU for The History Press.

CONTENTS

ACKNOWLEDGEMENTS

There have been many people who have helped me over the years, since my first book on this subject (*Mission Improbable*, 1991) and the several others in between, until this one. I don't doubt that the trail will end here, as the National Archives presently hold closed the Personal Files of eleven of these forty women and there are no files on four of the others.

As you may guess, this has caused much detective work through many other sources. When I began investigating my fifteen SOE WAAF women in about 1990, almost half of them still survived (including four who had been wireless operators). For various reasons only a few were willing to help, through the indefatigable Vera Atkins, whose memory was invaluable and to whom all thanks is due. It was, however, long before I envisaged covering all forty SOE women. One of their number warned me that they were 'dropping off their perches every day' – but they did seem long-lived. The opportunity for personal contact has now nearly passed me by, so I am trying to capture the essence of what remains.

One further spur drove me on, and I suspect may be shared by many readers in this subject. Whereas the male agent's role in a narrative is often given fully, female agents frequently appear and disappear in only a few lines, with little indication of their contribution in the gap between. Of course, they were usually a part of a team led by the male agent and working to the same objectives, but their assistance was peculiar to themselves and not inconsiderable. And sometimes circumstances forced them to work alone. These chapters may, therefore, I hope, add a little to each story and fill in the gaps.

Now I must express my thanks to all who have helped me over the years – there have been so many.

For moral support, I must thank my mother – alas no longer here – who often tried to alleviate, with her optimistic nature, what sometimes seemed to be an impossible task. Her lively but frequently frustrating diversions helped to keep me afloat.

Then I must thank my present brilliant typist Sue Bishop and her partner John, whose long-suffering patience and skills with the computer, together with the editorial team of The History Press, have helped smooth my rather bumpy path.

In the following list I must apologise for any whom I have forgotten to mention, but I have been sincerely grateful for the help they have given me. They include:

Hugh Alexander, Vera Atkins, Barbara Barrie, John Brown, Maurice Buckmaster, Yvonne Burney, Sonya Butt, Francis Cammaerts (Fr.), Jean Claude Comert (Fr.), Joanne Copeland (US), Yvonne Cormeau, Pearl Cornioley, Gervase Cowell, Sonya d'Artois (Canada), Howard Davies, Pat Escott, Major Farrow, Frank Griffiths, Major Hallowes, David Harrison, Queenie Hierons, Frankie Horsburgh, Robert Ibbotson, Ronald Irving, Liane Jones, Rita Kramer (US), Roger Landes, Bob Large, Louis Lauler, Sister Laurence Mary, John and Olga Leary, Peter Lee (SFC), Wendy LeTisier, Pierre Lorrain, Keith Melton (USA), Mrs Midgley (CWGC), Linda Morgan, Nora Mortimer, Lesley Nightingale, Molly Oliver-Sasson (Aus.), Yvonne Oliver, Claudine Pappe (US), Valerie Pearman-Smith, Alan Probert, Henry Probert, Mrs Raftree (MC), Norma Reid, Rosemary Rigby (of the Violette Szabo Museum), Prof. Barry Rolfe, Margaret Salm (US), Dee Scandrett, Wyn Smith (NZ), Faith Spencer-Chapman, Decia Stephenson (FANY), Duncan Stuart, Pat Sturgeon, Martin Sugarman, Roger Tobell, Terry Trimmer, Maddie Turner, Hugh Verity, Lise Villameur, Miss C. Walters, Jim Wilson and Christoper Woods.

INTRODUCTION

Birth of SOE

In the early 1930s Adolf Hitler began his schemes of conquest. In 1938 he occupied Austria and Czechoslovakia, while Western Europe desiring peace just talked. Then, in a vain attempt to save Poland from the same fate, Britain and France declared war in September 1939.

There was a short pause, known as the 'Phoney War', before Germany, in April and May of 1940, attacked and occupied Denmark and Norway, and then turned on Holland and Belgium.

So rapidly had the Germans advanced at this point that the French now faced a German onslaught on their own country. The Germans drove forward, easily outflanking out-of-date fortifications and tactics, until at last they caught the Allies trapped in a pocket around Dunkirk. The British and a large part of the French armies faced defeat.

Then came the miracle deliverance of the little ships, which from 26 May to 3 June 1940, evacuated about 338,226 soldiers – British, French and some Belgians to Britain – amid continuous enemy air bombardment, snatching a moral victory out of the jaws of defeat. Nevertheless, they left the beaches littered with all their heavy equipment and their casualties before Dunkirk fell, followed by Paris ten days later. Clinging to old conventions, the French Government resigned and Marshal Pétain, a First World War hero of Verdun, became President, to sign on 22 June 1940 a humiliating Armistice with Germany. It gave him an 'Unoccupied Zone', nominally freely administered from the town of Vichy by the French Premier, then Pierre Laval, while the Germans occupied and governed the larger part of France from Paris, except for a small area in the south held by the Italians.

The Armistice, of course, imposed other conditions too, which only gradually became apparent. France had to pay an impost of 400 million francs for every day the Germans were in occupation. In 1942 forced labour levies of French men and women were removed to work in Germany. An increasing part of their agricultural and industrial produce had to be sent there also. Hostages were to be taken and shot for any sabotage or killing of German soldiers. After a time, French Freemasons, Gypsies, Jews, Communists (after the pact with Russia broke down), Jehovah's Witnesses, homosexuals and others were rounded up and deported, and increasing restrictions on daily life, including curfews, passes and searches for all sorts of reasons were imposed. And yet the Germans behaved, on the whole, more fairly to the French than they did to their other conquered nations.

On the other side of the Channel, General de Gaulle, a little known French General who had escaped to Britain, set up an alternative to the French Government, organising his own Free French Forces in London. He broadcast on the BBC to France encouraging resistance: 'We [the Free French Forces] believe that the honour of the French people consists of continuing the war alongside our allies, and we are determined to do this.'

Meanwhile, Germany confidently expected Britain to accept its peace overtures. Even the President of the United States of America, not yet involved in the war, refused to help Britain, believing it to be wasted effort. However, in spite of this, with the remainder of Europe either neutral or hostile, Britain still refused to surrender. With German overtures rejected and only a few miles of Channel dividing German-occupied France from Britain, Hitler planned an invasion by air and then by sea. It was only the Royal Air Force planes in the Battle of Britain that thwarted his intentions.

This was the time, in the heat of July 1940, with defeat and victory so evenly poised, when the British Prime Minister of only two months, Winston Churchill, chose to give the management of the recently created* Special Operations Executive (SOE) to Hugh Dalton – his tall, bald and loud Minister of Economic Warfare. His instructions came with the order 'to set Europe ablaze'!

---

* The SOE's outline charter and name, was the last thing created by Churchill's dying enemy Neville Chamberlain, blamed by many for his policy of appeasement and the war.

The Organisation

SOE was to be a small secret organisation dedicated to encourage and aid resistance in any German conquered country. The F section was dedicated to aiding the liberation of France, and is the subject of this book.

SOE's home became a large office building, felicitously vacated by the prison commissioners at 64 Baker Street, unavoidably connecting the organisation with the memory of Sherlock Holmes. Peter Lee, Secretary of the Special Forces Club in 1991, in one of his many long helpful letters to me, wrote:

> The 'F' (for French) Section, like most of us started off in 64 Baker Street, but they moved over to Norgeby House in Autumn 1941, while our Security Directorate went to Michael House, more or less at the same time. The Free French were always at Dorset Square.

Nor was that the end of the moves for F Section.

During the war years its numbers grew and it quickly spread into other countries and counties with its different training schools, listening and deciphering stations, airfields, research and development facilities and other odd but useful places. Agents in the training schools used to joke that SOE stood for the 'Stately 'Omes of England', since many of these were requisitioned or on loan, because in their large buildings and spacious grounds agents could be trained in unusual activities, away from the public gaze. This was as well, since its role had widened, and also grown.

A short succession of energetic and high powered executives took over until 1943 when Colin Gubbins was put in charge. His military bearing was misleading and hid a very flexible and sharp mind. He was an enthusiastic exponent of SOE and had written several handbooks on the art of guerilla warfare, then out of favour. He had the overview of SOE's many divisions such as finance, supply, signals etc, as well as the country sections, one of which was France.

F section had been headed by Maurice Buckmaster since the autumn of 1941. Hitler is reputed to have said 'When I get to London, I'm not sure who I shall hang first – Churchill or that man Buckmaster'. Tall, with prominent blue eyes and a pleasant manner, his enthusiasm gave all in contact with him confidence in his choices and judgement, though his relationship with

Gubbins was always uneasy. In a letter to me he talks about the magnificent work carried out by members of the WAAF (Women's Auxiliary Air Force) agents in occupied France. He also commented in 1952 in his book *Specially Employed*, 'during the period March 1941–July 1944, we recruited over forty-six male and forty female officers for work in the field. It has always seemed to me surprising that there were so many British or Dominion subjects whose French was faultless, willing and anxious to undertake such supremely dangerous work.' He was ready to fight for his agents, always in a hurry and snowed under with work, as he was not very good at delegating. Thus he usually put in, with Vera Atkins (his right-hand woman), a good 18-hour day, and insisted on doing all the work himself. Frenchmen often called a network 'a Buckmaster', and his care of his agents set him to institute the Judex visits in October/November 1944 to thank resistants who had helped his agents.

His assistant* was Nicholas Bodington, who came from a public school and Oxford University background. In the 1930s he was working in Reuters in Paris. He was ambitious and attracted to the MI6 Intelligence Service but, never making it, seemed to take SOE as an alternative. His admiration of flying was reciprocated by Henri Déricourt, another young ambitious man who trained as a pilot, and the two became friends. During a short time in Paris before the war they also were acquainted with the elderly homosexual Boemelburg, then attached to the German Embassy but soon recalled. Now in SOE, Bodington visited France four times briefly between 1942–44 to investigate mistakes, despite the danger to agents like himself, who knew too much if captured. His support also cleared Déricourt, in his post-war trial for treachery in France.

Vera Atkins was officially nominated 'F Int' for Intelligence (amusingly she called it 'interference') but was really Buckmaster's assistant and was often Conducting Officer with departing agents, particularly the women. Her background was rather peculiar, but her work with SOE F seems to have been loyal and kind. She kept in touch with many of 'her' women if they finally returned, and helped them as much as she could. Directly after the war she spent over a year investigating the fate of about 117 agents, men and women, who did not come back, so that she could set at peace the minds of their families. She was the right hand of Buckmaster and had an incredible memory to which I can attest

---

* Buckmaster never called him his deputy.

from her letters to me. She later travelled all over the world to keep in touch with her 'girls' as she called them, consequently I found her often hard to track down. She also had a strong personality and did not suffer fools gladly. In 1991, after attending the dedication to the memorial at Valencay to the SOE F agents who had died in France, she said 'I could not just abandon their memory'.

After SOE sprang into existence, it should be of no surprise that – having such close ties with her gallant ally – France was one of the first countries to receive Britain's aid. It came in various forms, from Britain's meagre reserves of arms and sabotage materials and around 400 SOE F agents, (Colonel Buckmaster put the total at nearer 500). Numbered among those hundreds of agents were about fifty-one women, of whom eleven looked to de Gaulle's resistance organisation and were denoted the RF section. The other forty worked for London and were known as the independent F section.

Opposition to Female Agents

Previously the British people would not contemplate the idea of putting women in any danger and the authorities felt themselves responsible for the safety of its women.

In the services, from one of which fifteen F service women agents came*, there was agreement that no women should be involved in carrying arms, far less using them. Neither was it considered right, until nearly the end of 1944, that women should be employed abroad in time of war. At a pure chance meeting, the Head of the First Aid Nursing Yeomanry (FANY) – a uniformed organisation, which, being civilian, had no such limitations – offered her service as cover for SOE. It was, in any case, to be much involved in the communications and other services for SOE, and it knew and understood about the need for secrecy. Nevertheless, allowing women to be included as agents was initially fiercely resisted by the government, and only introduced into SOE F in 1942.

It turned out, of course, to be a very wise move, both because of the shortage of suitable male agents (under forties were vulnerable to German rafles**) and because of the large numbers of suitable women available.

---

* These fifteen women were from the WAAF (Women's Auxiliary Air Force). See *Mission Improbable* by Beryl Escott (P. Stephens, 1991).
** Rafles were the rounding up of men to work in Germany.

It was also assisted by the German male attitude to women, which was even more backward than that of Britain, therefore making Germans less suspicious of SOE's female agents. Moreover, in France, women, during the occupation, were often to be seen everywhere, travelling on all types of transport, especially on bikes with large baskets and carriers, seeking food and commodities, visiting or looking for members of families or working in the place of absent husbands as wage earners. Such women did not arouse suspicion and those acting as couriers slipped into the same role without difficulty, added to which, though no Mata Haris, they could deploy their feminine skills, and some were remarkably beautiful.

Yvonne Cormeau, one of the valiant number of the forty, stressed to me in her strongly accented English 'We were not spies*. Our work was sabotage'. It was indeed, but latterly it was to prepare the many resistance groups throughout France for the coming of D-Day and their part in driving out the occupying forces. Vera Atkins defined the task to me as 'to annoy, hinder and damage the Germans'.

The chief aim of SOE F was to support and encourage the French to secretly oppose the Germans. Thus its targets were mainly attacking communications and those industries supporting the German war effort by supplying such things as arms, weapons, vehicles, goods and spare parts of all kinds. Naturally, SOE F was always careful to avoid damaging such places as shops or markets, where people gathered to eke out their rigid rations, since SOE knew that attacking them would put at risk the lives of vulnerable and innocent civilians, whom it was part of its task to protect.

Finding the Female Agents

Generally, SOE recruited their male agents from the universities, with their 'old boy' networks, and in the upper echelons of the business and finance world. Such openings did not exist for women, as they rarely appeared in such places. Prior to the war, women were seldom seen in Higher Education or in the workplace.

The war was going to alter this forever. Men were away in the services and women often filled their slots in the workplace, went into new war industries, or, if young enough, joined the new women's services.

---

* Spying was the work of the SIS (Secret Intelligence Service).

As knowledge of SOE's existence was secret*, it faced unusual problems in recruiting its 'special' women, having no obvious 'networks' to tap into. The organisation, nevertheless, still managed to get around this problem. There was, of course, the already accepted cover of the FANY, where around half of its women were involved in work connected with SOE. They came very often from the higher social and leisured classes, and introduced other women from their acquaintances. SOE also tapped the existing pool in the three services, Navy, Army and RAF, added to which was the lower civil service. Here it asked to be notified if any of their recruits had special abilities, such as languages. It also circulated Customs and Immigration and the civilian offices doing the Registration for Employment of the general public, and received regular returns. Most interestingly, SOE issued a broadcast on the wireless, asking for people who had drawings or photographs of 'interesting' areas in Europe that they had visited in the last few years. It also advertised on appointments pages in certain newspapers and journals for interpreters in specified languages. Replies were to be sent to the Ministry of Economic Warfare (MEW). As a result, a surprising number of women agents, as will be seen, were drawn from the middle or lower middle classes.

Thus, among the women were shop girls, clerks, some from impoverished families, a doctor's wife, a commercial traveller, a newspaper editor's daughter, a hotel receptionist, a film impresario, a professional dancer, journalists, fifteen members of the WAAF, some Americans, an Australian/New Zealander, a Mauritian and others.

Female SOE agents were normally chosen for their language skills and their ability to mix inconspicuously among the French people. In many cases they had one parent who was French, or they had been brought up and educated in France or a French-speaking country. As a rule they were clever, articulate, quick-witted, good actresses and brave, putting an idealistic love for France and Britain, and hope to hasten France's liberation and end the war, above their own safety.

Agents were given officer ranks in the hope that if captured, they would be treated as Prisoners of War under the Geneva Convention. It proved a false hope.

---

*   Indeed, many agents had not heard of the name SOE until much later.

Interviews

Normally the assessment of men or women to be recruited for SOE was in the hands of Selwyn Jepson or Lewis Gielgud (brother of the actor), but the best 'talent spotter' of the women was Jepson.

SOE selection began when a woman received a note asking her to come to London and report to a building called the Inter Services Bureau. This may have been in reply to an offer she may have made of photographs she had taken of the French coast or some other area in very recent years. Or it could have been her noted ability to speak rapid French. One woman complained that she only came in answer to a 'wanted' advertisement for a French secretary or an interpreter post, and when she found it additionally required athletic exercises, was mystified.

The Inter Services Bureau seemed to move around a lot and was very discreetly hidden away. Sometimes it was through a side door in a rather dingy, squashed building, or in a large, cold, echoing place of several storeys. A doorkeeper would scan her letter and then send her to wait outside an office door. When it opened to let out a woman like herself, a voice from inside the room would call 'come in'. And so the interview that could change her life would begin.

There were usually two or three sessions, which would take place somewhere discreet and all with the same man. No names would be exchanged but he would have already found out a great deal about her. He would listen to her stories and draw out her opinions – they would, of course, be speaking fluently in French. Depending on her responses, he would hint at work in France – and not the ordinary kind. (Jepson writes that before he had proceeded this far in the interview with Odette Samson, she had guessed what it was about and immediately volunteered for SOE work. However, for most women he continued the process more slowly and arranged another interview.)

The next interview would be held at the same place and with the same man, but it would be much more serious. At this point the interviewer would test out the girl's family obligations*. He would emphasise the disadvantages and dangers of SOE work, and the possibility of death in France, where no one would be able help her. If she was still keen to go, she would be told that she must keep it secret (even from her family), but should sleep on it for a while before making a decision.

---

* Several of the candidates had young children at home, but this did not stop them volunteering, as long as satisfactory care arrangements had been made.

Then would come her last interview, where she would give her final decision and, among other things, sign the Official Secrets Act. (At this point few people refused to join SOE, so well had they been vetted beforehand.) Before or after this her 'job specification' would explain that she will first have to enlist with the FANY (quite an eye-opener for an inexperienced girl).

It is obvious that a number of candidates were refused, but for various reasons we have no records. However, I have one example, Valerie Pearman-Smith, an ex WAAF, who told me she was interviewed by SOE in the cellars of Whitehall. 'I thought it was for translation work like Yvonne Cormeau, but I was rejected, because my French accent was a Swiss one...' It obviously remained in her memory, and much later, when more was revealed, she realised what it was about.

Training

For SOE work, F agents were trained sketchily and briefly during the early war years but much more effectively later on. It was believed that Russian agents trained for five to ten years. SOE had no such luxury. Its agents averaged about four to nine months training depending on their type of work – a few in an emergency had even less.

There were approximately sixty special training schools in Britain, as well as in many other parts of the world. Training was divided into various groups: Group A was Guerilla Training, Group B acted as Finishing Schools and Group C was the Preliminary Schools. The majority of agents would go through all stages of training, but not all did.

Preliminary Training
Wanborough Manor, near Guildford, was designated a Group C Preliminary Training School in about mid-February 1941 and male agents would receive two weeks training there. Wanborough did not start the training of women until 1943 when it was carried out in mixed groups of men and women. By this time, it only housed those agents intended for France.

The first women of 1942 began training elsewhere and their whole course was much shortened to only a few weeks. The exception was Yvonne Rudellat in early 1942 who trained at Wanborough with the men and turned out to be better than most, as well as being the best shot of the course – appearances can be deceptive.

Wanborough students usually went through elementary military training and student assessment. The first involved physical training, cross-country runs, basic weapons training and unarmed conflict – (for women later these were modified). The main object was to improve physical fitness. They were also given an elementary introduction to wireless and codes and basic briefing on sabotage. They were watched day and night, though were probably unaware of this constant appraisal and its implications. Candidates were required to speak French most of the time and lapses could fail them, especially if they talked English in their sleep or drank too much and became garrulous. Reports were made on them several times, noting any special aptitudes or difficulties, and the decision made as to their continuing and in what line, or quietly being dropped from the course and returned to their earlier work.

Guerilla Training

If they passed this hurdle, then most went on to the area around Arisaig, a Group A school in the wilds of Scotland, where the weather could be as hostile as the environment beautiful. There they were introduced to guerilla warfare. They learned such things as making, mixing and using explosives. Far enough from habitation they could practise blowing up bridges or hayricks, and carry out various dangerous activities without causing trouble, though the canny highlanders usually knew what was going on. They learned to manage small boats without sinking them, how to use and load German, British and American arms – something Vera Leigh and Violette Szabo shone at – and loading slippery weapons in the dark by touch. They learned how to cross rough country without being seen, creep silently through undergrowth, how to avoid the sky line, wade rock strewn streams and how to live off the land, as well as how to tail people and avoid being tailed, and how to kill silently. Although good at most things, when Nancy Wake did kill a German sentry to save her life, it upset her for days afterwards. Their instructors were often jailbirds, poachers or commandos, and all found that a necessary quality in these activities, even in a gale and the pouring rain, was a sense of humour. Conducting Officers often trained alongside their candidates.

Special Training Courses

Wireless Operators (w/t)

In special schools like Thame Park in Oxfordshire, those who were to become wireless operators had a demanding and long course, unless like a few WAAF they came already from the trade, and even then they had to learn more. All messages had to be transposed into cipher or code, different for each operator, and the full message sent by Morse at a rate of at least twenty-two words per minute, together with special safety checks to prove them genuine. They also developed a 'fist' or 'style' by which whoever received the message could sometimes tell who was sending it – a kind of fingerprinting in Morse. Learning the skills or changing words into code was always difficult as no message was ever sent or received except in code. At different times different code methods were used – the playfair, double transposition and the best, the one-time-pad. They took time to understand and then learn, and speed was added to the complexity. Agents were also given a schedule (sked) of days and times for ordinary messages (except in an emergency) and told to keep them short, averaging no more than 12 minutes, but very often they took longer and proved to be the reason many agents were caught.

In January 1942 Leo Marks was called up and went to Bedford to train as a cryptographer. He was the only one of his intake not to be sent to Bletchley Park. This was because he cracked the code they had all been left to work out over a week in just one evening. Labelled a misfit, he was dispatched to Baker Street and SOE, and there he remained to become head of their decoding section. His rule was, 'There is no such thing as an indecipherable message'. Agents risked their lives to send it, so his section was honour bound to break it before their next sked.

Even those who had already mastered the skills of code and Morse, still had to spend time in the laboratories learning the composition of their set(s), fault diagnosis and how to repair it with makeshift materials when it went wrong. When receiving, there were other problems: atmospherics, oscillation, static, skip, dead spots, jamming and other details they had to know how to cure, as well as the mysteries of handling 70 foot long aerials, disguising and hiding sets and general security.

In addition, wireless operators had to be able to control the pressure and the loneliness of their work, together with the daily danger under which they lived. It was not surprising that this course might take well over four or five months or more, though sometimes an operator, urgently needed, might be sent out partly trained, occasionally with disastrous consequences.

Agents knew that once in the field their messages would, with the aid of their specially tuned crystals, go to a particular listening station in Britain – usually Grendon Underwood, where there were banks of receivers and relays of women – mainly FANY – who listened perpetually to receive their messages. Colin Gubbins referred to the work of the SOE wireless operator as 'The most valuable link in the whole of our chain of operations. Without these links we would have been groping in the dark.'

Parachuting

Another special school was set up for students who were to parachute into France – a method used by the majority of agents and preferred by SOE. Agents were accommodated at Tatton Park near Manchester and learned to parachute at Ringway Airfield, where all the troops were trained in parachuting. They aimed at doing up to five drops, at least one at night, and later, one with a leg bag for carrying equipment. Sometimes they were sent out into the field having had no more than one or two practice jumps.

Winifred Smith (a WAAF), was a parachute packer at Tatton for two years. She had clear memories of:

> ...seeing the girls preparing to parachute complete with lipstick and make up – otherwise it was hard to tell that they really were girls, what with their parachute suits, crash helmets and so on. We often watched them waiting to board their plane. It was like follow-my-leader. The girls were towards the back, but they were always laughing and we would wave and call 'Good Luck'.

Trainers sometimes said that they put the girls to jump first out of the aircraft into the grounds of Tatton Park, since they knew that the men would not hold back if a woman led the way.

Winifred also went into the training hangar:

> ...and saw them training on what we called The Fan. They were completely fearless. They learned to land properly and were quick off the mark in getting away afterwards. One had the feeling they didn't expect to come back from France, so they were living for the moment. When VE day was

over and we could talk more freely we all agreed that they had an inner strength and sheer determination which allowed them to do what was asked of them. They were inspired by something greater than the ordinary person.

Other Special Courses

At this point certain other short courses considered useful might be introduced. Thus some learned forgery, microphotography, picking locks, safe breaking and an element of industrial sabotage. There were other skills for certain agents intended for specific jobs – not usually assigned to women. Trainers for these other courses would be unusual people, often ex-burglars and felons. Nancy Wake was nearly thrown off her course for using one of these skills to break into a locked file at midnight to discover her training notes and thus what they thought of her!

Finishing School

Beaulieu

Last came a few weeks at Beaulieu in the New Forest in Hampshire, one of the Group B Finishing Schools (now the home of the National Motor Museum), which enabled students to catch their breath and enjoy the quiet of the abbey cloisters for a few moments when coming to the end of their training. Today a plaque in its wall records the fact:

> Remember before God, those men and women of the European Resistance Movement who were secretly trained in Beaulieu to fight their lonely battle against Hitler's Germany, and who before entering Nazi-occupied territory, here found some measure of the peace for which they fought.

This course brought students into the classroom, to learn the finer points of security or espionage. Housed in small 'mock' cottages, lodges or houses, formerly occupied by friends of Lord Montagu and his family, they looked quite homely.

As part of their security training they learned to recognise the ranks of the ordinary French Police and Darnand's more dangerous uniformed French Milice. They were to distinguish the different ranks of the ordinary German soldiers. It was hoped they would never encounter, but must know about the two wings of the two main German counter-intelligence bodies: the military Abwehr with its Paris headquarters at the Hotel Lutetia. The other body was the SD (*Sicherheitsdienst*) in its headquarters at 82–86 Avenue Foch – the French sometimes called it the Avenue Boche. This was the intelligence wing of the SS – the political, State Police, which also controlled the Gestapo, whose Paris headquarters was at 11 Rue des Saussaies. These two bodies were rivals and in spring 1944 the Abwehr was absorbed by the SS. French men often confused the SS and called their officers the Gestapo – though all were equally feared. Nevertheless you might be able to trust in any agreement being kept by the Abwehr, and your treatment by them was likely to be gentler – neither of which applied if you fell into the merciless hands of the SD or SS. But if not shot after torture, you might end in a concentration camp either way.

Agents were also given some useful pointers in what to look for in French recruits, and advice on keeping small groups secure. This independence would then safeguard the other members in case of an arrest. Also no list of members was to be written down to be discovered by an enemy (as in the case of the CARTE network, whose list was discovered by the Abwehr). In the same way personal relationships were not encouraged – especially for SOE women.

It was agreed to pay individual full time members of the group (and compensation/pensions given to their French families if one was imprisoned or killed). Money was also needed for bribes or living expenses of agents or members working for them. Extravagant expenditure would always draw attention from the enemy and was to be checked. The money supply, however, was one of the problems about which SOE agents never had to worry, and there are few cases of it ever being abused.

Then came other security matters – more on codes and the use of sending personal messages or receiving replies, other than through the signals. This was achieved very discreetly by the French station of the BBC, usually after the 9 o'clock news, to which most Frenchmen found a way of listening, to hear a true account – good or bad – of the progress of the war. The Germans had ordered the destruction of all radios in the home, but soon many owners found ways to hide them in unrecognised cellars, attics or cupboards.

It was only after D–Day that the agents began to discover the wholehearted support of people turning to the Allies and then the resistance grew. Until then, it was generally areas furthest from the main German centres of influence that were the resistance's strongest supporters. Otherwise support was small, secret and careful – save in groups like railwaymen, dockers and very often farmers, where the greatest opposition to the Germans appeared.

Contact was usually made with other members or agents through an intermediary, or by the use of a special phrase with an appropriate coded reply. There were also different means of warning that Germans were present or nearby, by agreed signs – one flower pot removed from a row, a drawn curtain on one side of a window, a book put in a certain place – the kinds of signs or symbols used in most secret societies. Those dealing with wireless learned how the enemy could track down the transmission, and to be aware that sometimes he could mimic their messages on a captured wireless.

All agents had to learn how to code and decode messages to help their wireless operator, and their task too was to arrange reception parties for an aircraft drop or landing, and the laying out of lights in a prescribed pattern to guide the pilots. Additionally they had to spot areas of land suitable for drops and, when checked, work out the co-ordinates on a map to pass to London, with an agreed message of confirmation or otherwise to be made after the 9 o' clock news, if the plane could come, weather permitting, on the selected date.

Finally the agent was given the last few pieces of her own jigsaw puzzle – her new code and cover name, the name of her network and her organiser – she might have even met him at this stage if he was not in France – information on her contacts, the part of the country where she was being sent, and a hundred other small details. Her personal identity was usually based on a real person, or mixed with facts that were as near as possible to her own experiences, and she was photographed to give a different appearance, such as with new hairstyles and taken from different angles for her new identity documents. She had to go over and over all her personal facts, until her new identity became second nature.

There was so much to learn and absorb, and all the time she was being warned to be careful of security, neglect of which could cost her life.

The Test
Agents usually had two tests - the first, during or after her training courses, especially after her wireless training, when she would be sent for one or two days to another part of the country. The second was normally near the end of her Beaulieu course, when, at some unearthly hour in the morning, like 3am, she would be shaken out of her sleep by a person in Gestapo uniform, and then, still befuddled by sleep, she would be dragged, none too gently, down to the cellar and surrounded by more men in Gestapo

uniforms and made to stand on a table, or alone face an interrogator with a lamp shining full into her eyes, to answer all kinds of questions on who she was, and why was she here – unlikely answers might get a slap and threats of torture would be made. If she stumbled, she would be roughly treated and the questions would come fast, leaving little thinking time, until she was nearly fainting. She would be repeatedly accused of all sorts of things and told that she had been watched ever since landing in France – until she hardly doubted that she was there. She would be bullied and offered an easy way to get out of the situation by telling all that she knew. This would seem to go on for hours, and yet they would keep her there and repeat the same things time and time again. Wearily, she would manage to keep to the same facts about herself.

Then, suddenly, the lamp would go out, the screen across the window would be drawn back and daylight would flood in. The Gestapo men would pull off their caps and laugh, perspiration running down their faces. She would be escorted out, mockingly, and in the corridor beyond her Conducting Officer would sit her down and press a cup of cocoa into her hands. After a while, when her hand was shaking less, she would have been able to drink it. One of the men questioning her would come out and she would recognise one of her training staff. She would be stunned – so this was the test she had heard they were to have!

After she had sufficiently recovered, she would go back to her bed for a short nap and later her test would be gone over in minute detail – so that if next time it was to be real, she could avoid any mistakes made in the practice interrogation. She would learn that this has happened to others, who had real experience of it in France, like Blanche Charlet, who said that this practice test had saved her life.

Finishing

When the training and test was over, the student was as ready as he or she could be. Not everyone passed even at this stage but now, because they knew too much, students who had failed this last stage had to be sent somewhere until their knowledge was out of date – the 'cooler' for most was at Inverlair in Scotland – very comfortable, but so disappointing.

Before the final decision of those failing was made, however, their report was considered by Buckmaster, who occasionally, after consultation, reversed it. This he did in a few cases, like that of Noor Inayat Khan, being very often influenced by a shortage of people in a particular role or of time for an urgently requested agent.

Then she would be whirled away to wait for her final destination – at Fawley Court perhaps or Gaynes Hall or a similar comfortable FANY-run kind of hotel. Here some time might have been spent tying up family business, or writing a dozen or so letters saying 'I am well and all is right'; these would be given to Vera Atkins to send to family at intervals – even after there was no news of the fate of the agent. The rest was just walks, entertainment, games, dancing or going over her new identity.

Finally the Conducting Officer would warn the agent, if there was time, 'next day I may turn up to take you to the port or airfield to prepare you for your journey'. At this stage there was usually a last visit to see Maurice Buckmaster, who would greet her with open arms in the sybaritic flat at Orchard Court, sending her spirits soaring with his compliments, and giving her a small gold or silver powder compact as a parting gift – 'in case you need to sell it or pawn it, if you need money in an emergency'. Now there was no more to do except wait to be called for her journey to France.

Travelling to France

There were a number of ways by which an agent could be taken in or out of France secretly. It was one of the agents, Cecily Lefort, who opened up a route once used by escapees fleeing from the French Revolutionary guillotines. By the early war years there were some specially adapted boats for various routes.

Sea

Breton fishing boats and motor torpedo boats from Falmouth and then Helford were used by the escape lines from the North of France, and they sometimes involved a borrowed Navy submarine. Inevitably, an occasional SOE agent could also be taken in by that route. However, the lines concern to carry in more stores limited their size and operations, and they became mainly the preserve of the 'Var' (DF) escape line, the RF service and the SIS.

Getting agents into the South of France by sea produced different needs. F service preferred to send its agents by plane or submarine to Gibraltar at the beginning. From there a pair of specially adapted feluccas (traditional wooden sailing boats) crewed by Polish seamen from the EU/P (Polish) Section, ferried agents in cramped and slow conditions to somewhere along the Mediterranean Riviera coast. Most operations were suspended here when the Germans took over the unoccupied Vichy Zone.

Air – Special Duties Squadrons

Sea Operations were much hampered by Admiralty Rules. SOE found quite early in its existence that air operations were its best option, despite the expected opposition from the Air Ministry.

In February 1941 Air Chief Marshal Charles Portal said 'I think you will agree that there is a vast difference in ethics between the time honoured operation of the dropping of a spy from the air, and this entirely new scheme for dropping what one can only call assassins*'. Later on, when SOE required help from the RAF for taking in agents and supplies for the French resistants, 'Bomber' Harris objected, not so much on the grounds of what the planes were carrying, but that he was losing the use of a few of his planes, when he was trying to find enough aircraft for his famous 1,000 Bomber Raids to weaken Germany by destroying its factories, power plants and railways.

Nevertheless two Special Duties Squadrons were formed. Squadron 138 of Whitleys, Halifaxes and Stirling aircraft, which parachuted in both agents and supplies, their airfield finally being Tempsford. Squadron 161 of Lysanders and Hudsons carried out mainly the landings of agents, although the Hudson was used in 1943–44 to carry between eight and ten passengers and some 'packets', with a range of 1,000 miles, but took longer to turn around. The Lysander was an excellent aircraft for short flights and secret landings. It had a fixed metal ladder at the side and normally carried one or two passengers, and because its range was no further than 600–700 miles it operated from the small airfield at Tangmere and only flew to the north of France. It was a little aircraft with a fixed undercarriage and was reputed to be able to land and take off on a pocket-handkerchief sized piece of land.' "The Lizzie", as it was fondly called, was the result of a concept already out of date by the time it was developed, and failed totally in the role for which it was designed. Nevertheless in the end it was to be put to other uses, in which moreover it was to excel' – Jean-Michel Legrand, author of *Lysander* (Editions Vario, 2000).

---

* Assassins - An example was the case of the bungled killing of the Jewish exterminator, the murderous Heydrich in Czechoslovakia in 1942. It was only vaguely connected to SOE.

Together with the little twin-engined Hudson, these lone aircraft were part of the Moon Squadrons, since they would only fly on the few moonlit nights of the month, and there were very few when the moon was not covered by cloud or storm. It was necessary, since the pilot hoped to fly below the eye of enemy radar, and, flying low, to find his destination to a tiny little pin-point of land. To do this he would have to sight-read his way across France, by following, as long as the moon picked them out, the shine of rivers and lakes, railway lines, steeples, roads and any recognisable objects. The 'Lizzie' could not carry radar or instruments, and passengers did not even wear a parachute if overloaded. The SOE agents had to trust the highly skilled pilot. Such men were few. No wonder Bomber Harris wanted them in his Pathfinder Force. And for delivering agents to France, there were other secret services seeking their aid – as this humorous verse by Robin Hooper indicates:

> The moon is sinking in the sky,
> We know we damn well got to fly
> Or get into a fearful mess
> With SOE or SIS,
> The messages come thick and fast,
> We've got a field for you at last,
> So come tonight and try your luck…

Frank Griffiths was a co-pilot for his first flight on a Halifax of Special Duties Squadron:

It was such a smooth and uneventful trip – it lulled me into a false sense of security. We crossed the Channel at 200 ft, then jumped the French coast at Cabourg at 4,000 ft. Nothing came up at us. Then down to tree level in bright moonlight. We called at two receptions east of Paris and dropped our loads, then off to Belgium to drop a Joe [all agents were called Joe] and his pianist [wireless operator] to a reception, then back around Paris to, of all places, a sewage farm just south-west of Versailles. A curious place to have a reception, but no doubt few people hang around a sewage farm at 3 o' clock in the morning! So back to Cabourg to jump the coast – then to Tempsford and bed.
…Walking back, I remarked on the lack of excitement! The way the moonlit countryside rolled by underneath and the water check points came up dead on time.

'That's the navigator', Jack said. 'If you don't get lost you don't get shot at'. How right he was. There were inevitable losses to crews and aircraft. It was dangerous even for the best pilots, and there were always accidents.

Professor M.R.D Foot states that in 1941, not more than five aircraft were available to the squadrons. By November 1942 there were twenty-seven and by spring 1944, thirty-six. Using the Lysander 258 people were landed and 433 taken off, while over 1,200 agent parachute drops were made into France – not a bad record for a few years.

After November 1942 a special inter-services unit called Massingham in Algiers (AMF) began dropping supplies to the south of France (too far for British-based aircraft) and later dropped agents and commandos. It was this way that agent Christine Granville arrived, and in a gale. In mid-1944 the USAAF (United States Army Air Force) Flying Fortresses made their first daylight drop near Dole.

Organisation of Networks

All agents were allocated to an area of France called a Network/Circuit/ Reseau, usually a collection of small clandestine resistance groups scattered sometimes over hundreds of miles. Each network had a codename to maintain its secrecy in wireless transmissions (similarly all agents had codenames, as well as cover names for their assumed identities).

Eventually three kinds of agents worked together in an F network. The Organiser was the leader, planner and recruiter. He was usually a man. A Courier travelled widely between the organiser, his wireless operator and his resistance groups, transporting things like instructions, messages, wirelesses and explosives. Often he or she chose landing grounds and assisted at receptions. Women were particularly useful for this work, being less suspect among a population where, since men were often absent, the women were the family mainstay and were to be seen cycling or travelling everywhere. Third was the Wireless Operator (later called w/t operator, and the wireless, a radio), on whose Morse messages in code to London depended the arrangements for where and when the requested supplies, if available, could be safely dropped into France by a British aircraft. Unfortunately operators were frequently encumbered with one or two large, heavy suitcases containing a wireless transceiver and various items of equipment, including their long unwieldy aerial. Then they used difficult codes and ciphers, rigid time schedules for transmissions (until London altered them rather too late) and had to beware of watchful German direction-finding and listening stations. These were among the things that made wireless operators the most vulnerable of all agents. Spending too long on the air could be a death sentence, so much so that by mid-1943 they averaged just six weeks before capture.

As time passed, large or important networks under one organiser sometimes had several couriers and wireless operators, together with occasional specialists for weapons training or a particular sabotage project. On the other hand, a few networks managed with only one or two agents in all the roles.

Other Agents in France

SOE F were, of course, not the only agents being sent into France. At the end of 1941, the United States of America entered the war and in 1942 set up its own Secret Service called the OSS (Office of Strategic Services). Unlike Britain, it combined intelligence and sabotage into one section. Many, including the Americans and even some Russians, were trained and transported by Britain. The Russians were part of the ubiquitous NKVD, present in France even before the Communist alliance with Germany broke in June 1941. Second in numbers to SOE F were the RF agents sent by de Gaulle's BCRA (*Bureau Central de Renseignements et d'Action* – Central Bureau of Intelligence and Operations). Unfortunately, Churchill sometimes withheld vital strategic information from de Gaulle until after the event, and in any case de Gaulle had to show the French that he acted independently from the British and was no puppet. This often made for very strained relations between the two leaders. Moreover, though both the Gaullist RF and the British F were trained by SOE in Britain, de Gaulle was annoyed by F's very existence, because it worked with Frenchmen who did not favour him. Again unfortunately, de Gaulle also fell out very bitterly with the Americans, for similar reasons.

SOE F had other branches – DF the escape lines run by F until 1942, EU/P for Poles and small ones for Czechs, Dutch and later other nationalities.

Before leaving Britain, F agents were usually warned to avoid tangling with the DF escape lines, the RF service, or the special (and much older) British intelligence service of SIS, who *were* spies. Though the masters of

RF and SIS disliked SOE intensely, inevitably F agents did occasionally touch on them, and found they worked together much better in the field than in London.

The Legacy of SOE F

Though these women knew they risked their lives by their work, they did not seek death, avoiding it with all the skills they had been taught, realising that it was a useless, coward's way out that would cause lifelong loss and pain to those left behind. For that reason they all refused the L pill (cyanide) offered to all agents before they left. Instead they worked productively to help and benefit the people around them. They particularly tried to avert the heavy air bombing which only caused avoidable civilian deaths, by encouraging other means of destroying enemy installations on the ground, through sabotage brought about by resistants in the network, and which if cleverly done, could occur without anyone seeming to be responsible. They suffered, often alone, trying to protect the civilians, resistants and fellow agents around them, and to unify a fractured country (often difficult, as resistants sometimes quarrelled quite violently among themselves). Whatever these differences, they still tried to help a long established ally to turn out her invader and they tried to prepare the ground to return France to the freedom to choose her own proper government and peace.

SOE's task was done when the war ended and it was closed down in early 1946.

★★★★★★

Books, films, documentaries and articles, drawn from many different sources, have been written about the small handful of forty SOE F women, some beautiful and romantic, whose lives or deaths have attracted attention, or whose records are easily found. Unfortunately only a little, or none, has been recorded of the others who remained in the shadows, and about whom information is hardest to find. Perhaps they lacked glamour, their deaths cannot feed the current taste for violence, or they worked undiscovered.

In the following chapters I have sought to cover each of the forty F women in a brief individual account, the little known with the better known, short though some must be. It will also give you an overview of the extraordinary variety of women who volunteered for such dangerous work, inspired purely by a love of France and freedom. Their accounts are given in the order in which they arrived in France and I have tried to update them in the light of present knowledge. So there may be a few surprises!

This brief narrative is therefore my attempt to celebrate their courage and their lives, to right a wrong of oblivion for many brave women, to adjust the balance, and pay a tribute to a small company, now rapidly fading into the past.

I

BEGINNINGS

It is notable that the first two women helping SOE in 1941 were not British. They went openly into France as civilians, under their own names.

They went there early in the war, but worked mainly in the less risky unoccupied zone, at a time when the Germans were trying to employ a charm offensive to win over the uncertain, confused and despairing citizens.

The first, Gillian Gerson – an innocent, who enjoyed playing a part – was moved to do so mainly out of love for her husband and to help France, but she did not stay too long.

The second, Virginia Hall, might be described loosely as one of the intelligentsia. She was moved by indignation at the German invasion, which she followed shortly with clandestine opposition, and she stayed in France much longer.

Both were protected by their nationality.

Whereas the first had definite objectives which she completed fast before leaving, the other came with a number of objectives, which changed and expanded during a stay of over a year.

They were the groundbreakers, preparing the way for others, and both proved very successful.

GILLIAN GERSON

Gillian Gerson was the first woman sent to France on behalf of SOE. She travelled there in May 1941, her role being that of a sightseer.

She was a young actress from South America, born in Chile in 1913, to a wealthy Balmaceda family, and because she married only a short time before the war, she still held a valid Chilean passport in the name of Gigliana Balmaceda Provasoli Gerson, with a visa for Vichy, France.

Her husband, Victor Gerson, born in 1898, the son of a wealthy Lancashire textile manufacturing family, had settled in Paris after fighting in the First World War, and opened a shop there to sell fine rugs and carpets. In the early 1930s his first wife and son died, and later in that decade he married Gillian as his second wife.

Gillian, just over twenty, newly married and settled in Paris in the Rue de Lisbon, fell in love with the city and its people. This brief but exciting new life ended abruptly when the Germans attacked France. On the signing of the Armistice in June 1940, Victor, who had already transferred most of his stock to Britain, where he had a house in Grove End Gardens, London, fled there with his wife. In London, he shortly discovered that the infant SOE organisation was interested not only in him but also in his wife, and particularly in her valid travel documents. When approached, she proved as enthusiastic in helping SOE as he was.

The result was that on 23 May 1941, Gillian left Britain on her own and travelled to Vichy and the city of Lyon, in the unoccupied zone of France, SOE making all the arrangements for her. Her journey went smoothly: no one questioned her travel papers. On arrival, acting the part of a visitor, she found that when she was at times a little lost and asked so many innocent questions, everyone forgave her for her brilliant smile. With her sharp eyes and the retentive memory of an actress, she wandered unrebuked into forbidden areas. She learned about the passes and papers citizens had to keep on their persons at all times. She watched for the extent of railway and bus controls and collected timetables and information on all kinds of transport. She discovered the legal and illegal ways of crossing between the occupied and unoccupied zones, the checks on hotels and lodging houses, the times of curfew and penalties for breaking it. She copied ration cards and noted prices of food and shortages of all kinds. In the cafés she tested the reactions of the French to the German occupation and cultivated useful contacts for the future.

Finally, loaded with information, she returned through Spain and arrived safely back in Britain around 24–25 August 1941, where she remained. As their dates may have overlapped, it might have been possible for Virginia Hall, the second of SOE's initial agents, to meet her briefly on her way into France.

In September 1941, Victor Gerson, armed with Gillian's intelligence, and now a trained SOE agent, parachuted with another man into occupied France. A resourceful businessman, he was on a mission to examine the creation of resistance networks to form safe and secure escape routes out of France. This DF Section* route was to become known as the 'Vic' escape line, which under his firm leadership and strict security, continued with only a few hitches until the liberation of France.

---

* DF escape routes only remained part of SOE until 1942.

2

VIRGINIA HALL

This brave and gifted American was both an authentic SOE and OSS hero of World War II.

Gerald K. Haines (American academic)

One of the greatest women agents of the war.

Denis Rake (agent)

Virginia was born in Baltimore, USA, on 5 April 1906, the youngest child in a well-to-do family of English-Dutch background. Her father, Edwin Lee Hall, owned a cinema there. She knew her French and English history before that of her own country. A talented linguist, she graduated from the best schools and colleges in North America and Europe. By then she was a tall, athletic woman with soft shining almost red hair and a strong mind, together with a burning desire to belong to the American Foreign Service.

However, from the time of her father's death in 1931, everything seemed to go wrong for her. Despite working in the American Embassy in Poland and then a Consulate in Turkey, her attempts to join her country's Foreign Service, except as a lowly clerk, were constantly frustrated by ill luck and inflexible rules. In addition, through a snipe shooting accident in Izmir, Turkey, in December 1933, the lower half of her left leg had to be amputated. She returned home for a year, where with an artificial limb and characteristic determination she learned to walk almost smoothly by lengthening her stride. At the end of 1934, undeterred, she was again in Europe as a clerk in a US Consulate in Italy, but in the following May, on hearing that she was due to start a further posting to Estonia, she resigned, and was caught in Paris when war broke out.

Shortly afterwards she joined the French Ambulance Service, but soon discovered that hopping in and out of ambulances did not suit 'Cuthbert', as she had named her new leg. Disgusted by the June 1940 Franco-German Armistice, she left her ambulance and made for Britain by way of Spain, ending up in the London US Embassy.

The start of the next year saw her proposing herself as suitable for employment in SOE – anything to return to her beloved France. In addition to fluency in European languages, she had another advantage to offer. Since America had not yet entered the war, her nationality would allow her reasonably free movement in France. These gifts, allied to an imposing figure, a quick and adaptable mind, a talent for making friends, fearsome drive and an unquenchable spirit, marked her out as ideal for a special agent. Maurice Buckmaster, shortly to be head of the F service, recognising this, took her under his wing. Thus in May 1941, at the same time as permission was granted for her to become a card-carrying Foreign Correspondent of the *New York Post*, she began a crash course at Bournemouth on SOE 'weapons, communications, resistance activities and security measures,' with a little extra coaching from Buckmaster himself.

Accordingly on 23 August 1941, in keeping with her apparent status as a journalist of a neutral country, she left Britain before being slipped quietly by air into Lisbon, where she joined a Lufthansa flight to Barcelona in her own name, completing her journey by train. Her first stop was Vichy, a town of which she had a poor opinion, though it purported to be the home of the French government of the area nominally unoccupied by the Germans. When she went to register at the Police Station on her arrival, she won the confidence of the gendarmes there. Nevertheless, the city of Lyon was to become the central base for her HECKLER network, and here she operated her own 'safe house'. Her cover name was Marie Monin, but she became Marie of Lyon to the resistance and later Philoménè, while the Free French knew her as Germaine.

However, her perceptive and informative accounts to the *New York Post* became fewer, while her work as SOE organiser and courier for the HECKLER network expanded and engulfed her. A bar in Lyon was known as her contact address and her activities were multifarious. Under an unflappable exterior, she was a whirlwind of activity, which ranged from advising, lodging and despatching newly arrived or lost agents, to passing others onto an escape line, once even arranging a sick organiser's escape from hospital. She recruited new resisters and holders of safe houses and stores, telling London of landing places, but not taking part in the reception parties for RAF drops of arms, sabotage materials and much needed money for forged papers and bribes. She also had to keep in touch with the Paris underground resisters. As Ben Cowburn, another successful agent whom she helped, observed, 'If you sit in her kitchen long enough, you will see most people pass through with one sort of trouble or other, which she promptly deals with.' She also became a regular visitor to the American Consulate and cultivated relationships with a motley variety of people from a gynaecologist, a factory owner, nuns and prostitutes, a brothel keeper, to an Abbé, as well as important individuals of all persuasions including Police chiefs, who turned a blind and sometimes benevolent eye on her many activities.

Although another task was the distribution of the rare and invaluable wireless sets to nominated agents, her handicap was having no wireless operator of her own to enable her to contact London with her requests and information, causing her to use others – and placing herself in real danger of compromising her security. She was indeed a grossly overworked spider in the midst of a gradually growing web, with, unfortunately, an undiscovered Abwehr spy in her network. Yet her work was key to getting numerous early F section networks started in France.

When Germany finally declared war on the United States in mid-December 1941, she had to be 'a little more careful'. She was already aware of the mounting problems of another agent, Pierre de Vomécourt and his AUTOGYRO network. His arrest in April 1942, through the capture of one of his couriers to her, was the death knell of his network and others around him. Untouched herself, but with her sharp nose for danger, she must have foreseen future disasters.

September 1942 seemed to presage the arrival of another agent to help or possibly replace her, as she had been requesting London. Alas, circumstances turned against her when the courier arrived, only to be lost to another network. However, the Allied landings in north-west Africa on 8 November 1942, precipitated the German occupation of her slightly freer Vichy Zone.

Tipped off that same night that the Germans were making for Lyon, she hurriedly decamped, much to the frustration of the Gestapo, hot on the heels of 'that Canadian bitch' (their geography was a bit hazy), also known as the 'Limping Lady' to the resistance. With three other escapees, whom she picked up on her way, she successfully surmounted the Pyrénées on foot in the depths of winter, in about 48 hours. This was no small achievement for anyone, let alone someone with an artificial leg – she had been told to eliminate 'Cuthbert' if troublesome by London. Bad luck saw the party arrested on the border of neutral Spain, and imprisoned in the notorious camp Miranda de Ibro, from where she was extricated by the American Consul in Barcelona.

Again in London by January 1943, it was not until May before SOE decided to use her again and sent her to Madrid, Spain, seemingly as correspondent for the *Chicago Times*, but really to gather information useful for the DF service on the escape routes. Bored with such inactive, mundane work, she was back in Britain by November, and eager to return to France.

Now she had two aims. One was to become her own wireless operator, the other was to be transferred to the Office of Strategic Services (OSS) of the United States, now that America had joined the Allies. SOE had felt that she was too well known to be safely employed in France, but seemingly OSS had no such fears. She achieved both her aims. She was accepted by OSS and had her wireless training at the SOE school at Thame Park.

On 21 March 1944, she was landed from a British torpedo boat onto the coast of Brittany near Brest, under the codename Diane, and the cover name of Mademoiselle Marcelle Montegrie, a social worker. Her messages were still sent through SOE, as OSS and SOE worked closely together in London, but this time she was to establish an OSS network called SAINT. Alongside Virginia was another OSS officer, whose discretion and reliability Virginia came to distrust, so she tried to shake him off as soon as she could. She then made her way slowly to the rural department of Cher, Nièvre and Creuse in central France.

Here as her own wireless operator and organiser, living in relative squalor posing as a peasant milkmaid, and still helping others, she held a roving commission, sometimes visiting Paris, organising drop zones, storage sites, safe houses and keeping in regular wireless contact with London from constantly changing haylofts. The Gestapo knew of her and tried to capture her, but she always managed to elude them.

After D-Day she was directed to move to the Haute Loire in the Massif Central, for similar work. Nevertheless it proved very different and difficult.

The mountainous terrain put maximum strain both on cycling and walking, and she was again continuously on the move. Worse still, she found her new Maquis hostile to her leadership, asking 'who the hell was she to give orders?' Often it fell to her to single-handedly organise drops and the distribution of money and weapons. Even so, in such unpromising conditions, trains were derailed, bridges destroyed, rails cut, convoys disrupted, Milice captured and several hundred Germans killed or captured.

In mid-August came the invasion of Southern France, and a three-man Jedburgh team* arrived to help her. Their aim was to assist in creating three battalions out of the Maquis for the Forces Françaises d'Interieur (FFI). These were intended to hinder the Germans and help the advancing Allies. Virginia now reported on German troop movements, such as the relocation of the German General Staff from Lyon to Le Puy. But with the scent of victory in their nostrils, the Maquis became even more rebellious and disruptive, ignoring instructions from any but the French political parties they favoured – and there were many – their leaders even ignoring orders from SHAEF (Supreme Headquarters of Allied Expeditionary Force).

In September 1944, a small still loyal group was absorbed by the French First Army. At this point Virginia was able to hand everything over and leave for liberated Paris, undoubtedly relieved to wash her hands of the seething cauldron of political bickering.

This was not the end for her, however. She and another OSS agent, Paul Goillot, (whom she married in 1957) were to head a new team to foment resistance in Austria. The rapid collapse of Germany saw the mission aborted, and instead they returned to Paris in April 1945 to make reports on those who had helped them. They also collected abandoned equipment. Task finally completed, Virginia resigned from the OSS.

Thus ended the war career of a fearsomely capable and quite extraordinary woman.

---

* Jedburghs were special forces units representing British, French and Americans in uniform, who usually comprised of a three-man team (two officers and a wireless operator), who would parachute into enemy territory and establish links with resistance groups.

3

YVONNE RUDELLAT

*She was amazing. So small and slight, controlling hefty middle-aged
men… When she said 'Jump', they all jumped.*

Frank Cocker (agent)

At the beginning, as in so many cases, Yvonne seemed a most unlikely
choice of agent, but in reality she proved very much the opposite.

Yvonne Claire Cerneau was born on 11 January 1897 at Maisons Laffitte
near Paris. Her father was a horse dealer for the French Army, and until
his death the family was fairly well-off. She was in her teens when she
left for England and tried a variety of jobs until 1920, when she married
an Italian waiter, while working as a salesgirl at the Galeries Lafayette in
Regent Street.

She was a vivacious, dainty charmer with dark hair and hazel eyes, whose
air of fragility was deceptive, but being an incurable romantic, erratic and
completely irresponsible, the marriage inevitably failed, though she did
have a daughter, became a grandmother and was on good terms with her
ex-husband.

In 1941, bombed out of her husband's lodging house, she became a
receptionist at Ebury Court Hotel, where her gift of unobtrusiveness,

together with her often repeated wish to do something to help France, was noted by one of the French agents using it.

In May 1942, having been selected for SOE, her first training officer derided her, but soon this 'little old lady' as he described her, with her chameleon personality, outshone the others. At forty-five, she was one of a strange mixture of women on the first women's course, which included Blanche Charlet (forty-four), Marie-Thérèse le Chêne (fifty-two) and Andrée Borrel (twenty-two).

She was flown to Gibraltar by daylight in a Whitley bomber, followed by a rough sea crossing in a specially adapted felucca called *Seadog*. One of her fellow passengers was Nicholas Bodington, Deputy Head of F section, who had come to investigate the CARTE network, about which SOE had its doubts. He, two other men and Yvonne, landed secretly in the moonlight of 30 July 1942, on the Riviera coast between Bijou-sur-mer and Pointe-Fourcade. Later that morning, Yvonne, on her own, took a train from Cannes to Lyon in the unoccupied zone, where she had to stop for a forged paper to be obtained from Virginia Hall, who was still resident there. Then she smuggled herself across the demarcation line* into occupied France in the coal bunker of a steam engine, and thus, she arrived in Paris. There she had to report to London, and saw her mother in the distance without drawing attention to herself, before continuing by train to Tours.

This was a prosperous, industrial university town of the Indre et Loire Department, in an area known as the garden of France. Here her cover name was Jacqueline Gautier, a refugee widow from Brest, but her codename was Suzanne. She was intended as a courier for agent Francis Suttill, known as Prosper, who was to set up a network in Paris to replace the AUTOGYRO network, which had just failed. But as he had not yet arrived, she had been sent temporarily to be a courier for agent Raymond Flower (codenamed Gaspar), the organiser of the MONKEYPUZZLE network based in Tours.

Once settled she worked hard, cycling everywhere, pinpointing suitable landing grounds, transporting wirelesses and explosives in and around Tours – possibly some in her voluminous bloomers – and taking messages by train to Bordeaux and at least three times to Paris. Wherever she went she had the gift of making friends, though what she told them varied, as she was given to romancing, which fortunately SOE did not know. Among the agents who appeared on her landing grounds were her former training friend

---

* The rigid boundary between unoccupied Vichy and occupied France.

Andrée Borrel and Gilbert Norman, both destined to join Suttill in Paris, Lise de Baissac to go to Poitiers, and Roger Landes for Bordeaux. They all landed in twos in September and October 1942, on a field near the farm of Boisrenard, a place recommended by Pierre Culioli. Culioli had wandered over France for some time, in fruitless attempts to escape to Britain, and finally having attached himself to the MONKEYPUZZLE network, had forged a useful partnership with Yvonne. Unfortunately Flower neither liked nor trusted either of them, despite their efforts, and was proving a most unsatisfactory leader who tried to incriminate them in his messages to SOE.

After a difficult time, on the advice of Suttill, who had now arrived, the two of them broke away and formed an independent sub-network of their own within Suttill's growing PHYSICIAN network. Culioli, with a wicked sense of humour named it ADOLPHE. It was in South Touraine, Central France, in a district of the Loire valley known as La Sologne, and initially worked very well.

Then, in November 1942, danger loomed, as a number of Suttill's helpers were now being watched. In that month also, the Germans had taken over the unoccupied zone. Meanwhile, in late 1942 and spring 1943, Yvonne and Culioli went out into the Sologne, whose centre was Romorantin, recruiting helpers. Here their sub-network grew, as the people were fiercely anti-German. Yvonne with her plastic explosives on the carrier of her bike, delivered them where they were needed or stored them overnight under her bed. At night, on her own or with groups of resistants, she was blowing up railway lines and high tension cables. Between April and June 1943, she took part in twenty parachute drops, which were mainly arranged through the wirelesses of Gilbert Norman or Jack Agazarian of PHYSICIAN, often using the same safe house. Her sabotage also extended to trains, a railway bridge and a food store in Caen. Thirteen more agents were received on her landing grounds, and finally in June 1943, two Canadians landed with wirelesses and letters to be distributed.

On 21 June, Culioli, with Yvonne, drove their rarely used Citroën to take their Canadian visitors to the railway station at Beaugency. En route they were stopped at a German roadblock, and although their papers were in order, there were some questions about the Canadians, who had to leave the car and walk to the Dhuizon town hall, which meant that they arrived much later than the car. Consequently Culioli left the engine running while he and Yvonne again went to have their papers cleared in the town hall.

Then they returned to the car, wondering what to do about the Canadians who were just arriving and would surely be discovered as their French and accents were very poor.

It was only minutes before there was a call for the agents to come back. Giving up all hope of saving the Canadians, who by now had disappeared into the town hall, Culioli pressed the accelerator and the car leapt forward, zig-zagging over the road, hotly pursued by three German cars. They rammed into another barricade and roadblock outside Bracieux, with shots flying in all directions. One hit Yvonne in the head and she fell unconscious across Culioli and the gears, who thinking her dead, purposely drove into a wall, hoping to kill himself too. The car, however, rebounded, and stunned but still fighting, Culioli was shot in the leg and captured. At the town hall the two Canadians were in chains, and the car was impounded with all the messages, letters and equipment the Canadians had brought. These soon started the arrests of many of the PHYSICIAN network in Paris to whom the majority of the letters were addressed, and some members of the ADOLPHE network were also incriminated.

Both agents were taken to Blois. Culioli was sent to a military hospital where he was stripped, chained to a bed and given minimal medical care. Shortly he was taken to Avenue Foch, Paris, and interrogated to no purpose, followed by imprisonment at Frèsnes and afterwards Buchenwald Concentration Camp, which he survived.

Whereas, Yvonne, still unconscious, was taken to a civil hospital and treated by a sympathetic specialist, who seeing that the bullet in her skull had not penetrated the brain, decided to leave it where it was, knowing that it might only affect her sense of balance and memory – perhaps an asset under the circumstances. So Yvonne awoke next day a bullet still lodged in her skull and an armed German guard outside her door.

Almost immediately the news of what had happened flashed around the network and, while those most involved took cover, plans to rescue Yvonne were made but postponed until she could walk. Interrogators arriving to question her, found her unconscious from injections given to protect her by the nuns nursing her. This situation might have continued, had a drunken member of staff not given it away, resulting in her being transferred to another hospital in Paris, where although now conscious, she exaggerated her confusion and memory loss.

Eventually in late September 1943, still almost too weak to walk, Yvonne was moved to Frèsnes Prison, stopping on the way at the Gestapo headquarters for more questioning but to no avail. At Frèsnes she shared a cell with two other women from the resistance. Though she talked freely to them, the Germans hesitated to question her, thinking her condition worse than it really was.

On 21 August 1944, after a six-day journey by train, Yvonne, now recorded as Madame Jacqueline Gautier, arrived at Ravensbrück, and was recognised by at least two women who had been in her network. Here she shared in the filthy, overcrowded and insanitary hutted accommodation with other prisoners, but on 2 March 1945, she was transferred to another camp – the worst of all – Belsen. It was a place of starvation, typhus, dysentery and death, where corpses, then too many to bury, lay around putrefying the atmosphere with an indescribable stench. But even here, though weak, she made friends.

On about 5 April, the camp was liberated by British troops. Yvonne was still clinging to life but so deeply sunken in her alias that she drew no attention to herself. A week later she was still alive, but too weak to move and barely conscious. Then the death pits for the essential mass graves claimed her – one unknown among thousands. Her death was given as 23 or 24 April 1945, and later confirmed by the indefatigable Vera Atkins.

Thus died an indomitable and courageous woman, whose personality and activities persuaded SOE that women, like men, could make successful agents. She was the third female agent to enter France for SOE's F service, and the first British woman agent to be infiltrated for this purpose.

4

BLANCHE CHARLET

My practice interrogations were responsible for saving my life.
Blanche Charlet

Blanche Valentine Charlet was born in Belgium on 23 May 1898, both her parents being Belgian. She was small, dark-haired and attractive, but she had never married. Before the Second World War she was living in Brussels and had been managing an art gallery there, and, being an intelligent woman with a wide clientele, she had picked up some languages, her English being 'passable'.

When war overtook her country she fled to London, where, although a refugee, she knew a number of contacts, and her expertise in Modern Art was recognised. Ebury Court Hotel with its mixed range of customers attracted her and eventually, when SOE began recruiting women, she became one of the first four to be trained. She signed on under the cover organisation of the FANY with Yvonne Rudellat, her Ebury Court acquaintance, Marie-Thèrése le Chêne, and, one of whom she did not approve, Andrée Borrel. She was a natural choice for SOE, not only because of her maturity, experience and fluency in French, but because she carried her forty-three, almost forty-four, years very lightly under a lively manner and quick understanding. What happened to her in France is an adventure story in itself, with some unusual twists.

Her training went well, but in view of her age and that of two of her fellow trainees, it was decided not to send them by parachute, but by sea, though not together. In late August 1942, she was flown to Gibraltar and then boarded *Seadog*, a specially adapted felucca with some surprising additions, including an unexpected turn of speed and hidden guns. The captain very generously gave her his cabin, although he later admitted to being quite disturbed by her tantalising presence, and as he recalled, 'If we both acquitted ourselves creditably, that was all due to her.' Close proximity over the days of the voyage must have been trying!

On a moonless night of 1 September 1942, *Seadog* dropped anchor near a small cove below Agay, on the Riviera between Marseille and Toulon in the south of France. The arrival arrangements worked smoothly enabling 'Madame Sabine Lecomte' (her then alias) to spend the rest of the night in a quiet villa on the coast. She was alone, but she had the contact name and address of another agent at Cannes. However, when she arrived there, it was only to find that he had been arrested the day before. She cast around for further contacts over the next few days, when finding none, and feeling vulnerable, she decided to go north to Lyon to yet another contact, who turned out to be Virginia Hall, who was expecting Blanche to be her replacement.

Unfortunately, this was not to be, and Blanche shortly learned that she was to join the VENTRILOQUIST network headed by Philippe de Vomécourt (codenamed Gauthier), whose second in command was Aron (codenamed Joseph). Sent to him by Virginia, he instructed her to find safe houses for their soon-to-arrive wireless operator, Brian Stonehouse (codenamed Celestin). This did not turn out to be easy, as the Germans were watching Lyon carefully, despite it being in the unoccupied zone, since they believed it to be a hot bed of resistance, which indeed it was. Vichy was also arresting resistants elsewhere, as in Marseille. Blanche soon realised too that de Vomécourt considered SOE agents as 'incompetents'. All he wanted from London were arms and money.

Stonehouse appears to have been the most unlucky of agents. After parachuting blind* at the end of June 1942, it took him days to reach his

---

* Parachuting 'blind' meant that an agent was dropped without a reception party and expected to make their own way to their contacts.

wireless set, suspended in a tree. Then he had technical trouble before he could contact London, in the middle of which he went down with dysentery just as his set finally broke down. He thus became Virginia's responsibility until his set and health were once again restored, and even then neither were perfect. Time therefore had passed before Blanche finally caught up with him.

Now, at last, the courier work for Blanche (now codenamed Christianne), could commence. It proved mainly to consist of carrying messages between de Vomécourt, Aron and Stonehouse. It did not take long before she and Stonehouse became dissatisfied, and wanted to change networks, mainly because of the attitude of de Vomécourt and Aron and his disorganised group. Stonehouse also was inclined to transmit his messages for too long periods, and he needed more than two houses to escape detection. Nevertheless he was, in her estimation, an extremely hard worker.

On 24 October 1942, Blanche was carrying a message to be sent to London from de Vomécourt. Stonehouse was in a house at Feyzin, which he was only using for the second time. As Blanche arrived she noticed two caravans or trailers at the side of the road. Uneasy, she put the papers she was carrying in an outside shed, but went back to fetch them after she found everything normal inside the house. Taking them with her, she went up to the attic where Stonehouse was working. She tried to tell him that one message was urgent, but as he was in the middle of a transmission he signed her to be quiet. She therefore put the papers on the table and began her usual task of coding. A few minutes later the lamp light went out. Stonehouse immediately broke off. 'Danger' was all he needed to say. He took up the set and she the papers, and they ran down the back stairs to the basement, where they hid them all in some soft sand behind the lift shaft. Then they agreed to exit by the door to the back garden.

It turned out that this was guarded by a German policeman, who arrested them. The house was then thoroughly searched discovering the papers and set, after which the two were separated and Blanche was taken to the Petit Depot St Jean in Lyon, on her way hiding her notebook of addresses under a car seat. At the Depot she and Stonehouse had a few minutes together when they managed to arrange their stories to make sense. Blanche was going to say that she didn't know what a wireless operator was, and that she was the mistress of a married man whose address she could not give away, so as not to hurt his wife. She kept secret, however, her codename of Christianne.

At the beginning of her interrogation, the French police tried to help her as a fellow citizen, even suppressing some evidence against her, particularly when Stonehouse told them he was English, but later when they discovered her codename, and with the Germans present, they became harsher. She pretended to faint and took on the role of a simple woman wanting to play a glorious part in the resistance, not understanding anything about it (though she did make some slips). The interrogation took place over several days, in between which she was imprisoned in a cell on the women's floor, but in the courtyard exercise period, she found a way to communicate with Stonehouse on the ground floor, so they knew what the other had said.

Eventually, after about twenty days, the Germans discovered enough evidence, and on 13 November 1942, she and Stonehouse were transferred to the prison at Castres, used for holding hostages to be shot for any attacks on the Germans. It contained about eighty-five prisoners, some French but the majority other nationalities like Yugoslavs, Czechs and Poles, many of whom had been there for up to four years. Conditions were poor, morale low and food the principal preoccupation. Exercise was only half-an-hour daily, but the Germans never visited the prison, so there were no more interrogations.

Blanche shared a cell with three other women with whom she got on very well, though she had to beware of 'stool pigeons' (informers) scattered among the cells. Discipline was fairly lax and often cell doors were not locked. Blanche made a point of making friends with some of the staff, especially one of the cleaners, a Yugoslav. On the evening of 16 September 1943, he appeared to tell them that they could have a free run of the prison for the next two hours, as prisoners had duplicate keys and pistols, the guards being locked up or tricked. On that night about thirty-seven prisoners made their escape, though about five were later recaptured and died under torture. In Blanche's cell two could not leave, so she went out with Suzanne Warren, another agent from an escape line. As the prison was in the middle of the town, they all left in little groups so as not to draw attention.

Blanche and Suzanne had a young boy to guide them to meet the others, but in the open country he admitted he was lost, and finally struck off on his own, leaving them to continue until next morning. Tired and hungry, they stopped at a village and asked the local priest for help. He sent them to a farmer who gave them food and let them sleep in a barn, until Blanche suspected that they had been betrayed, so they ran quietly away. Two days later, fearing to ask for further help but desperate as they had no food or shelter, on reaching Dourgne they saw in the distance a Benedictine monastery. Risking everything, they rang the bell. They were sent to a guest house in the grounds, where they met with the greatest kindness, despite the danger the monks ran by sheltering escaped prisoners. There they stayed for two months, even being put in touch with their British organisation. Their attempts to cross the Pyrénées failed twice, the second because the ice and snow on the passes in midwinter drove them back. At the beginning of January 1944 they were advised by a French escape line to go to Paris. There Blanche was sent to Lyon, which she wanted to avoid as she was known there, but she had to remain in the district for a month before moving on to the Jura. Here she did a bit of courier and escort work until April when SOE arranged for the two of them to return to England with another escape line.

This proved quite an adventure in itself. They were escorted north and west to Brittany, in a coastal area closely watched by the Germans, who were expecting an invasion. Picked up by an open-backed baker's van doing its delivery rounds, they shortly joined a roomful of other escapees waiting for a confirmation message after the 9 o' clock BBC news. Then a local fisherman led them in the dark, across the wild moors and through minefields for three precarious hours until they came to the beach. There they waited. After two in the morning, little lifeboats bringing in supplies and more agents, quickly picked them up and embarked them on the two larger mother ships standing out of the bay. When the engines started, German boats lying in wait fired on them, killing one sailor, but were soon left behind by the superior speed of the British boats. When it was light, RAF planes escorted them to harbour.

They landed in England on 20 April 1944 in the early morning, and after a good breakfast Blanche was off to London to make her report. Thus ended a rather unusual and eventful two years for Blanche with SOE.

5

ANDRÉE BORREL

She was the best of us all.

Francis Suttill (agent, codenamed Prosper)

Andrée Raymonde Borrel was born on 18 November 1919 in the suburbs of Paris. With her elder sister, she had a good education, but she left school at fourteen to work in a bakery and then a general store, as her mother was a widow and the family was poor. Still under twenty, the left-wing idealist in her briefly spurred her into action and she joined the Spanish Civil War. By this time she was a small, dark-complexioned, stocky young girl, very quick, athletic and determined.

Back in Paris at the beginning of the Second World War, she moved her mother from Paris to Toulon, where Andrée joined the Association des Dames de France, nursing wounded soldiers at the Beaucaire Hospital in Nîmes where one of her fellow workers was Maurice Dufour. Shocked by the Franco-German Armistice, she joined the French resistance and was drawn into the 'Pat'* escape line. It rescued downed pilots, prisoners of war

---

* Created by Albert Guérisse, a Belgian army doctor, under the name Lieutenant-Commander Patrick O'Leary. He was betrayed and imprisoned, and later provided identification of Andrée at the Natzweiler War Trial.

and the remnants of Dunkirk servicemen, and worked from the Belgian frontier, over the Pyrénées and into neutral Spain, in the face of severe German reprisals. She was credited with helping to save 600 pilots. After a while, Andrée, with Dufour, was sent to run one of the last safe houses before the Pyrénées, near Perpignon. But in late 1941, when part of the northern line was betrayed, they had to depart the same way as the escapees. Andrée then worked for a time at the British Embassy in Portugal, until her April 1942 flight to Britain.

Cleared by the Patriotic School, she offered her services to de Gaulle's Free French Service, but was turned down when she refused to divulge to them any secrets of the 'Pat' line. For this very reason SOE F service was more than willing to accept her, as it now, against fierce opposition, had been given permission to recruit its first non-British volunteers. It was also impressed by her war experience and current knowledge of French conditions. She was the first French woman, who having first worked with the resistance, chose to work with SOE F service after training.

On 15 May 1942, Andrée joined the first women's course for SOE F agents. They were an unusual bunch, Andrée being at least twenty years younger than the other three – Marie-Thérèse le Chêne, Yvonne Rudellat and Blanche Charlet.

They were trained under the cover of the FANY, a uniformed, civilian and unconventional organisation. Andrée being intense and rather frightening in manner, the others thought her a typical Parisian street urchin. She horrified Yvonne Rudellat when, asked how to deal with a sleeping German, she replied that with a pencil she would stab him through the ear into the brain – but, only she knew the reality of war. Marie-Thérèse le Chêne, however, saw through her assumed sophistication to the innocent beneath and tended to mother her. Eventually she proved a brilliant student, with no nerves and plenty of common sense. With men she would be a loyal friend – but no more.

After one failed flight, a Whitley of the Special Duties Squadron dropped her and another woman from the second course on the moonlit night of the 25 September 1942 into a field near Boisrenard, to a reception arranged by Culioli and Yvonne Rudellat, who had arrived a different way. Andrée was one of the first two SOE F women to be parachuted into France. They spent an uncomfortable night in a hut, before Culioli took them in a horse and cart to a farm, their first safe house. There the two women spent a few days to allow for Andrée to help Lise de Baissac (the second woman), as security had ensured that neither would know the other. Conditions had changed since

Lise's last visit, so she had to acclimatise herself to rationing, the daily sight of German soldiers, procedures at railway stations and many other minor things that would mark her out as a stranger. Then they parted never to meet again, Lise to travel to Poitiers and Andrée north to Paris. There Andrée was to have things ready for the arrival, on the night of 2 October, of her organiser Francis Suttill (codenamed Prosper), whose network was called PHYSICIAN, for whom she was to be a courier, codenamed Denise.

Their first meeting was to be at a café where Andrée's sister lived. Almost immediately she had to change her plans when she found that Suttill's French was not good enough to pass scrutiny. Since he was supposed to be a commercial traveller in agricultural products visiting the farms of the Île de France indicated in the list provided by André Girard (codenamed Carte), Andrée now had to accompany him everywhere, pretending to be his sister, carrying the money and doing most of the talking. In this way many new resistance members were also recruited.

It only needed Gilbert Norman's arrival in November, to be Suttill's wireless operator, for the PHYSICIAN network to be fully operational. It was unfortunate that Norman was sometimes called 'Gilbert' (his Christian name) by his friends, as this was the codename given to Déricourt, the Paris Air Movement Officer (whom Andrée did not like). This was to be a cause of confusion later.

By March 1943, Andrée and Suttill were widening their circle of contacts to Blois, Orléans, Romorantin, Melun, Beauvais, Compiègne, St Quentin and other places. Suttill relying heavily on Andrée – some resisters felt she influenced him too much – appointed her as his second-in-command, feeling her utterly trustworthy. Their efforts had resulted in recruiting about 10,000 men, divided into many smaller sub-networks, and the recipients of around 240 containers of arms and explosives, encouraging much sabotage, particularly in Paris. Almost every day a German soldier died in its streets, often the work of the Communists, who did not concern themselves about French hostages being shot in reprisal. Andrée herself was credited with the wreck of a power station.

But there was danger in the PHYSICIAN network growing too large and too fast. Too many people knew too much and spoke openly about it, growing overly confident. Even Suttill, Norman and Andrée ate out frequently, and played cards until late in Paris restaurants and cafés, sometimes dropping into English, sure that they would not be betrayed. Once they were seen showing the working of a sten gun to admiring resistants in Montmartre.

Another danger also lurked in the background. A list of supporters which was sent to Suttill and was lost, had fallen into the hands of the Abwehr, though none realised this at the time. Unfortunately many of Suttill's current members were on the list. Things started to go wrong from April 1943.

Sisters running a safe house in Paris were arrested, and Suttill's efforts to rescue them with a bribe, exposed others and failed. In May, Suttill was summoned to London for a short break and a briefing, but it was noted on his return that he seemed to be a very worried man. Resistants had a belief that many who were soon to be arrested carried a 'haunted look' and with this, Suttill was now credited.

On 21 June, Andrée, Suttill and Norman waited to see Culioli, Yvonne Rudellat and their two newly landed Canadians, one bringing Norman some new wireless crystals. They did not arrive, and Suttill and Andrée that night had to leave for another aircraft drop. Next day Suttill went to another sub-network near Gisors, while Andrée and Norman had dinner with friends in an apartment above a café until 11pm, and then travelled separately, she by Métro and he by bike, to Norman's new safe house. There they started coding Norman's next wireless messages.

Suddenly there was a loud knocking at the apartment door. 'Ouvrez! Police allemande.' Their hostess, thinking it was a joke, answered, only to find herself facing a revolver. They were all arrested and taken to the Avenue Foch for interrogation and torture. Andrée was kept apart, without torture, possibly because they already knew all they wanted and because she stayed silent, treating them with defiant contempt.

Suttill was captured the next day by men awaiting his return in his new hotel room, the whereabouts of which was only known to Norman and Andrée. Afterwards the arrests of resistant members of the network snowballed, and were eventually reported to London by the only wireless operator still free in Paris. Andrée, after a short stay at the Avenue Foch, was committed to Frèsnes Prison. Almost a year later, on 13 May 1944, Andrée was taken from Frèsnes back to Avenue Foch, where she met seven other women, all of them former SOE F section agents. After a few hours they were bundled into a truck to catch a train, all handcuffed in pairs. The journey lasted several days, until they reached the civilian women's prison at Karlsruhe in Germany.

Here they were separated and most of them shared a cell with several other German women, but their conditions were generally better than those in Frèsnes, and it was hoped that they would remain here until the end of the war, since all the prisoners now knew that D-Day was imminent and hoped the Allies would release them.

But this was not to be, and it was very early in the morning of 6 July 1944 that four of them including Andrée, were summoned to the prison offices, and their confiscated belongings returned. They were taken by the Gestapo in a covered truck to arrive at about 3 o' clock that afternoon at the concentration camp of Natzweiler – the only concentration camp on French soil. As it was a men's camp, and the women were brought there secretly, it was bound to arouse curiosity. A working party outside the walls saw them, and later two men who survived, spoke to them through an open window, one being Andrée's leader in the 'Pat' escape line. All male prisoners were ordered into their huts at about 8pm and told to close their shutters. When the women first arrived, they were put together into one cell, then separated into twos and finally each was left on her own.

That night between about 9.30pm and 10.30pm, the women were taken out one by one, accompanied by guards, up the short pathway to the crematorium hut, which they did not recognise. Each was conducted to a room containing eight beds. She was told to lie down and then injected with a very high dose of phenol – a fairly common disinfectant. A short interval afterwards she lost consciousness and a doctor certified her as dead. She was then stripped and carried to the furnace.

Some crematorium stokers, shut away in their tiny bunk dormitory, heard one girl ask loudly, '*Pourquoi*? [What for?]' and a reply in a man's voice, '*Pour Typhus*'. Some time later a groaning body was taken up the corridor and the crematorium oven opened. This happened four times, except, from the testimony of one of the stokers at a later trial, that one of the bodies struggled and screamed when being placed into the oven. Knowing the character of the four women, it is possible that it was Andrée, fighting to the last!

Thus ended the life of Andrée Borrel, a very loyal and brave woman. She was twenty-four years old.

6

LISE DE BAISSAC

I was very lonely… I discovered what solitude was. Having false papers, I never received a letter or a telephone call.

Lise de Baissac

Lise de Baissac was born at Curepipe on Mauritius in the Indian Ocean on 11 May 1905. The island, conquered by the French, was now held by Britain, so Lise grew up being bilingual, but her nationality was British. She had two brothers, one who later joined the British Army and the other preceded her into SOE. In 1919 the family moved to Paris, where her father worked in insurance, and after finishing her education, Lise remained there to work.

In 1940, after France fell they all left Paris and Lise went south into the Dordogne, in the area soon to be controlled by the Vichy. Ever strong in her opinions, Lise was ashamed of the Armistice, feeling it a humiliating slur on France. Vichy was soon full of refugees, and here Lise began her earliest resistance activities by helping them to escape.

Later the American Consulate arranged her travel to Portugal and on a British refugee liner in Gibraltar she met her brother Claude. Safe in Britain, Lise got a shop job in London, where she heard that Claude had joined SOE. As soon as the organisation started recruiting women he recommended her. Thus in May 1942, she went on the second course to be held for women agents, along with Jacqueline Nearne, Mary Herbert and Odette Sansom.

Lise was a mature woman of thirty-seven, small, slight, with black hair, light eyes and a very confident manner. Her trainers found her exceptionally intelligent, strong-minded and decisive, with a definite flair for organisation and better working on her own as an organiser, having the family characteristics of being difficult but dedicated. She was also clear-minded, imperturbable and reliable, preferring, despite the risks, to work without a courier or wireless operator, who might lead the Germans to her.

She was one of the first two women to be parachuted into France, jumping with Andrée Borrel. Her brother Claude had already parachuted in two months earlier, but unfortunately damaged his ankle on landing, so that his new network at Bordeaux was slow to start. The women did not leave until the night of 25 September 1942, on their second attempt. Andrée jumped first and Lise followed. They landed safely near Boisrenard to a reception organised by Culioli. Although Lise said she was never afraid, she found herself wanting a cup of tea after the jump, and to her disgust found someone had replaced the tea in her hip flask with rum – no doubt more suitable under the circumstances.

After a night in a woodland hut, Culioli, once the curfew ended, took them by horse and cart to their next safe house, where for a few days Andrée acclimatised Lise to the changed occupied situation, even taking her to the railway station so that Lise might see how things were now done. This brief respite over, they parted – Andrée for Paris, Lise for Poitiers.

In the sleepy university town of Poitiers, capital of the Vienne department, surrounded by wide fields of wheat, vines and woodlands, giving cover for clandestine operations, Lise (codenamed Odile) was to become Madame Irène Brisse, a widow seeking peace and safety, although in reality her job was to form a new network called ARTIST, and also liaise closely with her brother's network SCIENTIST at Bordeaux. She was to set up a safe house and help newly arrived agents.

A local auctioneer helped her find a two-room, ground-floor apartment near the railway station, and later found her an equally useful one next to the Gestapo headquarters. The work was lonely and energetic, taking her out on her bike by day looking for suitable safe flat landing sites, recruiting and contacting resistants, or taking the train for long night journeys to Paris, or shorter ones to Bordeaux seeking wireless operators to take or receive her messages. In Tours, she once sheltered in Yvonne Rudellat's room; in

Paris she only saw agent Francis Suttill (codenamed Prosper) in person once, her main contact being Andrée, although communication with her was limited too, and from her trips to Bordeaux she became friendly with fellow agent Mary Herbert, her brother's courier. She also saw her brother very occasionally, if she wanted to pass him a message in Bordeaux. In the evenings at Poitiers she sometimes entertained friends to a meal, excellent cover for night-visiting agents, who then drew little attention when leaving late. Of real friends she had few, except the auctioneer and a university professor giving her Spanish lessons.

Though she set up successful receptions, she was rarely present, as late departures and returns would spoil her cover story. In the new year she met another agent, Henri Déricourt, whom she liked, and he used several of the fields she had selected for receptions. By the end of May 1943, thirteen agents had landed on her fields, but the next month saw the arrest of Suttill and the destruction of the PHYSICIAN network, which was dangerous news for her brother, a frequent Paris visitor, since some members of his network worked there.

Then in August things started going very wrong for her brother, Claude. The Germans, raiding the apartment of his principal Bordeaux supporter, found the written details of many others, and later some arrests in her own network made Lise suspect that it had been infiltrated too. So on 15–16 August, London recalled Claude and Lise, collecting them from one of her own fields, the departure arranged by Déricourt. Claude left the SCIENTIST network damaged but still viable in the steady hands of his wireless operator Roger Landes and his courier Mary Herbert, but Lise, having no replacement, left only one little network in Ruffec still intact. Nevertheless, she found she had been very popular and left behind a core of friendships. Buckmaster considered her the bravest woman he had known.

In the interval between this and a second mission, Lise became a training officer for SOE. Unfortunately, while taking two agents on a parachute course, she landed badly and broke her leg, delaying her departure until 9 April 1944, and even then she had to be sent by Lysander as her leg was still weak. She was landed at Villes les Ormes, to become a courier for the PIMENTO network with its centre at Toulouse. Here many of the agents and resistants proved hostile to her, and she felt her time wasted on unimportant errands. Possibly, she was also affected by the additional problem that PIMENTO's socialist views were under the control of someone in Switzerland and not London, their interest being political rather than patriotic. Recognising their incompatibility she requested a move, suggesting her brother's new SCIENTIST II network in the south of Normandy. By the end of April she joined Claude, her cover changed to Madame Janette Bouvillle, and her new codename, Marguerite.

Claude had been working frantically since his return, seeking out large landing grounds for paratroopers and planes, ready for the invasion when it came. He must have been delighted to receive his sister as courier and virtually second-in-command to his work. She backed him to the hilt and despite a still painful leg, she was quite willing to cycle over 36 miles (60 km) daily on his errands. She was also good at managing awkward members of the Maquis or resistance, who became increasingly troublesome and more likely to act impetuously as more supplies and arms were dropped. Also, her brother's abrasive manner might have caused rebellion, but she was able to handle the tensions diplomatically. At least thirty receptions on Claude's fields produced 300 packages and 777 containers between April and May 1944 alone, which had to be distributed and hidden, while the men had to be restrained from frittering them away on useless acts of sabotage, which proved to be no small task.

Just before D-Day, Claude felt that SCIENTIST II was growing too large and unwieldy. He decided to divide it into two, sending his wireless operator and another assistant forward to the departments of Calvados and Manche, where they would be the most help to any invading troops, while he would remain behind the German lines to the south of Normandy in the Orne and Eure-et-Loir.

Early that May, another wireless operator joined them, Phyllis Latour (codenamed Paulette), who had been sent to them only partly trained as their need was so great. She became Lise's responsibility and lived with them during the busy times leading up to and after D-Day, when the sending and receiving of messages grew so numerous and urgent that there was hardly time to eat or sleep in between decoding and coding, in the latter of which Lise helped. Sometimes Lise also had to courier Phyllis's wireless, batteries and crystals with her, and there were several incidents when they were stopped at German road blocks, and vital pieces of equipment fell to the ground, fortunately unnoticed. Sometimes, Lise would strap crystals to her legs and waist. On one occasion she and Phyllis were cycling to another village to replace some parts needed for Phyllis's broken-down wireless, and despite both being frisked nothing was discovered.

Although Lise knew that Paris was growing more dangerous as the Germans became more nervous and aggressive, she still had to go there twice for Claude. She was on her second visit when she learned that the D-Day action messages had come through. It took her three days to return, though she hastened with all speed, sleeping in ditches and pushing through roads crowded with military vehicles and soldiers rushing west.

During the tumultuous days after D-Day they lived rough in the house of a local farmer, using three empty rooms with just straw to sit and sleep upon. Once Lise returned to her room to find that the Germans had taken it over and were sitting on her sleeping bag of parachute silk. This worried her less than the bags of English sweets in a kitchen cupboard, which the officer in charge fortunately had locked and given her the key, without looking inside. At another time they were sharing a school house with German officers, who came and went by the main doors, while Claude's agents slipped in and out of a side door. A bike too was absolutely essential to Lise's work, visiting their scattered groups of resistants and Maquis. Once, returning to reclaim it, she found it being requisitioned and wheeled away by a German soldier. She told him smartly that she would report him for theft to his commanding officer, whom she knew, and he would have to get his permission for taking it. When he returned, Lise and the bike had disappeared. At another time she is said to have slapped the face of a young soldier trying to remove the precious bicycle by force, and she got away with it. These and many other such incidents coloured her days.

In later June both Claude and Lise were busy. Lise trained as a fighter, helped to instruct the Maquis, and frequently accompanied them on sabotage missions, setting tyre bursters or mines on roads used by the military, or showing them where and how to cut telephone wires, underground cables and railway lines. At least once she took part in attacks on enemy columns. Her journeys also gave her useful intelligence information, which, although it was not her work, she would pass to Phyllis for her signals. Had she been caught, she would have been shot on the spot.

Eventually the Allies, aided by the resistance, broke through the German lines in the Mayenne. To Lise and Claude the war must have seemed to be drawing to an end, with the Germans now retreating eastwards, and Allied armies marching up from the south.

In August, Lise and Claude were seen, dressed impeccably in British Army and FANY uniforms, standing in front of the local Mayor's office, ready to welcome the advance party of a regiment. One soldier asked in amazement, 'Where have they come from?', 'Out of the sky!' shrugged the other, blissfully unaware of the accuracy of his comment.

7

MARY HERBERT

Mary was a tall, slender, fair-haired woman, who was naturally courteous and considerate of other people, generous and trusting, and in some ways naïve. She was attractive with an engaging smile, made and kept friends easily and her knowledge of art, literature and languages made her an interesting companion.

Claudine Pappe (a relative)

Mary Katherine Herbert was born in Ireland on 1 October 1903, the younger daughter of Brigadier-General Edmund Herbert of Moynes Court, Chepstow. She went to the Slade School of Art, took a degree at London University, and was fluent in several languages: French, Italian, Spanish and German, including a Diploma from the University of Cairo in Arabic. To these, in later years, she also added Russian. Before the war she did many things, at one time acting as escort to children at Farm Schools in Australia, and then taking a post in the passport control department of the Warsaw Embassy, before working at the London Air Ministry as a civilian translator.

On 19 September 1941 she joined the WAAF, training at Innsworth as a clerk (general duties) in the Intelligence section. There she remained until March 1942, when she was released at her own request to join SOE

F service in May, being given a pre-dated Section Officer commission for 15 January 1941, in the hope (it proved mistaken) that if captured she would be treated as a prisoner of war.

Mary was also given cover by FANY where being in a civilian body she could be trained in arms and be sent abroad, and so she joined the three other women on the second SOE women's course: Lise de Baissac, Odette Sansom and Jacqueline Nearne. At thirty-nine, she was quite tall (5ft 7in, 1.7m), slim, with short fair hair, pale face and, as far as SOE was concerned, the gift of being inconspicuous. She was also highly intelligent, patriotic and very religious.

In October, her course complete, she was sitting in the relative comfort of a flying boat in Plymouth harbour. At the last minute the flight was cancelled and a few days later, she shared the cramped accommodation of a submarine with two men and two women: Marie-Thérèse le Chêne, Odette Sansom and fellow male agents, Marcus Bloom and George Starr, their leader. At Gibraltar they boarded a felucca with a strong smell of sardines and an unusual head of steam. After several days they arrived at a cove near Cassis, on a moonless night, with only the phosphorescent spray breaking on the rocks and high cliffs. The felucca hove to with silent engines, leaving them to be propelled to the shore by cockleshell boats with muffled oars, landing on Halloween, 31 October 1942.

Next morning after curfew was raised, she caught the little coastal train to Cannes, where she met with the others at the back of a beauty salon in this holiday town. She took the train to Tarbes and then north towards Bordeaux. Still in Vichy, she had to cross the demarcation line into occupied France. This was dangerous despite her cleverly forged papers, so she crossed illegally on the night of 10 November, unaware that the next day German tanks would roll into Vichy.

Reaching Bordeaux in early December, sooner than expected, she finally met Claude de Baissac (codenamed David), the organiser of her new network, SCIENTIST. The port housed German submarines, which prowled the seas attacking Allied merchant ships, and it also held German ships which ran through the British blockade between Europe and the Far East. Most dock workers were strongly anti-German and a source of useful intelligence. No German dared to walk in that area alone.

She found that she was one of two new arrivals. The other was Roger Landes (codenamed Aristide), the wireless operator, whom she met briefly on the aborted flying boat trip, and she was introduced to Charles Hayes (codenamed Victor), a demolition expert. Mary was now known as Madame Marie-Louise

Vernier (codenamed Claudine) and contact to Claude de Baissac could only be made through her. She saw Landes rarely but de Baissac frequently. Though Buckmaster rated him the most difficult of his officers, Mary, fortunately, got on with him very well and worked hard for him, not only carrying messages but money, equipment and even wireless sets. Once she was struggling with a particularly heavy load when a German naval officer picked it up and politely carried it to the tram for her, oblivious of the incriminating contents. She also spent time looking out for potential safe houses, new recruits and suitable areas for receptions, many of which, at night, she attended.

The SCIENTIST network expanded rapidly and Mary found herself travelling through German controls in the Gironde, with its outriders of the network in rural Landes, near Angoulême, and even to Poitou and the Vendée. At Poitiers Mary met Lise de Baissac, who had been on her training course, and since Lise, out of security, rarely visited her brother, it became Mary's favourite stopping place, carrying both their messages. Often when Claude visited Paris, he took Mary with him, as it was better for him to be accompanied by a woman to avoid German identity checks and her errands took her to some of his own membership there. She soon found herself a quiet hotel in Paris, not too concerned with registration. This could prove useful, as when one of the transmitters in Landes's set burned out and the only replacement was with Suttill, Landes had to come to Paris with her to check and then carry back the new item.

In 1943 London became more generous with explosives and armaments parachuted to SCIENTIST, since it knew the potential for sabotage in that network. Thereafter, a huge blast shattered the radio station at Quatre Pavillions, a key centre for Admiral Dönitz and his Atlantic submarines; another demolition crippled the power station supplying the Luftwaffe airfields near Marignac; and the transformers at Belin (which powered anti-aircraft batteries and the the radar establishment at Deux Poiteaux) were damaged in the same way – the latter explosion timed to sour Spanish-German negotiations over trains running between Bordeaux and Spain.

The increase in sabotage and other activities attracted more German attention to the area and potential peril to the network, so in March 1943 Claude de Baissac was recalled to London for briefing and discussion. To many of the resistants, such a recall indicated that the Allied invasion of France was not far off, especially when he returned a month later.*

---

* Another wireless operator to assist Landes also landed in May 1943.

However, late in June, the Gestapo pounced in Paris and began rounding up members of the PHYSICIAN network, Francis Suttill among them. It was inevitable that from questioning and torture the Germans would discover the links between Bordeaux, and perhaps the two de Baissacs. Members of both networks were told to take cover, Mary among them. An unfortunate German search of a Bordeaux resistant's home revealed a list of network members. Mary, badly shaken by the news, moved to another apartment. She changed her appearance and adopted a new identity. De Baissac made a futile attempt to extricate some of his Paris members, while Mary quietly shuttled to and fro trying to hold together the fraying edges of the huge network. Then several arrests began in Lise's network. The danger was now creeping nearer.

At this point, London decided to call back Claude de Baissac on a mid-August Lysander flight. Many expected that he would take Mary too, as she needed a break, but instead, at the last moment, he took Lise, leaving André Grandclément in his place, as temporary leader of SCIENTIST. This was not a popular move, and no-one was surprised when London shortly named Roger Landes as head of the network, since it was decided to send de Baissac elsewhere.

The news that Claude was not returning hit Mary like a thunderclap. Fellow agent Charles Hayes saw her and she finally broke down in tears and told him, what he had for some time suspected, that she was going to have a baby and de Baissac was the father. He had promised her – and she had it in writing – that he would marry her and now he was not returning what could she do? Hayes passed on the news to an astonished Landes, who wanted to send her back to London, but she refused. She had cleverly hidden her state for months and thought that the baby would be due around November.

Initially, Landes did not tell London, as this was a bad time for the network, and there were worse problems to solve, but he urged Mary to cut off all her contacts, then stop working and take enough money to go to a quiet, safe house outside Bordeaux. Meanwhile, André Grandclément was found to have turned traitor after he had been replaced as leader by London, and he had even shown the Germans where the carefully collected arms dumps were hidden. Amongst a spate of arrests, Hayes too had been caught and shot. Realising the end was in sight, Landes gathered a small nucleus of resistants for the future; shockingly 300 resistants had been murdered through Grandclément's betrayal. He then took Mary to a small private nursing home at La Valence in a suburb of Bordeaux, before he escaped over the Pyrénées on 20 November 1943.

During the first week of December Mary gave birth by caesarean to a healthy girl, called Claudine, under her assumed surname Vernier, and when she left the nursing home, by an intentional oversight, she gave no forwarding address. Then she settled in one of the apartments Lise had used in Poitiers. Adept at disguises, she created another new persona for herself and with the money Landes had left behind, bought black-market ration books and papers to support her new identity and that of her child.

But two months later her luck ran out. On 18 February she was awakened early in the morning by the Gestapo and arrested. All the people in her block of apartments were given the same interrogation, but she was the prime suspect, as they believed her to be Lise de Baissac. The French Social Services stepped in to look after the baby, leaving Mary in prison concentrating on weaving an ingenious cover story for herself. Her knowledge of Arabic came to her aid in proving that she was a Frenchwoman from Egypt. Her German too, helped her convince the Gestapo, so that just before Easter she was released and went in search of her baby. The trail was long and difficult and often drove her to tears, but at last she found Claudine in an orphanage. By now she had made many friends and was offered a home in a small country house near Poitiers, owned by the de Vaselot family. There she managed to pick up the pieces and put her life together again.

The months slipped by. The Allies landed in France and eventually, in September, Bordeaux was liberated. Claude and Lise, having signed off from their new northern network, reported to Buckmaster, borrowed a service car and drove off looking for Mary, following her trail from Bordeaux to Poitiers. An accidental acquaintance finally led them to the house where Mary had found shelter, and there Claude saw his daughter for the first time.

They all returned to London, where on 11 November 1944, Claude Marc de Baissac married Mary Katherine Herbert at Corpus Christi Church, London. His stay in London, however, was short, as he had to return to General Koenig's staff until the war ended*, and Mary returned to her father in Monmouthshire with her little daughter.

---

* General Koenig was head of EMFFI the combined force of de Gaulle's French Forces of Resistance and RF, SOE and SIS (but not FTP).

8

ODETTE SANSOM

Of all the SOE women who died in France, she was the only one officially condemned to death.

Odette Marie Céline Brailly was born in Amiens on 28 April 1912 to French parents, the only girl of two children. Her father, a bank manager, was killed at Verdun in the First World War. Given a convent education, she was considered difficult, possibly due to a childhood punctuated by illnesses and temporary blindness at aged eight from which she took a long time to recover. By 1926 when they moved to Bologne, she had become a small, vivacious, pretty girl with light hair and eyes. At nineteen she married Roy Sansom, an Englishman in the hotel trade. She had three children, the last two were born in Britain. At the outbreak of the Second World War her husband joined the Army. In October 1940, Odette moved to Somerset for safety and to be near her mother-in-law.

Her marked patriotism for both Britain and France propelled her into SOE, despite leaving three young daughters behind, which she said was the hardest and most painful decision of her whole life. She joined the second SOE women's course in May 1942, along with Lise de Baissac, Jacqueline Nearne and Mary Herbert, where it was noted that she was excitable, rash, stubborn and unwilling to ever admit she was wrong, but also very energetic and likeable. Her greatest handicap occurred during her parachute training when she had a bad fall, which ruled out that form of landing.

The felucca that brought Mary Herbert and Marie-Thérèse le Chêne to the cove near Cassis on 31 October 1942, also carried Odette Sansom. At thirty, she was the youngest of the three women. She was intended to go north to Auxerre, Burgundy, in the occupied zone, but her first destination en route was Cannes. However, when she met agent Peter Churchill (codenamed Raoul), the dynamic organiser of the SPINDLE network, in the back room of the beauty salon there, her plans were to change dramatically.

Matters in the south when Odette arrived in France were in flux. Peter Churchill's mission was two fold. To build up a resistance network called SPINDLE and to work in liaison with André Girard (codenamed Carte), a difficult dreamer, at Antibes, whose plans had impressed Bodington earlier. SOE was attracted to Girard because he boasted of an army of 200,000 trained and armed soldiers, mainly taken from the Vichy Armistice Army. But towards the end of 1942 everything was going wrong. Girard himself quarrelled bitterly with his wireless operator who was unwilling to transmit the terribly long and wordy messages which Girard insisted upon, and he also quarrelled with Frager, his assistant, so much so that Peter Churchill was forced to send the former away. In addition, the organiser of the southern felucca landings, URCHIN, was captured, and on 11 November, the German occupation of the Vichy Zone extended their control over the Riviera coastline. Another misfortune occurred when Girard, to help Francis Suttill (Prosper) in Paris, sent him about 200 names 'in clear' (unencrypted) from his extensive card index of possible supporters, by his courier Marsac. These were stolen during Marsac's train journey from Marseille, and were now, though none of them realised it, in the hands of the German Abwehr. Then, to cap it all, on 29 November 1942 the Vichy Armistice Army was demobilised.

This catalogue of disasters caused Peter Churchill to move closer to his wireless operator, Adolphe Rabinovitch (codenamed Arnaud), and also left him badly in need of a courier he could trust. Since Odette had to wait in Cannes for more papers before she could proceed, she took on a tricky assignment to Marseille for Churchill, only to find when she returned that she had been re-designated as his courier. She was now Madame Odette Metayer (codenamed Lise) of the SPINDLE network in what she considered a most dangerous town, full of holidaymakers, informers and Germans, and where she was shocked by the careless attitude to security of their French supporters.

The only compensations were Churchill and Rabinovitch, whom she liked and trusted and who also prized secrecy. Rabinovitch, however, was in France illegally and had no ration cards, so she had to find food for him. In addition, because he was continually on the move, she was constantly having to find secure places for him to transmit his signals and to live.

She also had to organise and attend their few receptions for air drops, which sometimes went wrong. They were often carelessly placed, such as on ploughed fields, or near German airfields or barracks, and once she only just missed being hunted by German dogs. Nevertheless, they conducted some successful sabotage missions, and Odette, by train or bike, took Rabinovitch's wireless or SPINDLE's sabotage materials wherever they were needed.

Meanwhile, André Girard's organisation was crumbling and his disagreement with Frager reached boiling point. So in February 1943, Girard went to London to put his side of the story. Shortly afterwards SPINDLE members started being arrested in Cannes. Peter Churchill didn't hesitate, and he immediately took his little staff off to St Jorioz in the Haute Savoie, where the mountain folk and the hidden Maquis in the forests strongly supported the resistance. Here Odette felt safer; she and Churchill took rooms in the Hôtel de la Poste, and Rabinovitch resided some distance away, where he could get better wireless reception.

Then the Abwehr decided to move against some of the addresses Marsac had lost and they had found, starting with Marsac himself. In prison Marsac was visited by Sergeant Hugo Bleicher, the Abwehr's most skilful interrogator, who pretended to be 'Colonel Henri', an anti-Hitler, anti-Nazi German, who wanted to end the war. 'Colonel Henri' requested arrangements be made for him to travel London and discuss his plans. Marsac was taken in by Abwehr's charade and suggested that in order to pass on such an important message, as he did not know the wireless operator's address, he could give him that of Odette and Roger Bardet, a new recruit, who would be able to help.

With a note from Marsac, 'Colonel Henri' sought out Odette and Bardet, with the same story. Odette was suspicious and asked London for advice, which was almost contradictory when it arrived and offered her no clear course of action. It was unfortunate that at this time Churchill and Frager were in Britain and not due back until mid-April, leaving her with no-one to turn to, but she trusted Marsac, though uncertain about Bardet. Nevertheless, she intended to leave her present hotel and told 'Colonel Henri' that he could be picked up on 18 April, knowing that Peter Churchill was due to parachute in on 15 April. Rabinovitch moved again, but Odette was so busy that she delayed her move, thinking she had at least two more days before 'Colonel Henri's' departure date, and that she and Churchill would have some time to consult together beforehand. She did not know that Bardet knew the true dates of Churchill's arrival or that London had warned Churchill before he left against Bleicher's story and told him to keep away from Odette, who might be watched.

In the interval, Odette found a good dropping ground on a flat mountain top, and cycled everywhere warning the resistants to take cover.

On time, Churchill parachuted in safely and Odette was at his reception. At their warm reunion all warnings were forgotten and they made their way back for a night's rest at the Hôtel de la Poste. So it was there on the night of 16 April 1943, that they were arrested by Bleicher in his real persona as a member of the Abwehr, together with the Italian police, since they were in an area nominally controlled by the Italians. Churchill immediately requested that they went into Italian custody, which only delayed their handover for a few weeks, but disconcerted the Germans.

Thus they were shunted from prison to prison in Italy and France, and on the occasions when Odette saw Churchill she told him that she would say they were married and that he was the Prime Minister Winston Churchill's nephew and that his presence with her was her fault, as she had persuaded him to join her against his wishes. When she came to face her questioners, both then and in the future, her overwhelming personality easily persuaded them to believe her, with the result that when they were handed over officially to the Germans in May 1943, and taken to Frèsnes and afterwards to the Avenue Foch, Peter Churchill was interrogated far fewer times than Odette, who was questioned twelve times. In addition she said that she had had to withstand torture. Her attitude remained defiant and she continued to hide the whereabouts of Rabinovitch and the arrival of Cammaerts, and repeatedly said, 'I have nothing to say', except for her story about her marriage to Peter Churchill.

Meanwhile, her conditions of imprisonment were quite different from most of the other SOE prisoners. At Frèsnes, she was put into a solitary confinement cell with hermetically sealed windows and so little food that it was hardly surprising that she fell ill several times. In June 1943 she was recalled to the Avenue Foch to be informed officially that she was condemned to death as a French resistance worker and an English spy. However, it seemed to alter things very little, except that she was moved to a warmer cell in Frèsnes, with two occupants and no more questions (no doubt her knowledge in any case by then would have been out of date).

On 12 May 1944, she was collected by a van and locked into a room in the Avenue Foch with seven other women, some no doubt looking as ill and miserable as she felt. She soon found out that they had all belonged to other SOE networks. The room was large and rather impressively decorated and the day sunny. They were offered tea in china cups and given cigarettes. They were evidently awaiting further transport to take them to a Paris railway station. They were then taken by train to Karlsruhe prison for civilian women. There the women were separated and put into cells, which they shared with two or three ordinary German women prisoners, ranging from prostitutes to black marketeers, or those condemned because they had been critical of the government. Odette was held here until 18 July 1944, when she was sent for a short time to Frankfurt and then Halle before she ended up at the women's concentration camp, Ravensbrück, where instead of being treated like other prisoners, she was put into an underground isolation cell in the punishment block known as the Bunker. This was intended as a reprisal for the Allied advances into France and her supposed connection to Churchill.

Though she was not interrogated or tortured again, she could hear the screams and executions of others nearby. The temperature of her cell could be raised and lowered at her jailer's will, stifling or freezing her, but the methods she learned in training and the blindness that afflicted her childhood, taught her the survival techniques she now used to will herself to live. Her main motivation was to see her three daughters again. Despite her strength of mind, she fell ill with scurvy, dysentery, tuberculosis and other chest problems. Incredibly, it seemed that the camp commander wanted to keep her alive, so in late 1944 she was moved to a ground floor cell, given a short exercise period daily and hospital treatment, though still in isolation.

After nearly a year at Ravensbrück in April 1945, saved from the mass extermination of the other SOE prisoners, the Camp Commander, believing her story about Churchill, drove her to the nearest American lines, using her as a hostage for his own life, telling them who she was as he handed her over. Thus ended her long ordeals.

She had survived by a mixture of pluck and luck, without ever letting her will be crushed, although she had to spend a long time in hospital after her return to Britain, overcoming the legacy of her imprisonment.

Later, with becoming modesty, she accepted awards for her bravery, which she saw as a symbol of the bravery of other SOE women who had worked and died for the freedom of France.

9

MARIE-THÉRÈSE LE CHÊNE

A woman full of common-sense and humour.

Peter Churchill (agent)

Marie-Thérèse was born at Sedan in the Ardennes on 20 April 1890, the eldest of a family of three, out of which one of her two brothers was also to work with SOE. A large part of her life was spent in London with her husband, Henri le Chêne, who was a British subject and a hotel manager.

She was the last of the four women on the first women's training course for SOE F agents, having beforehand refused to join de Gaulle's own secret service (BCRA). Her connections with the hotel trade had given her wide experience and taught her to get on well with those around her. On her SOE course she took Andrée Borrel, the youngest, under her wing, mothering her and helping to advise this Parisian 'urchin' on her general behaviour.

Marie-Thérèse was landed from a felucca near Cassis on 31 October 1942 – her age preventing her parachuting. Out of the three women in this party, she did not know the others, who came from the course after hers. When she had recovered from her trip at Cannes, her instructions were amended to tell her not to make her way to Lyon, where she had been supposed to join her husband Henri le Chêne (codenamed Paul), now the organiser of the PLANE network, to act as his courier. She also learned that her surname was to become Ragot and her codename Adèle.

Unfortunately, Marie-Thérèse had only been in the Vichy-controlled zone just over a week when the Germans crossed the demarcation line and took over the area, targeting Lyon, where they knew there was a nest of agents. Warned of this in time, Virginia Hall, before her hasty departure, had left accommodation for Marie-Thérèse in an insignificant corner of Lyon city. It turned out, however, that Marie-Thérèse had little time to use it, as the scope of her work had altered when she met Henri and learned of the reasons for the last-minute change in orders and the new dangers facing them.

Henri had arrived in France in April 1942 prepared for a tour of sabotage and propaganda, but after his first visit to Virginia Hall, he had decided that Lyon felt unsafe and changed his area and work. He still kept his eyes and ears open for information, helpers and suitable landing and dropping zones for aircraft, but most of these were far outside the city, in the less populated areas to the west between Clermont-Ferrand and Périgueux. Here, by moving and splitting his network into two he could use either town as his new headquarters. This change of plan had worked quite well and he found that there was much more support for spreading propaganda in the smaller towns and villages, since they provided the workers for the area, with the added benefit of being able to recruit elderly women of between fifty–sixty into the network, who made the best couriers, as they tended to arouse less suspicion. When he heard that London was sending his wife in that role, he was not pleased, as he said he could recruit any number of suitable women on the spot. Later he commented wryly that he joined SOE to get away from his wife, but that she had followed him into it.

Marie-Thérèse's work changed from courier to distributing anti-German leaflets and tracts, many of them printed under the very noses of the Germans. Of course, there were messages as well, and she was often heavily loaded by bags and parcels, which grew larger and heavier as her travels grew longer. It was helpful that the main-line passenger trains still ran on time, though there were fewer of them, and she soon set herself to find friends at most destinations, where she could stay safely overnight after curfew. Then, chatting in the big fire-lit kitchen with the family, picking up useful information from them, they would often bring out their forbidden and carefully hidden wireless to listen to the French news on the BBC and follow the course of the war.

Some of her travels took her down to Marseille, where she was fortunate to find an active escape organisation skilled in good forgeries of Spanish papers. Through them she heard of contacts in Cannes, Toulon and Antibes, who came from the CARTE network.

As she passed through Clermont-Ferrand, she kept her eye on the Michelin Rubber Works, which her husband assured her was not only distributing her propaganda leaflets but turning out inferior tyres for the Germans, which not only needed constant replacement or repair, but kept the workmen employed and paid, thus avoiding forced labour in Germany. Clermont-Ferrand, the capital of the Auvergne, was a busy industrial town and railway centre, whose workforce strongly favoured the resistance. However, Marie preferred the Dordogne, with its richly wooded landscape, fields and farms, and a flourishing black-market in scarce commodities, especially in its larger towns where shortages were acute. The town of Domme in central Dordogne produced her husband's best landing ground, which he used for collecting sabotage materials and London-produced tracts. The hillsides surrounding it were pock-marked with caves, which proved perfect for storage of supplies.

On one occasion, Marie-Thérèse visited Paris, with her market basket on her arm, innocently carrying sheaves of papers to known helpers in that city. It was here she met her sister-in-law in a café, who later left on record a description of her as a small, grey-haired woman with sharp determined features. She was also surprised to find in that city so many Communists, members of the Francs-Tireurs and Jews in positions high up in the organisation of the networks, who did not always agree with the sentiments expressed in her leaflets, but who had put their differences aside in favour of the liberation of France from the Germans.

Back in Lyon, a busy centre, she was helped by the engineer in charge of the tramway marshalling yards, near one of the railway stations, whose workmen enthusiastically distributed her leaflets among themselves and many of their passengers, giving them a very wide circulation; their popularity was hardly surprising, as most of the leaflets had been produced on these workmen's premises. In this way she spent a satisfactory, if tiring, first few weeks in her husband's network.

In December, her isolation and the bad weather began to tell on her, an effect increased by terrible news from the next door network SPRUCE. Pierre (codenamed Gregoire), her husband's younger brother, who had parachuted in shortly after Henri and become the wireless operator for

SPRUCE, had been caught by the Germans at his set. This triggered off several more arrests, and made Henri afraid of what would happen to PLANE, and indeed, in January arrests began in his network. Henri, who was already beginning to question the value of their work, with so many listening to the BBC, realised it was time to wind up his operations and escape. Marie-Thérèse, now strained and worried, was not well enough to leave over the Pyrénées as he intended to do, but was found a safe house with good friends until she could leave another way.

When she had recovered, she visited Paris to see if she could arrange her own evacuation, and there met Henri Déricourt, the new Air Movements Officer (who organised drops, landings and pick-ups), whom she liked. He explained his schedules were full, but he would contact her when he could take her. Later, back in Lyon, she met agent Robert Boiteux who had taken over the SPRUCE network and was asked if she could do a little courier work for him, since he had moved into the hills north and west of Lyon, an area and people she knew well. Frustrated with inaction, she was eager to help and did so, being involved at least once with a sabotage mission on a canal and railway in the locality. She also told him about Déricourt's work. This proved useful, when Boiteux, feeling he had done all he could in SPRUCE, and knowing that the Germans were closing in, was able to ask Déricourt if he could arrange to pick up all the agents from his network. Marie-Thérèse's exact references for a field near Angers suitable for landing proved the catalyst, and the second moon landing for a Hudson was arranged for the night of 19 August 1943.

That night, after confirmation on the French service of the 9 o' clock BBC news, ten hopeful passengers gathered on the field for the 2am pick-up. Unluckily, the field was found to be filled with horses and cows, which frightened Marie-Thérèse even more than Germans. More worrying was the non-arrival of Déricourt, who should have been there to see to the lights and arrangements, including the cattle. He eventually arrived with two assistants at 11.15pm, offering no explanation for his lateness. Dividing the passengers into three groups, he set about making things ready. After a nail-biting wait the Hudson landed. One man leapt out of the plane and bags of mail were exchanged. Then the passengers were escorted through the rear door. The engines, which had never stopped, speeded up, the plane ran down the field and was airborne. Now, except for enemy planes or anti-aircraft guns, they were away.

Next morning, after an uncomfortable and unremarkable flight, they landed at 6am to have an un-rationed breakfast of bacon and two eggs, and then were taken to be debriefed. Marie-Thérèse also met her husband, who had arrived back in Britain in May after imprisonment in Spain following his escape over the Pyrénées.

Her brief two months of activity in the field had covered nearly half of France, touching roughly ten networks and bringing her in contact with at least twenty agents. It was found that she had spoken to a friend about why she had been away. This was to cause the internal security department great concern, even though she could not be returned, as her network was blown. She was given a stiff warning, with the threat that she might endanger future activities or agents. Unfortunately, it appeared that she did it again. It was a pity that a few boastful and indiscreet words of gossip in Britain should mar a short but successful tour as an agent in France.

However, there was one satisfactory outcome from their ordeals. Her brother-in-law, Pierre, survived his imprisonment and later returned safely.

SONIA OLSCHANEZKY

One of the most beautiful women I have ever seen.

An SOE agent

Sonia Olschanezky was one of the few women agents who had not been trained in Britain, and yet worked for a time for SOE F service.

Sonia's parents were secular Jews: her father was a Russian from Odessa, who became a chemical engineer; her mother was from a moneyed family in Germany. Unable to return to revolutionary Russia after the First World War, they settled in Chemnitz in east Germany, where they had three children. Sonia, the last and only girl, was born on Christmas Day, 25 December 1923. Three years later they all moved to Bucharest in Romania, where her father managed a prosperous silk stockings factory. Growing anti-Semitism saw her father being swindled and led to another move for the family, this time to France, where her father was again defrauded, plunging the family into poverty.

While a schoolgirl of ten, Sonia joined a theatre dance company and planned to become a professional dancer to help the family fortunes. She was a small, slight graceful girl with dark hair and eyes, who was highly intelligent, energetic and capable, as well as resourceful and with steady nerves – as later proved when acting more or less alone for half a year.

The Second World War changed everything for the family. They were stateless, as their father had lost his Russian citizenship, and with so many refugees fleeing to France, jobs were hard to find. Sonia became an underpaid au pair and her brothers joined the Army to gain French citizenship. In 1942 after her father's death, German anti-Jewish laws of May 1942, sent Sonia to be interned at Drancy, where she volunteered to care for the orphaned children, while awaiting transport to the death camps in Germany.* Fortunately, someone intervened and she was freed, with false papers declaring her to have economically useful skills for Germany.

Before her arrest Sonia had become involved in a French resistance movement, and occasionally had helped Jacques Weil, a Swiss businessman with contacts in the French and British Secret Intelligence Services. Her French patriotism too had drawn in the rest of her family. On her return to Paris in autumn 1942, she became more active in a Jewish resistance movement. Mainly she carried messages for this small organisation that Weil was gradually building up, but she was found to have many other gifts, particularly her ability to pick-up useful information from sources as varied as cafés, to the countryside surrounding the city – these snippets often dovetailed with other pieces of intelligence. She had also proved good at organising things. Weil's Prosper (Francis Suttill) contact, through Andrée Borrel, brought him much-needed money from London, and in November Sonia became a paid agent and her work widened.

Now more help was needed, and it came in a reception organised by Andrée Borrel and Suttill, when Jean Worms (another agent) parachuted down on 22 January 1943 near Chartres. Worms had been an old hand at intelligence gathering in Paris in late 1940, and in 1941 had undertaken many tasks, such as investigating ports like Bordeaux, used by blockade runners trying to evade the British watch set to prevent supplies of raw rubber reaching the German war machine. In October 1942, he had been taken to Britain to undergo SOE training.

In this reception party for Worms was also Jacques Weil, his old business friend, and Sonia. Jean Worms, knowing their proven abilities, appointed Weil as his second-in-command and Sonia as his main courier. Weil's earlier resistance organisation now became an official SOE network, sometimes referred to by Jewish resisters as Robin, but called JUGGLER by the British. This gave them easier access to Prosper's wireless operator Gilbert

---

* Her mother had been granted Romanian protection.

Norman until their own wireless operator Gustav Cohen (codenamed Justin) arrived.

Now JUGGLER's task was changed from intelligence gathering to sabotage, mainly on the German troop trains operating in and around Châlons-sur-Marne and other places in the upper Marne area and Châlons itself, concentrating particularly on the important electrified lines, powered by the great pylons south-west of Paris. Additional targets were engineering sheds and locomotives, although sabotage attacks were extended across north-east France to the Channel coast. It helped too in that railwaymen were some of the keenest resistance supporters.

Sometimes Sonia herself took an active role. Once she was assigned to smear abrasive onto a machine vital to the production of industrial belting, of which there was a shortage in German industry. She had to join the workforce of the factory and gain their confidence. It took her weeks to do, and was tricky and very dangerous. This was only one of her daring exploits, until Weil stopped her. Now she was codenamed Tania and Weil had become her fiancé. Sonia, too, had changed her address and adopted a new cover name, Suzanne Ouvrard, but, like Worms and Weil, she remained in Paris. She became even busier, extending her range of travel to St Quentin in the north and Châlons to the east. Because of this she came to know well Gilbert Norman and Andrée Borrel of PHYSICIAN, Garry of CINEMA, and Gustav Bieler with Yolande Beekman the wireless operator of MUSICIAN in St Quentin, as well as many others.

Then disaster struck. Overnight, Andrée and Norman were arrested, quickly followed by Suttill the next day, 24 June 1943. This was followed by the rounding up of other members of PHYSICIAN's network. Since there were so many sub-networks connected with PHYSICIAN, the others took cover and waited with bated breath. A quiet period followed. On 27 June, Worms asked London if he should take over the fragments of what remained of the PHYSICIAN organisation, but this was immediately refused. He was treading on eggshells. Regardless, he called a meeting of surviving organisers on 30 June to discuss security, despite the fact that he hypocritically took no further precautions, even continuing to eat at the same Paris restaurants as before.

Predictably, he was captured at this restaurant on 1 July. Weil, due to meet him but a little late, saw Worms' arrest. With only time to warn Sonia and the wireless operator Gustav Cohen, he escaped to Switzerland and safety. Sonia decided to remain where her family were, although it is believed she accompanied him to the Swiss frontier before turning back. Cohen sensibly hid, eventually escaping over the Pyrénées. Meanwhile, Sonia tried to hold things in JUGGLER together but achieved little.

In mid-January 1944, she heard that Bieler and Yolande, her main route for messages, had been arrested. Later, she heard that another agent was landing to arrange for her to leave her dangerous post, and she was to meet him at a certain café. London had said he was coming in February, but a later message made the appointment for 22 January. Perhaps her delight in receiving help overrode her natural caution. She turned up and was arrested by a man accompanied by the Gestapo; her arrest was followed that night by the arrest of her barman brother.

Interrogated at the Avenue Foch, she gave nothing away. As a courier, she held much information on other networks and members, but she stayed silent. Afterwards she was sent to Frèsnes Prison. On 13 May she joined the seven other women agents in the Avenue Foch, of whom she knew at least two, as they waited for transport to take them to Karlsruhe in Germany, a civil prison for women.

Less than two months later, on 6 July, four of them, including Sonia, were again on the move. This time their destination was the men's concentration camp at Natzweiler. In this group Sonia only knew Andrée Borrel. On arrival, as the women went along the path where some prisoners were digging trenches for a pipeline near the gate, a man later recalled that they looked white and strained, but not starved. Also, with a photographic memory he was able to draw their faces a few years later.

They first were escorted to a room in a hut, where through an openable window, two of them spoke to some prisoners in a nearby hut. The women were seen brushing their hair and talking. Then they were separated and at about 10pm they were taken one by one to another hut, which was the crematorium building, though they did not know it. There they were told to lie down on one of the eight white beds in a room, and given a lethal injection of phenol. Afterwards their bodies were dragged to the ovens and cremated.

For many years it was believed that Noor Inayat Khan, who fitted a similar description to that of Sonia, was the fourth woman who died at Natzweiler. Much later it became a 'mysterious' person. It was not realised that this fourth victim was Sonia, as she was not a listed SOE agent, until the investigations of Elizabeth Nicholas in 1958 proved it, and gave Sonia a place among the brave women who had worked for SOE F service in France and died tangled in the fatal web around PHYSICIAN.

I I

JACQUELINE NEARNE

I think her one of the best we have found!

Maurice Buckmaster

Jacqueline, born at Brighton on 27 May 1916, was the second child in a family of four, with an English father and a mother of Spanish extraction. The children spent most of their family life in France, where the two girls were educated in French convents. They all lived for some time in the Pas de Calais and then Nice, and at eighteen Jacqueline became a commercial traveller for a firm. After the Germans invaded France, Jacqueline with her sister managed to escape through Gibraltar to Britain in 1942, where she joined the FANY, and because of her fluent French was passed on to SOE. There she went into the second group of women training as F section agents, along with Mary Herbert, Odette Sansom and Lise de Baissac, the latter becoming her great friend. Her sister Eileen underwent the training for a home-based wireless operator, as Jacqueline was opposed to her being an agent, on the grounds that she was too young. Later she withdrew her opposition.

Jacqueline had mixed results on her training course. She was found to be very good on the practical work but poor at the theory. She also acquired the nickname of 'Jackie Red Socks' when she found that French and English knitting was so different that the Germans could recognise it. She therefore set herself to knit several pairs of socks in red wool for her fellow agents. Nevertheless she was passed to be a courier and joined with her organiser, Maurice Southgate (codenamed Hector), to form a new network in the middle of France called STATIONER.

They flew in on the night of 25 January 1943, and parachuted 'blind' (without a reception party) near Brioude in the Auvergne, and were so disoriented in the shadows, that Jacqueline nearly shot her organiser, thinking him a German. Later, Southgate, uncertain of their direction asked a woman cyclist the way 'in English', which Jacqueline hastily covered in French. They finally found their safe house in Clermont-Ferrand and started work seeking out their contacts.

Posing as Josette Norville, the representative of a chemical firm, enabled Jacqueline to travel everywhere freely, and as a result, despite being shy, she began to gain confidence. She was small, dark and slight, with a rather chameleon appearance, fitting in unobtrusively wherever she went. At first she stayed in hotels when away, until, staying for a week at a hotel in Châteauroux, she was interrogated twice in routine checks by the French Police. Fortunately she had just received some new identity documents, though she did wonder if they might question why they were so new, but they never did. This taught her never to stay in hotels again except for meals, though in any case shortly she found that the Germans commandeered many of them. After that, she turned to establishing bases for herself for overnight stays, such as in rooms at Clermont-Ferrand or La Souterraine, or an apartment in Paris, if not staying with resistance members, or in a small farm before her pick-up in April 1944. Her security training in Britain was always uppermost in her mind.

Southgate initially started by collecting up small resistance groups, already in existence, mainly around Clermont-Ferrand and Châteauroux. He then took in a small active group in Tarbes and Pau, near the foothills of the Pyrénées. He encouraged all of them to have their own leaders, answerable to but rarely meeting him, except through intermediaries and with carefully coded words of recognition. Many of the most active members were Communists, who worked well with him. When either Jacqueline or Southgate visited these groups, their contacts were usually different and with different codes.

With so widespread an area, Jacqueline had to make long train journeys on the still good railway network, though Southgate once apologised for having sabotaged one of her routes the day before. The fast expresses were subject to searches and controls, whereas the slower trains were relatively free from these. Such travel might take her occasionally to Paris, and then Châteauroux, Clermont-Ferrand, Poitiers, Montluçon, and Limoges in the Auvergne, and then as far as Toulouse, Tarbes and Pau in the Midi Pyrénées, to mention only a few of her destinations. In addition she had to meet Southgate at least three times a week, and he was constantly on the move. Also there were frequent calls on other networks with wireless operators, including Jones of HEADMASTER, until their own wireless operator, Amédée Maingard (codenamed Samuel), at last arrived. From that time Jacqueline acted as courier between him and Southgate, or on other networks which had lost their operator. Maingard had to be constantly on the move too. It became easier when he at last stayed with a trustworthy family near Montluçon. These incessant journeys gave her little time for sleep, except on the overnight trains.

Inevitably, many of her messages concerned receptions, and though she rarely saw them, a number of male and female agents arrived for other networks on Southgate's fields. In September 1943, Pearl Witherington (codenamed Marie) landed to be a fellow courier to Jacqueline, by which time Southgate had begun to take an interest in a number of Maquis groups. Because he was always very careful of security, Southgate only included Jacqueline in one reception with him, which was in April 1943, when Maingard arrived. Normally Southgate preferred only to employ people outside his organisation, but if the fields for a reception were on a farm, the farmer himself often preferred to be involved. Southgate had many reception grounds and would use a good one for as long as it was safe. Generally the only difficulties he encountered were if London told him a wrong number of packages, the Gestapo often picking up the surplus, and by this discovering the landing ground, making it unusable in the future.

Once, outside Tarbes, the planes dropped the loads for two receptions at the same time and the place was covered with parachutes. Consequently, when the Gestapo arrived next day, Southgate was hurrying away containers by one path, while the Germans were doing the same on another.

In October 1943, Southgate was recalled to London for further briefing, and in the interval three disasters befell the STATIONER network. Southgate's principal assistant, Octave Chantraine, a local farmer, who had been with the mainly communist FTP (the Francs-tireurs et Partisans) since 1941, was arrested. At Christmas, Maingard fell ill and could not see properly. Around the same time Pearl was held up in Paris with a bout of neuralgic rheumatism, the result of long nights sleeping in cold trains. Jacqueline, having no one else to rely on, had to lean on Maingard, and he struggled on, never letting her down. With the new year of 1944, they had more or less recovered and were all greatly relieved when on 28 January, Southgate returned. He heard that the Germans had put a price of 1 million francs on his head. He also announced that his objectives had been changed. He was to concentrate less on sabotage and more on working with the Maquis.

In the past, part of Jacqueline's task had been to find suitable landing grounds, safe houses and ferrying various bits of equipment around with messages. Consequently, although sabotage was low key, some successes had been achieved, with attacks on factories at Limoges, the aluminium factory at Lannemezan, several small-scale attempts on the Michelin factory at Clermont-Ferrand and the munitions factories at Montluçon and Tarbes; an attack on the hydro-electric dam at Eguzon was also under consideration.

While in Paris in late 1943, Jacqueline had noticed that the German attitude to the French population was changing for the worse, and that the seasoned troops in the towns were being replaced by younger ones. There were more informers too among the people of whom she had to be careful and there was a big growth of the much-hated Vichy Milice, whose cruelty had alienated many. The increasing impatience of the Germans and the more frequent rafles, also had resulted in adding to the numbers of young Frenchmen leaving their towns and villages to hide in the woods and hills. They formed small groups of outlaw-like bands who joined up with the existing Maquis and became some of the fiercest resistance groups, although they were not very effective until organised, trained and armed. Such groups had existed since the invasion of France, but were now growing larger and stronger, and it was these that SOE and the Allies were realising might be forged into a valuable asset under the right leadership, to aid the Allies in their liberation plans.

These were the bodies that Southgate had been instructed to foster and help. In his area there were three particular Maquis groups at Bistro, Terracon and Souterraine (the latter was where Jacqueline had one of her rooms). These were to be supplied with arms and supplies, which were being dropped in increasing quantities. In February 1944, another agent arrived to take over and train some of the southern groups, thus lessening some of Jacqueline's travels. Later, another new agent arrived to take over the receptions.

As these relief positions were put in place, Jacqueline learned that London wanted her back for a rest. Though the message came in January, she could not manage to leave until February, due to the increasing number of drops that had to be dealt with. Then in March, the ground chosen for the Lysander pick-up proved unsuitable. It was, therefore, April before her departure could be arranged. Even then it was difficult. She had to wait three days in a farm, near the intended field. On the third day she had to hide in the hay of a barn when the labourers came to work. Eventually the plane arrived in the dark, she embarked and next morning, on 10 April 1944, she arrived safely in Britain for a long convalescence.

12

FRANCINE AGAZARIAN

*Germans were everywhere, especially in Paris; one absorbed the sight of them
and went on with the job of living and applying oneself to one's work.*

Francine Agazarian

Francoise Isabella Andre was born in Narbonne, south-east France on
8 May 1913 to French parents. As an English-speaking secretary, when
France joined the war she planned to go to Britain, and used a marriage of
convenience to a Sergeant in the Signals Corps, who said he was an escaped
prisoner of war, to enable her to gain entrance to Britain. When she arrived
there in September 1941, she discovered he was already married, so instead,
in late 1942, she married her former fiancé, a naturalised British citizen, the
handsome RAF officer Jack Agazarian, and later followed him into SOE.

A serious-minded pretty young woman, she was intended to act as
courier to her husband, Jack, and to work with him on his signals. He had
been in post as an SOE wireless operator since the end of 1942, sent to assist
Gilbert Norman, who was working for Francis Suttill of the PHYSICIAN
network in Paris. Unfortunately because of the shortage of wireless
operators, Jack found that he was sometimes handling messages to London
for other agents from as many as twenty-four different networks, as well as

those for Suttill, and later in 1943 for Henri Déricourt (the Air Movement Officer for SOE's northern networks). This increased his difficulties, since, like Suttill, he was fiercely concerned for his safety in such a dangerous milieu as Paris. In order to maintain security he had to keep moving his wireless transceiver regularly from place to place, to escape the ever-watching German Direction Finders.* Despite Francine's frail appearance, and somewhat temperamental personality and her often possessive nature, it was felt she would work well with her husband.

Thus, she became one of the four passengers in the double Lysander landings south of Poitiers on 18 March 1943. It was the first flight arranged by Déricourt. After a short rest during the curfew, Francine (codenamed Marguerite), now known as Francine Fabre, spent the early part of her first day travelling in a very crowded train from Poitiers to Paris. Sitting on her small suitcase in the corridor, she was crushed against a German soldier, who, fortunately for her, could not know that the suitcase at their feet contained a revolver and ammunition and, wrapped securely around her waist, under a wide black cloth belt, were bank notes, blank identity and ration cards for Francis Suttill, while hidden in her sleeves were some more crystals for her husband's wireless.

These little quartz crystals were an important component of the wirelesses, or as they became known 'transceivers', which could be used to send (transmit) and receive messages. They were small and breakable, and were usually packed in a little box. The crystal would determine the wavelength of the transmission and the best way of controlling the stability of it. The receiving stations for the Special Forces in Britain were tuned to the transmissions from particular transceivers. These British receiving stations were manned by people often from FANY who had signed the Official Secrets Act and were not allowed to speak of their work. They were located at Grendon, Poundon, Bicester and Dunbar. The signals, which were, of course, in code were then passed on to be decoded (translated). In time, after much use on certain wavelengths, the crystals would need replacing, and these were what Francine was bringing for her husband, Jack.

In Paris she found her way to the Champs Élysées, where another agent Julienne Aisner, had her offices for her normal daily work. Francine stayed there for the rest of the day and spent the night in its little studio apartment before setting out to find the furnished apartment in the Rue de Colonel

---

* Teams and equipment set up to track signals from wireless communications.

Mol which Juliennne had rented for them. Jack joined her there, and they lived there in the intervals between his disappearing to other parts of the city, often several times a day, to transmit his signals.

Later, since Francine worked more as Suttill's courier than Jack's, she would carry his messages and instructions, either by bike or train to various people, not just in Paris but to many more distant places of the widely dispersed sub-networks or others impinging on their own, in towns, villages or rural areas. She often also transported wireless parts and demolition materials (including grenades on one occasion) in her innocent-looking shopping bag. Always present were the Gestapo and police, controls and check-points, stops and searches, and everyday activity to meet, whether on bike, tram or train, questions and more questions, and papers that had to always be perfectly signed and correct. She soon grew very familiar with these, as Suttill would send her to the town halls of various districts to take time-expired ration cards or local papers (actually clever forgeries) to exchange for the real thing. As she knew her way around the people and places of officialdom in Paris, this proved to be a very useful function, and one which saved the unmasking of many agents and resistants.

Very rarely did Jack and Francine have a quiet time together in their apartment. The concierge had been told that they were escaping a jealous husband, so she didn't interfere or ask their names. However, work often interfered, for there was the coding and decoding of messages for Jack, which was part of Francine's task. Therefore, it was a rare pleasure when they could go out for meals to restaurants they could trust, or the homes of other network members, and occasionally they took coffee in cafés, where they met with Suttill, Andrée Borrel and Gilbert Norman to play poker, or if they felt safe to discuss present or future problems, or plans – sometimes in English, while quietly alongside them in the corner Francine carried on coding and decoding Jack's messages.

The work seemed unending. Suttill's network was growing too large and too fast, in the opinion of many, despite all his attempts to maintain security. Later it proved too, that one of his most trusted collaborators was a double agent. One problem occurred not long after Francine arrived, when in May, Suttill left for about a month in London. In the interval, the Germans, who had already gained control of the SOE networks in Holland, sent two spies to Paris, posing as Dutch escapees, asking for a flight to London. They were meant to meet Déricourt or Norman, but Jack happened to see them instead, and wanting to be helpful, and knowing Déricourt's flight schedules (which Jack often arranged for him), Jack advised them to return on 9 June, when he could tell them if it could be done. When they arrived in a café as arranged, one seemed to be picked up by the Germans – leaving a plane seat empty. At the same time negotiations were continuing on Suttill's behalf to release two women held by the Germans – exposing other resistants to the Germans.

Meanwhile life for Francine was still a whirlwind of activity and occasional arrests in the network, but the continuous travelling, the dangers and the stresses were gradually wearing her down, as she already had a frail physique and low stamina. She had always been thin and grew thinner, fearing that any minute a mistake might cause her or Jack's capture. The excitement of adventure in the heady atmosphere of Paris had faded, leaving her pale drawn and nervous. Jack, of a more robust constitution, could see this and grew so concerned that after three months he requested SOE to have her returned to Britain. She wanted to carry on but was overruled (as a tired courier was a danger to the network) so it was arranged.

Also, all was not well among the close-knit group of agents in PHYSICIAN, and the main trouble seemed to emanate from Suttill and Jack, neither of whom liked one another. There were many reasons, but principally that Suttill did not fully trust Jack, and by the time Suttill returned on 12 June he was sure that Jack was exceeding his position. There was no room for two leaders. Jack, on the other hand, did not trust Suttill's judgement, especially in regard to Déricourt.

Therefore, when the double Lysanders left on 17 June they carried, not only Francine Agazarian, as expected, but in the spare seat, Jack Agazarian. Francine, torn between her loyalty to Suttill and the network, was only too glad to feel that she and her husband were both returning to the relative sanity and safety of Britain. Neither could have known that they were leaving only just a week ahead of the break up and mass arrests of the PHYSICIAN network.

13

JULIENNE AISNER

*For one and half years she sheltered more than 50 officers British and
French being sought by the Gestapo, taking daily risks in cold blood...'*
From citations for Croix de Guerre

Julienne Marie Louise Simart had a colourful and exciting life. She was
born in the village of Anglure near Troyes in 1900, one of three children
of French parents; her father was a policeman in Châlon-sur-Marne. She
grew up to be an exceedingly beautiful and attractive woman, small and
full of energy with a round face, softly curling dark hair and large liquid
dark eyes.

In about 1924, she married Lieutenant M. Lauler of the US Marine Corps
and went to live in Miami, Florida, where her son was born. In 1927, her
husband was killed in a car accident, so in 1929, with her son, she rejoined
her parents, who were now posted to Lebanon. On her father's retirement
they all moved to Hanoi to join her sister, whose father-in-law owned a
chain of cinemas. As the climate made Julienne ill, she returned to France
in 1933, and worked as a scriptwriter to a film studio. She married Robert
Aisner in 1935, with whom, helped by her Hanoi contacts, she became a
partner in a small film company.

From her Paris office, overlooking the Champs Élysées, she was a daily witness, after the German occupation in 1940, of the shooting of hostages, the rounding up of citizens for deportation and the growing cruelty of the Gestapo. With her husband in the Army, and her son sent to an aunt in America, she was free from reprisals on her close family when she helped the French resistance. However, slapping the face of a German officer, who made improper suggestions to her, landed her in the Cherche-Midi prison for two months. Shortly afterwards, in June 1941, her divorce from Robert Aisner came through, giving the film business to her.

In January 1943, she was visited in her office by a tramp, who turned out to be Henri Déricourt, a former lover, who was now living with his wife in Paris. He had been appointed by SOE as their Air Movements Officer for the north of France. He trusted her, and because of her local knowledge and her useful contacts he wanted to employ her to help him, and she agreed. Over the winter months he travelled widely, looking for suitable landing sites, which he reported back to London through agents, Gilbert Norman or Jack Agazarian in the PHYSICIAN network, meanwhile forming a very small and separate network, FARRIER, with Julienne and another resistant member as his assistants. Julienne's chief task was to look for suitable rented apartments (seven in all) for his incoming and outgoing passengers – the rent paid by SOE money. She was also to collect various false identity documents and other papers, assisted by her cousin's husband, who worked in the town hall at St Ouen. She additionally helped to acclimatise new agents to occupied Paris.

On 18 March 1943, Déricourt called her down to Poitiers for the first landing of two Lysanders, the only reception in which she actively took part. In a quiet farm field, the planes arrived one after the other to land and pick up passengers. One of the former was Francine Agazarian, for whom she found an apartment with her husband Jack. Seeing how efficiently Julienne had managed and how well they worked together, Déricourt sent her to be given SOE training on 15 April, she having told her business partner and staff that she was taking a month's holiday. A month later, on 14 May, Julienne, now codenamed Claire, returned in a double Lysander reception at Azay-sur-Cher, accompanied by another female agent, Vera Leigh, for whom she allocated an apartment, as she did later for Noor Inayat Khan.

In Paris Julienne was warmly welcomed back by Jean Besnard, another resistant, a barrister, and her present fiancé and future husband, whose contacts had proved very useful.

She learned also that while she was away Déricourt had Jack Agazarian transferred to him as his wireless operator. This set her another task, since Jack was a young man and thus risked being taken in the rafles for forced labour (STO) in Germany. Her solution was a retouched X-ray showing him to have an ulcer and a forged hospital certificate, detailing that he was waiting for a room for his operation. This and other ploys she used for later visitors were an important part of her role in keeping agents working safely below the radar, as well as sheltering aircrew, whom she housed or acclimatised to their new surroundings.

One difficulty was Madame Gouin, wife of one of General de Gaulle's ministers, who had to be smuggled out of France quietly. Her problem was that the wife had too much luggage, which she would not leave behind. As the lady was very well known in Paris, Julienne did not dare to bring her there until the very last minute, but getting her to the train was almost bound to attract attention, with Julienne and Madame Gouin in one velo-taxi, followed by two more loaded with luggage. Fortunately, Julienne got away with it.

A different kind of problem was when her business partner's tuberculosis symptoms seemed to increase. She advised and sent him for a stay in the mountains at Briançon, in a hospital which had previously given him treatment. The suspicious Gestapo found his hospital address and came to collect him, but discovering him in bed with a high temperature, they, with surprising consideration, went away. The next day they came back, only to find that, tipped off, he had disappeared and joined the local Maquis.

One problem that was soon solved, as it turned out, was Jack Agazarian. In June, he was flown out with his wife but leaving Déricourt again needing to use other wireless operators. The arrest of Suttill in late August 1943 and many in his PHYSICIAN network, must also have shaken Julienne and those in Paris. Déricourt had merely shrugged his shoulders, remarking that this was why it was so essential that they (FARRIER) remained an independent organisation, as breaching security was one of the risks of growing too large.

Due to the upsets in the PHYSICIAN network, Jack's replacement, Adher Watt, did not arrive until October. Watt and the Besnards became very friendly, and to make it look normal Julienne sometimes invited him to join them at dinner in a restaurant or at the theatre. Beneath his rather foppish manner, Watt hid a sharp mind and Julienne nicknamed him their 'pocket radio' as he was even shorter than she was. On the same flight came another helper for Déricourt – Rémy Clément, who became his second-in-command and thus made up the full staff for FARRIER.

On 2 July 1943, a month after the PHYSICIAN network was destroyed, Bodington, deputy to Buckmaster in charge of the SOE networks in France, flew out to investigate what had happened in Paris. Bodington also brought along Jack Agazarian, whom Julienne had seen off a month before. At the toss of a coin, as Bodington later explained, Jack was chosen to visit the address thought to be Norman's. As he never returned, Bodington feared him arrested and Julienne moved Bodington further away.

A few days later, fellow agent Vera Leigh called at Julienne's office requesting an immediate interview with Bodington. He saw her and, calling Julienne as witness, they discovered that Vera had said that Henri Frager of the DONKEYMAN network was accusing Déricourt of being a traitor. Bodington then asked to see Frager. The result of this meeting was that Bodington wondered if Frager himself was a double agent or mad. Déricourt naturally was told, but nothing was decided by the time Bodington left on 15/16 August. A peculiar event occurred much later in October when Vera again appeared at Julienne's repeating the accusations and warned Julienne that the Gestapo planned to remove her as she was distracting Déricourt from fully co-operating with them. At this Julienne wrote to London for advice, sending her letter through Déricourt, as he carried all the surface mail to and fro on his landings.

Another event in Bodington's colourful August visit was his approval for Julienne to buy a small café, called the café Mas, through which all Lysander requests or contacts for the escape lines could be made. As the patronne of the bistro, she would call in daily and collect any messages, often hidden in a box of candies. This seemed to work very well.

October 1943 threw up more confusion; Roger Bardet was trying to arrange, through the café, to fly his organiser Frager to London. Julienne's meeting with Bardet on the day before the flight aroused her suspicion, so she warned Déricourt beforehand. Finally, on the field itself there was a mix up about who was taking the flight. In the end Frager did. London later informed Julienne that Frager would not be returning, and that it had complete confidence in Déricourt. Much later, when she saw Bardet again he told her that Vera had been arrested, and as he had lost his wireless operator, would she please pass a message through Watt to London. However, Watt later reported that Bardet appeared to have already sent the message. Julienne wondered who had taken it.

Things then went quiet for a while. Winter weather prevented some flights until February 1944, but March proved to be a puzzling month.

Besnard, who had supported Julienne in all she did, began to feel that they were being followed and that their telephones were being tapped. Also London reported that Bardet had been arrested, yet a few days later Bardet reappeared in the café with another man. Then two men, who looked like policemen, wanted to see the patronne, and a day later another man turned up asking openly about escape lines. Bardet, too, returned to the café asking to see Julienne in case he had more messages. Even Besnard, in his office, had a warning from a client that he was about to be arrested.

At the end of the month, Julienne, Besnard and Watt took council, and the next day, while Watt tried to contact Clément to tell London, Julienne closed the café Mas. Then she and Besnard went to their offices as usual. In the evening, instead of going home, each separately took a train to the suburbs and the safe house where Watt was living. Afterwards they all travelled by Troyes and Amboise to their Lysander pick-up arranged by another agent. Julienne also sent a letter to the concierge of her apartment in Paris, telling her to continue to look after it. The flight went smoothly and they arrived in London safely on 6 April 1944. Later they learned that the Gestapo had not visited and searched Julienne's apartment until July. The Besnards finally returned to it after Paris had been liberated.

Much later a number of pieces of information concerning Déricourt emerged. He had been withdrawn by London in February 1944, because of uncertainty over more accusations of betrayal, but he had arranged seventeen successful operations involving twenty-one aircraft. In 1948, he was tried in France as a traitor but acquitted due to lack of evidence, his chief supporter being Bodington, who in his London office had pencilled a note on a file on 23 June 1943. It said 'We know he is in contact with the Germans and also how and why'. In addition, from some of his own words, it seems he had been 'leaned on' by the SD – his wife was living in Paris. With the SD it appears that he had reached an agreement that they would not interfere with his friends or his operations, and that he would pass to them copies of all the mail his planes carried. There is no doubt that he *was* a double agent, but, nevertheless, he had protected those with whom he worked, like Julienne. Inevitably, his actions cast a shadow of suspicion on Julienne, who was so closely associated with him throughout this period. How much did she know or guess – or was she an innocent? And what about Bodington? How did his support of Déricourt fit in with the truth?

14

VERA LEIGH

She had lodgings quite near me. For months I would watch her, so busy so
affairée. She was of no interest to me; so long as she kept out of my way,
she could play at spies.

Sergeant Hugo Bleicher (Abwehr)

Vera Eugènie Leigh had an unusual background. She was born Vera Glass on
17 March 1903 in Leeds, but was adopted as a baby by Eugène Leigh, a rich
American racehorse trainer with a stables near Maisons Laffitte (a racecourse
near Paris). After her adoption, Vera became Vera Eugènie Leigh. As Eugène's
wife was English, Vera spent her early years around his stables in England
and France and became a fine horsewoman. When Eugène died, his widow
married again and had a son, who always remained friendly with her adopted
daughter. After college Vera gained experience as a dress designer in Paris at the
house of Caroline Reboux. Then, aged twenty-four, she founded with two
others La Grande Maison Rose Valois, noted for its '*hâute couture*', where she
proved good at business and took her place as a smart society woman.

On the German occupation, she fled Paris for Lyon to join her long-
time fiancé Charles Saissaux, the managing director of a Portuguese film
company, with the intention of making for England, but was sidetracked

into helping the French resistance, guiding downed aircrew on the 'Pat' escape line and meeting with the American Virginia Hall. In 1942, with the Germans on her trail she crossed the Pyrénées on her own but was caught by the Spanish and imprisoned at Miranda de Ebro, this was a prison very like a concentration camp, about 40 miles (64.4 km) south of Bilbao. She was released by the British Embassy and sent to Britain by way of Gibraltar. There, as a Frenchwoman very familiar with Paris, she was snapped up by SOE and responded magnificently to training, despite being forty years old. She had a pleasant manner, was easy to get on with, of supple mind and body, very confident and the best shot of her group.

In the early morning of 14 May 1943, she arrived on a double Lysander landing, masterminded by Henri Déricourt, on a field east of Tours. Her assumed identity was Suzanne Chavanne, a milliner's assistant (codenamed Simone); her mission was to act as courier to her organiser Sidney Jones (codenamed Elie) of the INVENTOR network. He was the liaison officer to Henri Frager of DONKEYMAN, mainly centred in the Yonne, both forming sub-networks to Francis Suttill of PHYSICIAN. Other passengers on the Lysanders were Marcel Clech (codenamed Bastien) their wireless operator, and Julienne Aisner (codenamed Claire) freshly returned from training, with whom Vera became very friendly, visiting her almost every day, despite SOE's security rules, perhaps because she may have believed that these applied to her working rather than private life.

At 3am on the morning of their arrival, leaving the men to deal with the fourteen suitcases, the two women cycled together through the moonlit fields and lanes, a good 6.2 miles (10 km) cross-country to catch the 8pm train, well after the curfew was raised.

Once arrived in Paris, Vera went to the first of Julienne's flats, one in Neuilly-sur-seine, later followed by one in the rue Lauriston, near what turned out to be the headquarters of a notorious underworld spy gang in the pay of the Germans. She stayed there quite a while, finally turning it over to an agency and finding her own flat in the rue Pergolese and Marbeau, on the doorstep of the Gestapo headquarters and neighbour of Sergeant Bleicher, an investigator of the Abwehr. She seemed to be strangely unfortunate in her choice of locations. In London an acquaintance described her as 'not very pretty and less of a Parisienne than she believed herself'; she was certainly not cautious enough.

The INVENTOR network had been fairly active in late 1942, being credited with setting fire to fifty goods wagons shortly after the German occupation of Vichy, and although its actions ceased in winter, in the summer of 1943 with DONKEYMAN, its tentacles began to stretch east of the Ardennes and even down to Marseille.

Settled in Paris, she now threw herself enthusiastically into her new work as courier to Jones, oblivious, it seems, to its dangers. She was regularly carrying messages to and from their wireless operator, Clech, at his living quarters in the suburbs, and had pre-arranged meetings in cafés with Jones and his bodyguard, since so many of her messages and visits concerned him and he was not always to be found in Paris. She also transported, or had helpers take, wireless pieces or sabotage materials and arms to eager resisters both inside or outside Paris, where single German soldiers were daily killed in its streets, with the usual hostage reprisals. All of this activity entailed long train journeys for Vera.

Paris was a great, elegant city, especially as the surrounding villages, parks, townships, estates, working class suburbs and woodlands had been swallowed up to form one vast conurbation, that seemed to separate it into many independent neighbourhoods linked only by the roads, the railways and the Métro. It was easy to be unaware of things that were happening only a few blocks away, unless someone made you aware of them. Thus it was that Vera seemed hardly concerned by the almost cataclysmic arrest and fall of Suttill in late June and the gradual disintegration of his PHYSICIAN network and followers. Perhaps she simply had not heard about it. This must be the only explanation of her behaviour after the news must have filtered through – the distance between them was very small – making her either hardened, not very bright or exceedingly brave, indeed others in the sub-networks around her behaved much the same, equally unperturbed by the unfolding events. Did they not realise the danger?

This can be the only explanation of her actions, barely a few weeks afterwards, when it appears that, as well as carrying out her normal courier work, she began to try to pick up some of her earlier life, visiting shops, theatres and even her previous hairdresser, simply ignoring the danger of being recognised. She also found safe houses for a few downed aircrew, renewing some of her earlier 'Pat' escape line acquaintances.

Possibly informed by Julienne during one of the calls, she knew that Bodington was visiting from London in July 1943, and soon after he arrived, she appeared in Julienne's office white-faced and upset, asking to see him urgently. He arrived and was later joined by Julienne, to whom she revealed that Frager was accusing Déricourt of being a double agent.

Naturally Bodington wanted to see Frager, and when Vera brought him, Frager was able to explain why he thought this. There was a heated exchange, after which the two men parted.

Things went quiet and then in October Vera returned to Julienne with yet another warning from Frager, even suggesting that Julienne herself was in danger from the Germans because she was distracting Déricourt from his work, but Julienne only laughed. Soon afterwards Frager flew out to London and did not return, leaving Bardet in his place for DONKEYMAN. Meanwhile, Vera herself was receiving warnings from several other people, including Bardet, that her own life was in danger and that she should leave Paris immediately, but she took no notice. Nevertheless, by late October it was evident that she was under pressure, and a visit to a doctor diagnosed her with suspected tuberculosis and an appointment for an X-ray was arranged. She did not turn up for the appointment.

On 30 October, she came for a meeting with Jones's bodyguard at the café Mas, a favourite gathering place for many agents, especially those requiring a flight through Déricourt, as he was often to be found there. They were both sitting enjoying their coffee, and had no doubt exchanged messages, when Bleicher of the Abwehr arrived and arrested them.

They were taken to the Avenue Foch, where there was little need for more than a brief interrogation, as the Germans appeared to know all they wanted. Vera had made too many mistakes. Then she was packed off to the women's floor of Frèsnes Prison, to stay in the crowded bleak place, lost to her world. Exactly a year after her arrival in France, she was awakened early, and with three other women escorted to a prison van for a short drive to the Avenue Foch.

There, in the faded splendour of a drawing room, they were joined by four other women. They all had one thing in common: F service of SOE. Contrary to what they might have been expecting, they were not interrogated. Instead, they were served tea in china cups. Later they were driven to a Paris railway station and in one compartment of the train, handcuffed to one another, taken on a long journey to the civil prison at Karlsruhe. Here, separated from each other but sharing a cell with other women, Vera was more comfortable and better fed than at Frèsnes. She also learned from her fellow prisoners that the Allies had landed in France and liberation had begun.

Two months later, in July 1944, awakened early and handed back her belongings by a wardress, Vera, with three others, was driven in a locked van to the men's concentration camp of Natzweiler-Struthof, where she was recognised by at least one prisoner. They arrived in the afternoon, and at first were put together in the same cell, where Vera evidently asked for a pillow. Shortly afterwards, she and the others were separated. A later investigator believed that she was then brutally whipped and probably raped.

Late that evening she was escorted to another block. There she was given an injection of phenol; she was told this was to protect her from typhus. Her death would have been quick, and when certified, her body was cremated and reduced to ashes. She was forty-one years old.

15

NOOR-UN-NISA INAYAT KHAN

A splendid, vague, dreamy creature — far too conspicuous — twice seen, never forgotten'

A London friend

Noor Inayat Khan's brown hair and skin, hazel eyes and slightly foreign accent made her noticeable. She was timid, gentle and unworldly, terrified of loud noises and heights, but was possessed of great sweetness and unexpected firmness. A fellow airwoman described her as 'fey'. A loner, she was surely a most unlikely person to be an SOE agent, but at a time when the organisation was desperately short of wireless operators, she was an already trained and particularly good one, as well as being eager to do anything to help liberate France. Her bravery, shining innocence and idealism impressed everyone.

Born in the Vasco Petrovsky Monastery of Moscow in pre-revolutionary Russia, on New Year's Day 1914, she was the eldest of the four children of an American mother of British descent and an Indian musician and religious teacher of the mystical Sufi sect, a branch of Islam. Noor could claim Tipu Sultan, the last Mogul ruler of Mysore, and an American senator and an evangelist in her inheritance. This made her a princess and of British blood.

In 1920, after a few years in London, the family moved to the quiet suburb of Suresnes in Paris which became her father's headquarters and their home. As they were very poor, only living on the charity of her father's followers, it fell to Noor at thirteen to fend for them, after her mother's breakdown following her father's early death.

She was a talented scholar. In 1938, she took a Psychology Degree alongside other studies, including six years of training on music and harp. She wrote children's stories in French and English, several of which were published and broadcast in France and Britain.

This promising career was interrupted by the war, and in 1940 the family escaped to Britain where her eldest brother joined the Royal Navy and she the WAAF. Her records show that she entered as Nora Inayat Khan, and, by a strange quirk, was registered as Church of England. She was trained as a wireless operator, but because of chilblains her Morse key had a wide gap, causing her to be nicknamed 'Bang away Lulu'. Despite this, she was so good that she was sent on an advanced course, raising her Morse speeds.

Her fluent French led her to SOE, and she began training in February 1943, with Cecily Lefort and Yolande Beekman, the latter from her WAAF wireless course. An earlier operation excused her from parachute training, but she spent longer on codes and misunderstood her instructions on 'filing her messages after use', which she thought meant 'keeping' instead of destroying them. This was to prove disastrous, although others tried to correct her. The head of SOE's codes section hoped she would not be sent into the field as 'she had no security sense'. Another difficulty proved to be her inability to lie – her solution was to say nothing. It was reported at the end of her course that she was too temperamental and unsuitable for the field.

Despite knowing the dangers, she still asked to be sent to Paris, which at that moment happened to be urgently appealing for another wireless operator. Although her security course was unfinished, because of the critical shortage of operators Buckmaster overruled the uncertainties, so she was to be the first female wireless operator of the F service sent to France.

On the night of 17 June 1943, she landed at Vieux Briollay, north-east of Angers, on a double Lysander reception masterminded by Henri Déricourt. With her came Cecily Lefort, Diana Rowden and another male agent. Noor was now to be Jeanne-Marie Renier, a children's nurse, codenamed Madeleine. Paris was the centre of many sub-networks to PHYSICIAN, its premier one organised by Francis Suttill. Noor was to be the wireless operator to a sub-network called CINEMA/PHONO, active in the Sarthe and the Eure-et-Loir, south-west of Paris, with its headquarters at Le Mans. Its organiser was Emile Henri Garry, a local man, not trained in London. The network was named CINEMA because of the resemblance of Garry to a current film star, but later, SOE, fearing it might identify him, changed it to PHONO. Several others lodged in his apartment – his fiancé, sister and another agent, and Noor spent her first night there.

On 20 June she was taken to the Agricultural Institute at Grignon, near Versailles, where in its grounds she met Gilbert Norman, Suttill's wireless operator, who let Noor make her first transmission on his set in a greenhouse in the grounds. It was also her chance to meet Suttill. A later parachute drop brought two A Mark II wireless sets in their heavy suit-cases for Noor, sent to Grignon, then Le Mans, and finally in July retrieved by Noor.

Then, just after her arrival, Andrée Borrel, Norman and Suttill were arrested, followed by others even closer to her network. Noor, seeing the danger, went into hiding, but on 29 June she still managed to attend Garry's wedding, as she had promised, before he left for Le Mans. On 2 July the Germans started arresting people at the Institute, and Noor calling there, saw it was in German hands and left. Now that she had at last got her wireless, she told London of the disaster that had engulfed the whole of the PHYSICIAN network. Indeed, as all the other operators were captured, she was the only one left in Paris. Nevertheless, she was still seeing agents and arranging a few drops, infuriating the Germans, who were trying to catch her.

Déricourt tried to get her on a July flight to London but failed. When London finally realised Norman's wireless was under German control, it was Noor's wireless that arranged Bodington's return. London now wanted Noor to return, but she refused saying that she was trying to build up PHYSICIAN herself, while arrests of resistants mounted into many hundreds.

However, she was living on borrowed time, with several near misses. One night a young German soldier helped her loop her 70 foot (21.3 metres) aerial onto a high branch of a roadside tree outside her apartment, without realising what it was for. Another time, lugging her heavy suitcase with her to the Métro, two suspicious German officers challenged her on what was in it. She told them it was a cinema projector, and their ignorance saved her. She took it with her when needing it for a transmission, together with her notebook with all her messages and codes.

In September 1943, the Germans were picking up her signal loud and clear, but they could not pinpoint the exact spot from which it came, as she kept on the move. Once her wireless broke down and a resistant repaired it. Again she helped a Gaullist agent, who had lost his two operators, by making a deal that she would 'send' for him, if he took her in his car into the countryside. Her underworld friend also drove her out into the suburbs, which must have annoyed the patiently listening Germans. London tried repeatedly to recall her, but knowing that she was probably the only SOE F wireless operator free in the whole of Paris, she still refused. Then London arranged a daily watch for her messages at its special listening stations. Also in September she was told to see two Canadian aircrew needing to be put on an escape line, as she had worked closely with the escape lines previously, helping about thirty Allied aircrew. However, she became suspicious of these Canadians when she met them, and later found it was a trap, which she had narrowly escaped. She was really doing exceptionally and unexpectedly well. Nevertheless, from the Canadians, the Germans now had a full description of her and knew they were looking for a woman, codenamed Madeleine, and put a reward of 100,000 francs on her head.

As the blazing hot summer dimmed into autumn, Garry returned to Paris, and Noor sent a summary of captured agents to London. Breathless, running everywhere when not on her bike, she lost weight and had a hunted look about her. A feeling of impending disaster drove her to seek the solace of her old home area of Suresnes and some former friends, though she warned them of the danger of harbouring her. Once she broke down in tears saying, 'I wish I were at home with my mother', and she was deeply touched when one London message ended, 'May God keep you'.

At the start of October, she disappeared for a few days, sent out of Paris by her underground friend for safety. A short time later she returned, her sense of duty driving her. Later she told those around her that she would soon be leaving for London, which she firmly believed would be on 14 October.

Meanwhile, the German SD headquarters received a tip off. A woman called and said that she would give away Noor's hiding place for the reward, which proved to be very much less than they were prepared to pay to catch her. Next day, Ernest Vogt, the SD civilian interpreter, was shown around Noor's apartment, seeing her notebooks and wireless. On the morning of the 13 October their informant told them she was out, but would return shortly. One man was left in the apartment to make the arrest. Noor, coming back, saw some suspicious men lingering around and gave them the slip, but was caught inside the apartment. In fact, she fought so fiercely that the man inside had to call for reinforcements. They arrived, including Ernest Vogt, who appeared to be the only one able to calm her, so that she could be taken quietly to their car and the Avenue Foch. The woman who betrayed her was probably Garry's jealous sister.

So began Noor's imprisonment. Taken to the attic fifth floor of the SD headquarters, Noor demanded a bath. To calm her it was allowed, but no sooner was she in the bathroom than she was out of the window and half way around the building, despite her fear of heights, before she was hauled back trembling inside. No torture was used, but she refused to answer Vogt's gentle questions, only saying she was a WAAF officer and her name was Nora Baker (her mother's maiden name). When Vogt showed her copies of all her personal correspondence, though shaken, she stuck to her story. At night, prisoners in the adjoining cells could hear her sobbing. Kieffer, the SD's Officer in charge of SOE investigations, also had a hand in her thorough questioning but learned nothing new from her. Dr Goetz, the SD wireless expert, got nothing out of her either. After his first and only interview with her he returned her to Vogt saying, 'She is impossible. I have never met a woman like her.' However, his operators with her wireless and notebooks found a way to imitate her style so effectively that London was hoodwinked, and supplies and seven further agents were dropped straight into German hands. In the five weeks at the Avenue Foch she did gradually soften under Vogt's sympathetic questioning and talked about her home life, believing it a safe subject, though it enabled them to answer some trick questions set by a suspicious London. Garry too was captured when the Germans revisited the apartment to pick up clothes that Noor had innocently requested.

Once, at midnight, Noor and two prisoners managed to escape through loosened bars in their skylights, and would have made it had their cells not been found empty when the jailers were alerted by a British air raid. The prisoners were re-captured, and Noor, who could not tell a lie, refused to agree that she would not try to escape again. On 26 November 1943, she was transferred to Germany. On the way, it is said that she tried to escape a third time. The Karlsruhe officials, as their prison was full, sent her to Pforzheim, a nearby political prison, ordering that, as a particularly dangerous prisoner, she was to be chained hand and foot in a solitary confinement cell on starvation rations, with no-one allowed to speak to her. However, the elderly Governor of the prison was impressed by her brave and cheerful manner and relaxed her conditions, until reprimanded by Karlsruhe, after which her cruel conditions were restored. Nevertheless, much impressed by her frail courage, the Governor continued to come and talk to her, and she received messages, scratched on metal food bowls from other prisoners.

On 10 September 1944, Noor was taken to Karlsruhe, again by direct orders from Berlin, and met three other SOE women, of whom Noor recognised one. They were taken by train on a journey punctuated by stops for air raids, and at midnight arrived at the concentration camp of Dachau, where they were locked into separate cells. There is little doubt that early in the morning of 12 September they were all abused and badly beaten before being taken out and shot – except Noor, who was again singled out for the worst treatment. During the night it seems that this quiet, gentle young woman was abused, stripped and subjected to the most brutal, degrading and sadistic treatment of kicks and blows all over the body, because of defying her jailer by not giving in. In the words of one writer, she was later left on the cell floor, 'a bloody mess', while her jailer had a short rest. In the morning he repeated the same actions, until he delivered a single bullet to her head. Even then, Noor's love for France shone out, and she is said to have died with the word '*Liberté*' on her lips.

Noor's is a pitiable account to relate. Her very nature seemed against her, and her mistakes cost a number of lives, yet she remained free against all expectations. Gubbins said, 'For months she held the principal and most dangerous post in France', and she maintained this very successfully. She also showed incredible courage during her captivity. She was, however, out of her depth in France, and should never have been sent.

16

CECILY LEFORT

She would have needed more courage than most to screw herself up to go to France.

Francis Cammaerts (agent)

By a strange twist of fortune, Cecily Lefort started training in SOE with Noor Inayat Khan and shared her love of sailing with Diana Rowden, both of whom were her fellow passengers in the double Lysander flight that brought her to the field of Vieux Briollay near Angers in France, in the early morning of 17 June 1943.

Cécile Margot Mackenzie was born in London on 30 April 1900, to a prosperous family of Irish descent, who moved between their properties in Ireland and England. She grew up to be fond of sport, becoming, among other things, a proficient yachtswoman. In 1925, she married a wealthy French doctor, Alix Lefort, who had an apartment in Paris and a villa near the fishing village of St Cast on the north coast of Brittany, where they shared a love of yachting, using the little sheltered bay below the villa for sailing.

In 1940, when the war was going badly for France, British nationals were advised to leave, advice reinforced by Alix Lefort, though he remained in Paris. Anxious to contribute to the defeat of the Germans and help to liberate the France she loved, Cecily in Britain in 1941 joined the WAAF and became a policewoman. Her French was remarked upon and brought her to the notice of SOE in 1943, which trained her to be a courier.

During this time, Cecily heard that someone in SOE was looking for good landing beaches in France, and mentioned to an agent that she and her husband had a secure, hidden bay in Brittany now unused. This news was passed to another agent looking for a place to land and take off agents from Falmouth. Armed with an antique Irish ring which she loaned him, he could show it to the caretaker of their villa near St Cast, proving that he had her permission to use the bay. In this curious way the 'Var' escape line of DF section was successfully established, unknowingly using the same route as the Scarlet Pimpernels of the French Revolutionary era.

On her night flight to France, Bunny Rymills, the pilot of her Lysander, was not very impressed by her French. To him, 'it didn't seem that hot'. He also thought privately that she looked rather like a vicar's wife. But knowing her errand, he concentrated on being kind and encouraging, which may have been the reason why he accidentally left on his transmitter just after they crossed the channel into France. As a result, the following Lysander could hear, but not stop, his conversation with his passenger.

'Now, Madame, we are approaching your beautiful country – isn't it lovely in the moonlight?' Back came the answer in soft accented tones, 'Yes. I think it is heavenly. What is that town over there?' He replied and continued pointing out all the local landmarks as they passed over them, a running commentary for which the listening Germans, if there were any, would have been most grateful. As they reached their destination, he fell quiet, concentrating on his landing.

After Cecily climbed down the short ladder of the Lysander on 17 June 1943, she and the three other agents who had landed with her on the other Lysander rode the bikes kindly supplied by the reception party to the railway station to catch an early morning train. When in Paris Cecily may have taken her only opportunity to visit her beloved husband. However, she was not to stay in Paris or the North, but had to make her way to join the JOCKEY network, which her organiser Francis Cammaerts (codenamed Roger), a most security-minded agent, had formed in independent groups along the left bank of the Rhone valley and areas behind the Riviera coast. With so large and widespread a network, he had asked for more assistance, and in June 1943 Pierre Reynaud (codenamed Alain), a sabotage instructor, was parachuted in to him along with Cecily (codenamed Alice) to act as his courier with the cover name of Cecile Legrand.

She met Cammaerts at Montélimar. Here he outlined her work, and the long distances she would have to travel by train or bike. In an average week he would visit Toulouse, Clermont-Ferrand, Agen, Lyon and Digne, dropping in on other small groups on his way. It was quite disconcerting. Later Cammaerts described her as 'rather a shy person with a perpetually surprised look about her. She, I fear, never lost that conviction of despair... with little belief in survival'. Not perhaps the best attitude for such a busy workload.

In early July 1943, the Allies invaded Sicily, in preparation for their next move into Italy. This prompted London to increase supplies to the south-east of France, which previously, because of the distance and limited stocks, had been much neglected. A big parachute drop was therefore arranged for the night of 13 August. And once the message of confirmation came in, it was part of Cecily's task to be at the field near Beaurepaire, which had been carefully reconnoitred and prepared to receive it. With an excited but quiet group of resistants, ready to remove and hide the supplies quickly, Cecily carried the principal light, which among others helped mark the drop zone, and she flashed the Morse identification letter to the approaching pilot to tell him it was safe to drop his loads. At last the plane arrived and the large canisters swung down on their parachutes, to be either broken up into more manageable pieces (each weighed around 4 hundredweight/203.2 kg) or carted away whole. Cecily counted seven canisters. It was a good night's work.

Their arrival signalled a new outburst of sabotage over the JOCKEY network. Bigger dislocations appeared on railway lines, a few on those between Valence and Grenoble. Power stations and various industrial targets were damaged with little loss of life. Cecily was glad to be involved with Reynaud in the sabotage. This activity inevitably drew German attention to the area, redoubling their efforts to find the perpetrators and especially their leaders. Cammaerts warned everyone to be very careful, mentioning certain places to avoid, particularly Montélimar, his former headquarters.

Ignoring the warnings, Cecily and Reynaud, on 15 September 1943, called on the house of Raymond Daujat, a prosperous corn merchant and leader of a local resistance group in Montélimar. The Germans, perhaps from a tip off, surrounded it and sent some SS guards in to detain anyone there. Cecily was inside resting, Daujat and Reynaud were talking in the garden. Hearing the commotion, Cecily, instead of trusting that her papers might prove her innocent, went to hide in the cellar – almost sure proof of guilt.

Daujat and Reynaud, hearing the noise or seeing the guards, ran off and escaped. Cecily was found and taken to the Gestapo prison at Lyon, where, none too gently, they broke her alibis and sent her off to the Avenue Foch in Paris for further interrogation. In the face of harsher questioning she fell silent. Cammaerts, away on one of his many visits, rushed back and tried to mount a rescue, but it was too late. Nevertheless, the system of security he had set up held and enabled the JOCKEY network to survive.

Eventually, the Gestapo, unable to extract any information from Cecily, sent her to Germany before the end of 1943 and the endless journey to the concentration camp of Ravensbrück (50 miles/80.5 km north of Berlin), which was referred to by the French as '*L'Enfer des Femmes*' – the Women's Hell.

During the routine admission examination came a surprise. A doctor diagnosed cancer of the stomach, which Cecily had suspected but to which she would not admit. In the hospital block he operated on her successfully, and then was sure he could cure her on a post-operative special diet of a type of thick porridge and vegetable soup, on which she appeared to thrive until she was returned to the main camp.

Gradually conditions there deteriorated until after about eighteen months, in February 1945, Cecily was given a pink card, declaring her unfit for work, and she was sent to the Jugendlager, believed by the prisoners to be a rest camp. Mary Lindell, a nurse in the general medical block, formerly involved with escape lines, found a way to send forms recalling Cecily and two friends to join a Polish Knitting Group. Unfortunately, one of Cecily's friends refused to leave, and while Cecily was away, trying to persuade her, their transport left and her one chance of escape vanished. The Jugendlager was really an extermination camp, where inmates were either poisoned or sent to the gas chambers. Others attributed her death to an overdose of the sleeping powder frequently administered by a senior prisoner. So Cecily died and the doctor never found if his cure for cancer had been successful.

It was to turn out that the three women on Henri Déricourt's June Lysander were all captured and killed. They may have been followed to their destinations – Cecily to Montélimar, and her movements watched to see if she might lead them to the leaders of the network. If so, it failed, because of Cammaerts' tight security, and the Germans certainly lost track of the supplies dropped to the network. Cecily's big mistake was to visit Montélimar against Cammaerts' orders, where she played straight into German hands. This one slip was her last.

17

DIANA ROWDEN

Jeune fille Britannique, volontaire pour des missions en territoire occupé, fut envoyée en France... et continua avec courage a remplir ses fonctions de courier.

[A young British girl, who volunteered for missions in occupied territory, was sent to France, where she courageously carried out her work as a courier.]

From citations for Croix de Guerre

Diana Hope Rowden, daughter of a Major, was born in London on 31 January 1915, but spent her early years at Cap Ferrat and along the Italian Rivièra, where her mother rented a villa and a yacht. There this turbulent tomboy spent most of her time running wild with her two brothers or sailing, at which she became quite proficient. The yacht was called *Sans Peur* (the Fearless One), a name that would prove to be equally suited to Diana in later life. Despite appearances, it was not an entirely happy existence.

When Diana was about thirteen her mother sent her to a boarding school in Surrey, where she resented the restraints on her freedom, becoming self-contained and withdrawn, though on the surface she remained poised and sophisticated. At seventeen, her mother took her back to France. She was now a quiet, gentle, diffident and rather stocky woman of middle height, with reddish hair and pale complexion.

After a course at the Sorbonne she embarked on a career in journalism. On the outbreak of war in 1939 she joined the French Red Cross, but the German invasion separated her from her mother who escaped to Britain in a coal boat. In 1941, advised to leave, Diana organised her own escape through Spain and Portugal, and found her mother in London. Almost immediately she joined the WAAF, where her fluent French and striking character promoted her to the Intelligence Branch. Later, after a serious operation, a fellow patient recognising her language skills and devotion to France, recommended her to SOE, which she entered in March 1943.

Her training school reports were adequate but mixed, noting that she had plenty of courage and intelligence but was suppressing a lot of hate (perhaps due to her troubled childhood). Soon afterwards she was one of the three women brought by Henri Déricourt's double Lysander landing on 17 June 1943 to act as a courier (codenamed Paulette) to the ACROBAT network in the large region of Franche Compté, where locally she was to be known as Juliette Fondeau. Harry Rée (codenamed César) joined them as a senior leader in the network.

Diana travelled to the Jura to meet her organiser John Starr (codenamed Bob) in a hotel at Lons-le-Saunier. He felt that she was still recognisably English, so assigned her to living accommodation in the beautiful Château Andelot in St Amour, where Cuthbert Young (codenamed Gabriel), his wireless operator, with Newcastle-accented French, was hidden. She still acted as courier by bike and train to as far south as Marseille and to Paris, as well as nearer Lyon, Montbéliard and Besançon.

Her journeys were beset by many dangers and many narrow escapes, once she just missed a police check on the train by taking refuge in a vacant toilet, and even more hair-raising was an incident when she was actually arrested at a checkpoint, but managed to slip away when the soldier's attention was diverted for a minute. Sometimes she was in contact with groups of the Maquis, for whom the Jura mountains were a safe retreat. She was also present for at least five supply drops and the cancelled attack on the changed route of the train carrying Field Marshal Rommel in July.

Then came the news of the arrest of Starr. By this time, Harry Rée, who had had a troubled relationship with Starr, had already been sent to Belfort and formed a new network there called STOCKBROKER. With Starr gone, Rée immediately took over ACROBAT and sent a warning to Diana and Young to take cover. Young took his transmitter to a sawmill at Clairvaux and Diana lodged above the village shop in the tiny village of Epy. During their three weeks of hiding, while the Germans were searching for resistants, she was once arrested on suspicion but was shortly released, though on her return she moved to Clairvaux to be with Young in his sawmill.

The sawmill was isolated and surrounded by woodland. It formed a cluster of buildings where several families who owned it lived. The Pauli family house was where Young lodged, though he kept moving his equipment around. The Juif house where Diana stayed resembled a Swiss chalet with a wooden balcony over-looking a steep slope. Between the houses was a cobbled road. The Juif family suggested some alterations in Diana's appearance and her codename was changed to Michelle, but to the outside world she masqueraded as Marcelle, a cousin recovering from a serious illness.

From here she resumed her contacts with resistants, and they received some more supply drops from the air. She also helped Rée with several of his sabotage plans, including a new one: blackmail. In this way he arranged a little internal accident with the foreman of the machine shop, abetted by the Director of the Peugeot car factory now making tank turrets and engines for the German Air Force planes. This resulted, on 5 November, in a massive explosion, putting the factory out of use for three or more months. Unfortunately, this disaster drew German attention to Rée, who then fled to Switzerland.

This meant that ACROBAT needed another organiser. It is uncertain whether, on the morning of 18 November, it was the new leader, Maugenet himself, who came to Clairvaux, or a German impersonating him. He met Diana and Young, passed the safety checks, including a welcome letter from Young's wife, and promised to return that night with his suitcase of explosives. In conversation at the Lons café earlier where they introduced him to some more contacts, he had asked Diana if she were afraid. Laughing she shook her head. Young, meanwhile, felt uneasy and moved his wireless in the Pauli family's house several times. Then they waited.

At about six that evening Maugenet again arrived and Diana escorted him up the road, unaware that he was flashing his torch behind his back. They went to the house of the Juif family. Another resister, late for the meeting, hesitated on the balcony outside. From there he saw three cars with twenty German Field Police stop in the yard in front of the house. He immediately jumped off the balcony and ran down the slope to warn the other resistants.

Inside the house, Diana, Young and Maugenet were arrested with all the family, but Diana managed to hide Young's wireless crystals inside the mattress of the cot where the baby was lying. After some brutal questioning they were taken to the Lons Police station, where Diana could hear Young in the next door cell being tortured. Later that night, Maugenet, in German uniform, returned to the sawmill and led the search for Young's wireless, which the resistants had now removed. The family were interrogated, beaten up, their belongings stolen and one of them was sent to Ravensbrück.

On about 20 November, Diana was sent to the Gestapo Headquarters at Avenue Foch for further interrogation, as they could not extract any information from her at Lons. Here she had a shock, meeting her former organiser Starr, apparently free and employed by the Germans. Diana's interrogators soon realised there was nothing to be learned from this polite, serious young woman. She was therefore on 5 December packed off to Frèsnes Prison.

On 13 May 1944, looking white and drawn, she met with seven other women in the drawing room of the Avenue Foch to await further transport to take them, handcuffed in pairs, to the prison at Karlsruhe.

At the beginning of July, Berlin realised that they were political not civilian prisoners and under the '*Nacht-und-Nebel Erlass*' (Night and Fog Decree*) ordered four, including Diana, to be moved, just over 100 miles (160.9 km) back to a men's concentration camp in Alsace. They may have been told they were being sent for agricultural work.

It was on the afternoon of 6 July 1944 that they arrived in close secrecy at the Natzweiler-Struthof men's concentration camp, and were taken straight to the Bunker. Together for a short while, the four were finally separated. Diana was wearing a short grey flannel skirt and a finger-tip swagger coat, which made her look even more English. Her short fair hair was tied with a cheerful tartan ribbon.

About 10pm, Diana was called out of her cell and escorted to an isolated hut, which she may have taken to be a hospital, but was actually a crematorium. In a room with eight white beds she was told to lie down for a typhus injection – really a massive dose of phenol. She died almost immediately and her body was then taken to be cremated.

Thus died a very brave woman. She was twenty-nine years old.

---

* The 'Night and Fog Decree' was a directive from Hitler issued on 7 December 1941, which resulted in the kidnapping and forced disappearance of political activists, resistants, and anyone found guilty of endangering the 'security or state of readiness' of German forces. Hitler intended it as an instrument of terror, intimidating the local population into submission. It is unknown how many people were victims of this programme of extermination, but certainly SOE and other agents working behind enemy lines were at risk from this treatment.

18

ELAINE PLEWMAN

Because she was born in France to an English father, she had the option of choosing French or British nationality. She and her brothers had chosen to be British.

Rita Kramer (an American author)

Elaine Sophie Browne-Bartroli was born in Marseille on 6 December 1917, to a Spanish mother and an English father. She had two brothers, one of whom preceded her into SOE. Her early schooling was in Marseille, then with her brother, Albert, in England, before being 'finished' in Spain. After college she worked in a Leicester importing firm, handling correspondence in French, Spanish, German and English. On the outbreak of war she was sent to the British Embassy in Madrid and then Lisbon. In July 1942, her talents had taken her to Kensington, London, working for the Spanish Section of the Ministry of Information, and it was at this time that she married Tom Plewman, a newly commissioned Army officer.

She was a vital, brilliant woman, with a heart-shaped face, dark hair and eyes and a fair skin, whose presence lit up the room wherever she went. It is hard to imagine anyone who looked less suited to war work. Her devotion to France, her intelligence and her cool, balanced attitude made her an obvious choice for SOE. It is also possible that her brother, by now already in the service, may have recommended her. She sailed through her training, and after a failed first attempt, she finally found herself dangling on the end of a parachute on 14 August 1943, 20 miles (32.2 km) away from where she was supposed to land in the Jura.

Her parachute had drifted towards a farm, whose dog kept barking at her as she hung above his head. Trying to avoid the creature, she landed badly and sprained her ankle. Burying her parachute, she hid her bag containing 1 million francs in some bushes (later the bag was returned but the money had gone). Until her ankle was strong enough, she went into hiding, her reception party counting her lost, and when she was able to investigate a few of her contacts, it was only to find that they had all been arrested. It was not an auspicious beginning.

Consequently, it was nearly two months before she found fellow members of her network, MONK, including its organiser, Charles Skepper (codenamed Bernard) and his wireless operator, Arthur Steele (codenamed Laurent). Their main centre of operations was Marseille, making this network a surprising choice for Elaine, as it was her former home ground, where there was the risk that she would be recognised. Albert, her brother, also had his wife living there, who was very kind to Elaine and gave her what help she could. However, Elaine felt that her brother was too rash and careless, so she found different safe places out in the countryside for young Arthur Steele to tap out his radio messages. In public Elaine passed as Madame Prunier, but her codename was Gaby.

She travelled widely but mainly between Marseille, Roquebrune and St Raphael. Occasionally she went with messages and sabotage materials by train or by a Gazo-lorry driven by a resistance member, who often gave lifts to German soldiers, who sometimes unwittingly sat on boxes of arms and dynamite, which he was bringing back from an air drop by the RAF. The area was heavily defended with 240,000 German troops, artillery batteries and gun emplacements, in preparation against a possible Allied invasion. Elaine also helped in the training of resistants, in particular in sabotage on the railways. Once, her brother, meeting her in Marseille, was horrified to find her carrying a bag of heavy plastic explosives to sabotage a line single-handed, and insisted on carrying it on and off the train himself, muttering that they were working her too hard. Actually, in January 1944, the MONK network succeeded in damaging thirty trains, as well as de-railing the main line train to Toulon inside a tunnel and then destroying the first breakdown train sent to repair it, causing a hold-up of four days. Afterwards MONK's work slowed down, with a last spurt of sabotage in March, damaging thirty more railway lines.

On one of her many journeys by train, Elaine was standing in the corridor packed with German soldiers. As she also spoke German, during a conversation with the German officer beside her, he asked for a light for his cigarette. Elaine was in a dilemma. She had two boxes of matches in her bag. One carried a message from a resistant – the reason she was on the train – but they both looked identical. She had just lit her own cigarette from one, so she couldn't deny having any. Reluctantly she handed one over to him and then with his cigarette alight, he pocketed the box. Did he know? She was surprised to leave the train undiscovered. Back at base, with shaking hands she poked at the matches in the remaining box. Nothing! It dropped to the floor and a twist of paper fell out. The message. All was well. Such heart-stopping incidents were part of daily life for an agent.

On another such occasion she was afraid that she had mislaid her handbag with money, identity cards, ration books and keys. A fellow resistant let her climb onto his shoulders to reach her open apartment window, where she was lucky to find them.

She was not alone in her lucky escapes. Once, a fellow network member, suspecting that Germans were searching inside his apartment, called on a barber, living and working in the apartment below his. In the middle of his enquiry, he found himself whisked into the barber's chair, swathed in towels and his face smothered in shaving soap, just as the Germans entered the shop.

Yet again, a special Christmas Eve dinner with friends was long delayed by the non-appearance of Steele, the wireless operator. At length Elaine found him hiding in the garage, dishevelled and out of breath. He had been chased by SS dogs and only escaped by diving through prickly bushes, and so was in no fit state to be seen by the other diners, who were ignorant of his double life. The diet of another agent required Elaine to hunt for foods in short supply, and only obtainable in the black market. This was ultimately to be the cause of their undoing, for the man who supplied their needs shared a mistress with a man who worked for the Gestapo, and it was this mistress who betrayed them. Even when Elaine sensed the treachery, she refused to leave her post, although her brother's wife did escape in time with her young child.

On 23 March 1944, Skepper was arrested in his apartment. The next day, unaware of this, Steele and Elaine called to see him with messages, and they too were captured by the Germans, who had been lying in wait for them.

As this was such a small, closely knit network*, the news of this capture travelled quickly and plans for their rescue were contemplated, but the three were moved so swiftly after their arrest that it was too late.

Elaine was transferred to Les Baumettes Prison, where she was cruelly treated, beaten about the head, tortured perhaps with electric shocks so that some later hardly recognised her, her face was so swollen. Through it all she told the Germans nothing, except only that she was her organiser's mistress. Indomitable as ever, she was often heard singing in her cell at night. After about a fortnight of interrogation, realising there was nothing to be gained from her, the Gestapo sent her to Frèsnes Prison, and then on 14 May, with seven other SOE women, she was moved to Karlsruhe.

On 12 September 1944, with two of the remaining SOE agents from Karlsruhe and one from Pforzheim, she was sent to the concentration camp at Dachau. Here, they were separated, brutally beaten and kicked. Three of them were taken out in the early morning, where, in the narrow yard beyond the crematorium, a single shot through the head ended their suffering. The fourth died in her cell. They all knew too much of German treatment, and perhaps of the PHYSICIAN debacle, to be released to the advancing Allied armies.

---

* The network remained relatively small, despite acquiring some of the members of Francis Suttill's PHYSICIAN network, who had been able to escape its collapse.

19

YVONNE CORMEAU

The question of not going did not arise. I was ready to go. I'd steeled myself… There was constant fear, but you just had to live with it.

Yvonne Cormeau

She was always incredibly precise in her activity under conditions of great strain without a single miscode.

Maurice Buckmaster

Beatrice Yvonne Biesterfeld began her adventurous life in Shanghai on 18 December 1909. Her mother was Scottish and her father a British consular official. When he died in 1920, the family moved around France, Belgium and Scotland, where she was educated. She married Charles Cormeau, an English chartered accountant, in 1937, and they had one child. When war broke out he joined the British Army and in 1940 was wounded and sent home, only to be killed during the Blitz; Yvonne's life was luckily saved by an overturned bath. She sent her young daughter to Bristol and then onto a convent near Oxford, before Yvonne became an airwoman in 1941. Soon her fluency in German and French saw her moved into Operations and Intelligence, and in the beginning of 1943 SOE claimed her.

She struggled with her decision to become an agent for SOE and she had an agonising few weeks over the risk of leaving her daughter an orphan, but in the end she decided France needed her. Once decided she did not look back.

Her sensible attitude, quick wit and intelligence were coupled with plenty of strength and independence of character, which all helped when she started training as a wireless operator alongside Noor Inayat Khan and Yolande Beekman.

The SOE wirelesses used for sending and receiving messages were properly called transceivers, all needing crystals to tune them to the British receiving station. Most could be powered either by mains electricity or a heavy glass battery, which Yvonne preferred. She ended up with an A Mark III weighing only 8.8 pounds (4 kg). All messages were in a code, hidden in a false lining of the briefcase she always carried. She learned all this and a great deal more during the sixteen weeks of her wireless course.

Finally, on the night of 23 August 1943, she parachuted down near the hamlet of St Antoine du Queyret, 75 miles (120.7 km) from Bordeaux in the south west of France. Her three wireless sets had been dropped beforehand, but only one survived. With this she managed to contact London on the day after her arrival. However, having only one set, she was forced to take it everywhere with her for the next few months, despite the risks. Horrified by the noise and confusion when she arrived, she borrowed a bike to leave for her first 'safe house' at Pujols, learning that a spy had caused many arrests. Later she found that he was among her own reception party, so that the Germans already knew that a small, dark-haired, green-eyed British girl, codenamed Annette, had come to be a wireless operator, and there were soon posters of her face everywhere, with offers of 5 million francs for her arrest! George Starr (codenamed Hilaire), the organiser of the WHEELWRIGHT network and the brother of John Starr (codenamed Bob) of ACROBAT, whom she had met before, did not want a woman, but quickly recognised her worth, and they soon had complete confidence in each other.

Because Starr had been without a regular courier for a long time, Yvonne often had to perform this role as well as being a wireless operator. She travelled far and wide looking for safe houses from which to transmit her messages, never staying more than three days in the same house, nor even then 'sending' from the same spot, loft, barn or field. Vineyards were good for hiding her 70 foot (21.3 metres) of aerial, and farms in the region were so isolated that they were her preferred safe spots, as it was hard for the Germans to get a 'fix' on her signals.

September 1943 was hot. One morning Yvonne suddenly awoke. The cows that she had been tending as part of her daily 'job' for a local farmer, were patiently standing waiting at the gate. After a hectic period sending and receiving messages, it was so good to relax. She ran and herded the cows into the milking shed. Somehow five had become six as she explained to the farmer, just ahead of another angry neighbour arriving and accusing her of stealing his cow. It must have come through a hole in the wire to join its sisters. She was fired.

At other times in different houses or farms giving her a brief shelter, she tried to help. Sometimes she posed as a district nurse with her X-ray equipment, the large heavy suitcase strapped to the carrier of her bike. Once she only just avoided arrest by the Gestapo late in the night, by leaping from her bed through a window in the dark and making off into the fields, evading their shots. Little wonder she often had butterflies in her tummy, as she put it, because she knew that most radio operators at that time lasted about six weeks before capture. In fact she lasted thirteen months, with 402 messages carefully tapped out in coded Morse in no more than 20 minutes each, without a single miscode. Almost a record! No wonder the women in the British receiving station would compete to be the ones to take her messages.

Since WHEELWRIGHT was such a large network with its centre in the Gers department (though it touched on ten other areas), her travels could take her from the Dordogne to the remoter areas of Gasçony or up into the Pyrénées. At first she went by train or bus, but later she turned to her bike, because of increased German surveillance on public transport. On some days this meant cycling as much as 62 miles (100 km) through all kinds of weather, her wireless eventually being transported by local people. Little wonder that her weight went down to 87 pounds (42 kg). Her hosts knew what she was doing, but never once did they refuse her a bed or betray her, despite the risk to them.

In August 1943, she went on air about three times a week, according to her pre-arranged schedules (skeds), but this increased towards December, when London wanted to try out the effectiveness of the resistance. Thus the December instructions produced a satisfactory outbreak of sabotage all over the south of France, and there was a more generous drop of supplies after each mission. As it was Yvonne's calls that brought them, none would let her near the drops for fear of harming her 'magic fingers'; she was known as the 'pianist' who played the 'piano'. Then in spring 1944, the rigid timing and wavelengths of her 'skeds' became more flexible and varied.

On 4 January 1944, two more agents were dropped to join WHEELWRIGHT, Anne-Marie Walters as courier and Claude Arnault an explosives expert. It was just as well, since during the early spring Yvonne had strained a muscle in her leg cycling, which was so bad that she had to be hospitalised for some weeks.

Around this time the Germans learned from a Spanish prisoner that Yvonne might be found in a village called Castelnau, only to discover that there were eight villages of that name in the area. The Germans searched several, dismissing the only one where she was, because it was so small, up a steep hill, had no mains electricity and no running water.* This village was called Castelnau-sous-l'Auvignon, where Starr often lodged and had been elected Deputy Mayor, a testament to the trust that the people had in him.

As Yvonne's wireless could be switched over to 'receive' as well as 'send', she could listen and decode at night in comparative safety, and travel by day. This non-stop routine played havoc with her sleep.

There were also messages broadcast in ordinary French language on the BBC World Service, listened to in secrecy by many French families, after the 9 o' clock news. On the evening of 1 June 1944 came the long awaited 'A' message from the BBC – '*Les-sanglots lourds des violons d'automne*'. It was the general alert to the French in her area, preparing them for Allied invasion. Yvonne knew that when the 'B' message came, which was the second line of the intentionally misquoted poem by Paul Verlaine, '*Bercent mon coeur d'une languer monotone*'**, it would be the evening before the landings. On the evening of 5 June, it was broadcast and followed by about 300 action messages to the resistance all over France. The Germans, of course, knew something was about to happen, but not exactly what. Arrests immediately began.

Yvonne, recovered from her leg injury, had moved to Castelnau to be nearer Starr. She also took another radio operator with her to help in handling the stream of messages now passing through her hands. The Maquis groups that Starr had nurtured and trained soon joined with others in the area. Starr's headquarters at Castelnau overflowed with recruits.

---

* The Germans were convinced that the English loved their baths and would not deign to stay somewhere where there were no such facilities.
** The 'A' and 'B' messages for D-Day were taken from the well-known French poem *Chanson D'Automne* by Paul Verlaine, one word in each line was changed as a deliberate mistake to alert resistance and SOE agents across France of the landings. 'A' message translates: 'The heavy sobs of the autumn violins' and 'B' message, 'Lull my heart with its tedious monotony'.

On D-Day +1, the attacks and ambushes set up by the resistants organised by Starr were holding up the 2nd Panzer Division, the Das Reich, based in the neighbourhood of Toulouse, which was attempting to join the hard-pressed German troops in Normandy. Starr had ensured that the Toulouse power stations and telegraph lines were rendered useless and its petrol dumps blown up, while a nearby network destroyed its trains and railway lines. The Das Reich was thus compelled to take to the roads and march, constantly harassed by the resistants as it passed through one network to another, effectively under attack by forces that melted away as soon as they turned to fight and delaying its arrival in Normandy until D-Day +17.[*]

Later, a German spotter plane was seen over Castelnau. Immediately, Starr ordered the evacuation of the village, so that the German attack, when it came, was met by only a handful of Maquis. Yvonne stayed as long as she dared and then, collecting her equipment, she made off down the fields and paths, assisted by the local doctor with his medical case. On the way a bullet caught Yvonne's leg, spattering her briefcase with blood.

About midday they heard a huge explosion, indicating that the Maquis had blown up their army stores, and that the village would soon be in German hands. Yvonne and the doctor took refuge in a wayside farmhouse, where she was able to send her news. Later, rough estimates of the battle, which had involved about 800 Germans and 150 Maquisards, reported that the Germans lost 240 men and the French, twenty.

Yvonne finally joined up with Starr and the remnants of his Maquis, which, with the aid of some Jedburghs and other Allied parties, eventually became the Armagnac Battalion, which was often involved in skirmishes with the enemy. Yvonne lived uncomfortably with this new group. When they travelled, she went too, her wireless an invaluable link. She was transmitting everywhere.

August brought the invasion by the Americans and the Free French on the south of France, west of Cannes. These forces quickly drove north to join up with the northern forces coming down near Dijon. Caught in the maelstrom, Yvonne became busier than ever. Once she was trapped on the plateau of Lannemezan. Ignoring the battle raging around her, and being machine-gunned on the ground and strafed from the air, she kept on

---

[*] The Das Reich were so angered by their experiences with the resistance that they perpetrated the massacre of Oradour on their route.

sending her messages for as long as possible. She never took unnecessary risks, but her coolness and courage saw her through.

When the Maquis finally took over Toulouse in late August 1944, she and Starr were in the liberation cavalcade. Suddenly, a loud bang rang out and everyone scattered for cover. It turned out to be a bald tyre bursting under Yvonne and Starr's car. Laughing, the Maquis heaved the vehicle up and they were borne bodily into the square on the shoulders of the men.

They both returned to England on 23 September 1944. In November Yvonne accompanied F section's Judex mission to the WHEELWRIGHT area. They were tasked with investigating, rewarding and trying to assist, in a small way, the French who had helped SOE. Unfortunately, many who had deserved the most recognition were either dead or still in concentration camps, but Yvonne did her best. Finally she returned to her daughter in time for Christmas, leaving behind many friends and, as Annette, an enviable reputation.

20

YOLANDE BEEKMAN

After the war I shall come back in my uniform and we will celebrate the Liberation together.

Yolande to Madame Gobeaux (her host)

Yolande Elsa Maria Unternahrer was born on 28 October 1911. Her Dutch mother described her as a gentle, self-effacing child with a core of steel. Her father was a businessman of Swiss/French origin, but a Londoner by adoption. She spent, with her sister, a happy uneventful early childhood in Paris. After an education in Paris, London and Switzerland she ended up speaking English, German and French with a slight Swiss accent. This cosmopolitan background produced a young girl who was good-humoured, kind and rarely ruffled, but with a surprisingly homely English appearance.

Her first marriage to Beekman failed, so in 1941 she joined the WAAF and became a wireless operator. In February 1943, her ardent love of France, her wireless skills, her languages and personal qualities took her into SOE, working alongside Noor Inayat Khan and Yvonne Cormeau in her further wireless training. Unexpectedly, she also fell in love again and married one of her instructors, Jaap Bateman, who hoped that their marriage might stop her being sent to France, but it didn't.

Until mid-1942, SOE had to rely on SIS for its wireless communications, but by June 1942, it had its own radio networks. Starting in 1943 as a wireless operator, Yolande was given the sturdy B Mark II transceiver, commonly known as the B2 set. Completely equipped in its dog-eared suitcase, and therefore not likely to draw attention, it weighed about 32 pounds (14.5 kg), quite a weight for a woman to carry around, but it was considered comparatively compact.

It came in four compartments. The left contained the accessories such as aerial, Morse key, headphones etc. The middle top part held the transmitter and the bottom the receiver, while the right side carried the power fittings. Should an emergency crystal be necessary, provision for that was also allowed for. In addition, it could be rapidly switched from mains electricity current to battery during a Gestapo tracing episode. The B2 was liked and trusted by its operators and continued in use until well after the war.

The letters A and B indicated the power and range of the transceiver. 'A' meant that about 400 miles (644 km) might be its limit, as much as from Britain to northern France, though some sets did do better than that. 'B' sets could reach up to 1,500 miles (2,414 km), and so might reach from Britain to southern France easily. Mark numbers indicated the latest developments in either A or B sets. There were slight variations in many types, and of course there were other sets used by other organisations in France.

It was on the moonlit night of 18 September 1943, that this short, plump, dark-haired woman arrived with three men in a double Lysander landing organised by Henri Déricourt, north east of Angers, near Vieux Briolay. She was supposed to join Michael Trotobas (codenamed Sylvestre), head of the FARMER network in Lille, but instead a signal had preceded her, changing her destination to St Quentin, where Gustav Bieler of the MUSICIAN network was asking for a wireless operator. He was a French Canadian who had damaged his back so badly parachuting down in November 1942, that ever afterwards he walked with a limp and was in constant pain. His network at St Quentin was the centre of the industrial canal and railway system of the area, as well as providing many airfields for German bombers and fighters.

Yolande (codenamed Mariette) and Bieler (codenamed Guy) got on well together, as they were both intelligent and quick to see what was needed. They made an excellent team. At first she lodged in St Quentin under the cover name of Madame Yvonne de Chauvigny, but later she stayed variously with a schoolmistress, a pharmacist, a farmer and latterly above a café. Contrary to her training instructions, which advised her to keep changing the places for her wirelesses, she kept hers in the attic of the same house in St Quentin for nearly three months on her regular three a week transmissions. Did she think it was safer to use the one safe house than risk looking constantly for a new, perhaps not so safe, one?

On the prescribed evening for her transmissions, she would let herself into the house with a key, and then stretch herself out on a wide brown velvet divan, cradling her head in her mittened hands – it was so cold in the attic – and wait for the correct time to start transmitting.

Yolande's arrival to the network speeded up the RAF drops of supplies to MUSICIAN, and there were about twenty big deliveries of sten guns, bazookas, arms and explosives; she was often present at the receptions for these supplies, afterwards seeing the contents fairly distributed to at least twelve well-trained and armed Maquis groups in the MUSICIAN network. Bieler preferred concentrating on bigger projects, though he did allow the men to try out a few newly arrived explosives on blowing up a bridge or two and a few petrol pumps. The railway men co-operated with the resistance, being particularly pleased with sabotage operations that used abrasive grease that wore away the parts it was supposed to lubricate, so that by autumn ten locomotives were put out of action. Damage was also caused to individual lengths of track, points, signal boxes and shunting sheds, with satisfactory delays for repair. Thus, for nearly a year the resistants caused chaos over 115 miles (185 km) of railway between Paris, St Quentin and Lille, and thirteen times between Paris and Cologne.

For a long time, Bieler had considered ways of blocking the St Quentin canal, which was used to ship delicate and heavy submarine parts for midget submarines active in the Mediterranean. Then came the answer – limpet magnetic mines to blow the lock gates. An expert was sent to help, but was captured by the Germans. On the same night, Bieler, with a small dedicated team, did the job himself. The team got safely away and, better still, the limpet mines worked. A huge explosion jammed the lock with its broken gates for weeks and nearly 100 barges carrying delicate parts were sunk. This success encouraged the resistants to repeat the action several times.

Meanwhile, Yolande's friends in St Quentin reported seeing German direction finding vans* in the neighbourhood – even on Christmas Day. In the week before New Year's Day, her hostess saw one actually pass the house.

---

* Used to identify and track wireless signals.

She ran upstairs to warn Yolande, who immediately broke off her transmission with a warning signal, packed up the set and the two women moved it to another house. Yolande also bleached her dark hair and took a new alias.

On 12 January 1944, before curfew, she pedalled her bike through the frosty streets to the outskirts of the city and an ugly grey brick building standing near a canal bridge. It was the Moulin Brulé, the Burned Mill, a small wayside café where she was to lodge. On the next morning, she came downstairs to a pre-arranged meeting with Bieler, where they were joined by another man and the café owners. As they talked two cars drew up outside and Germans came in to arrest them all, handcuffing them and dragging them to the waiting cars. Someone had betrayed them, though it appeared that they had been watched for some time.

They were all interrogated at the Gestapo headquarters in St Quentin, where their interrogators concentrated on Yolande and Bieler. A few days later Yolande was taken to the local pharmacy to ask for money supposed to be kept there. The owners pretended that they did not know what her escort was talking about, but later they told friends that they could see from her badly swollen face that she had been tortured. A rescue attempt failed. Torture had not shaken Bieler, who so infuriated his interrogators that in a few weeks he was taken away and shot.

There was no such quick ending for Yolande. Because her skills with her wireless might be useful to the Germans, she was sent to the Avenue Foch and its wireless experts. It proved a waste of time. She was then sent to a solitary confinement cell in Frèsnes Prison.

On 13 May, looking white and drawn, she joined a convoy of eight captured SOE women, all couriers except herself. They travelled to Karlsruhe women's civil prison, crowded but no longer alone.

On 11 September 1944, Yolande joined two others from her May convoy and awaited a third, Noor Inayat Khan with whom she had trained, and who was being sent from Pforzheim. The four travelled all day, and came to another concentration camp at midnight, where they were taken to separate cells. It is likely that, as was the normal practice here, Yolande was beaten and badly treated before she and two others were dragged out next morning. In a narrow space between huts, she was then shot by a single bullet in the back of the neck, her body being reduced immediately to ashes in the nearby crematorium.

The camp was Dachau. The date was 12 September 1944. Yolande was thirty-two years of age.

21

PEARL WITHERINGTON

Femme admirable… le vivant example de l'abnégation et du plus pur patriotisme… exposant sa vie sans cesse… un bel example pour nos combattants du Maquis.

[A wonderful woman… a living example of self-sacrifice and deep patriotism, continually risking her life… a great example to our Maquis fighters.]
From her Légion d'Honneur citation

Cécile Pearl Witherington was born on 24 June 1914 in Paris, the eldest child of English parents. She attributed her success in managing the Maquis and her network in the Auvergne to a difficult childhood, where, because of a rarely seen, feckless father and an ineffectual mother (who produced eight children in nine years, of whom only four daughters survived), she had to provide and fight for all her family throughout her childhood. Nevertheless, with only four years of schooling she became a typist in the Paris British Embassy, and was engaged to Henri Cornioley before he joined the Army on the outbreak of war.

Fleeing from the German occupation, with many adventures, she led her mother and two sisters across Europe to Britain, arriving in July 1941. Here, her sisters joined the WAAF and she worked in the Air Ministry, until she learned that her fiancé was an escaped prisoner of war and back in France. Then, against strong opposition from the Ministry, in 1943 she joined SOE to be trained as a courier, with excellent reports on her training. Pearl was tall and good looking, with delicate features, her fair hair plaited around her head like a German housewife, with an air of calm and steadfastness about her. She had a photographic memory too and writing was quickly memorised and then destroyed, so never on her person.

On 23 September 1943, she parachuted down from a Halifax bomber, landing near Tendu in the Auvergne, slightly off course, to be met by Maurice Southgate (codenamed Hector), her organiser for the STATIONER network, who reunited her next morning with Henri Cornioley, who, in the future, was to work closely with her, although he was based in another organisation at that time.

In the STATIONER network she joined Jacqueline Nearne (codenamed Jacqueline), Southgate's first courier since January 1943 and Amédée Maingard (codenamed Samuel), their unflappable wireless operator from Mauritius. Together with Southgate they made a strong quartet for the network which was spreading from the Indre almost to the Pyrénées, where SOE's task was to form small groups of resistants everywhere, so that on D-Day they could expand their operations quickly.

She and Jacqueline travelled over different areas, with Maingard at Châteauroux the hub between them, as well as Southgate seeing them separately and frequently. Pearl's area was to be the Auvergne. Her codename was Marie and her cover name Marie Jeanne Marthe Verges (a real woman who had completely disappeared.) Despite Pearl's clear skin, untouched by cosmetics, her constant journeys were as a travelling sales representative of Lancray Beauty products. Thus she travelled, usually by night, in unheated trains – less likely to be challenged – to such cities as Paris, Montluçon, Châteauroux, Poitiers, Lyon, Limoges, Toulouse and Tarbes, often with no more information of her destination than Southgate deemed necessary.

This lack of information sometimes proved to be dangerous. Once, at Poitiers, had she not been stopped by the concierge of the building, she could have walked straight into the arms of the Gestapo. At another time she was nearly shot by the resistance when sent to collect money from another sector, only saying a 'Robert' – unknown to them, had sent her.

It was soon obvious to Pearl that she was right in the middle of a Gaullist area, spread over four or five departments of which no-one had informed London (and London had told her always to avoid such territories). There were other bodies operating in the area, such as the FTP Communists.* All, except SOE, were ultimately hoping to take over power after the Liberation. Southgate, on the assumption that whoever was against the German occupation was with SOE, kept friendly with everyone and Pearl was sent to meet the organisation's leader, smooth any ruffled feathers and arrange some supply drops for him. During her time with the Maquis in the midsummer of 1944, Pearl usually had to resort to her bike to reach them. Whenever hot, dusty and thirsty she stopped at a farm and asked for a glass of water, the farmers would insist on giving her wine. At first she gave in, but afterwards she found she could hardly stay upright, let alone pedal the bike. Later, when they became determined to press the wine on her, she became just as determined to refuse, often nearly quarrelling with her over-generous hosts in trying to get at the precious water – little did they know that the ghost of her alcoholic father still haunted her. They couldn't understand her foible but with a Gallic shrug usually gave in.

She had hardly begun to know the places, houses or people to contact, before she found that Southgate was being recalled to London, leaving on 7 October. So, she and Jacqueline continued on the lines worked out by Southgate. About this time too, Maingard began training a few other civilian wireless operators in case of mishaps.

At Christmas this really did happen, when he fell very ill. Pearl also was kept in Paris by an attack of neuralgic rheumatism, the result of too many nights in cold trains. A further disaster followed soon afterwards with the capture of Octave Chantraine, one of their leading members. This increased the strain on everyone, but once Pearl recovered, she soldiered on, consulting with Cornioley, now often at her side. Unfortunately, their three attempts at sabotaging the Michelin rubber and tyre factory at Clermont-Ferrand failed. In late January 1944, Southgate returned, full of energy, knowing that D-Day was approaching soon and pleased at the way things had been run

---

* SOE was keen to avoid confusion and confrontation with some of the key resistance organisations operating in occupied France, such as the Gaullist groups, who supported Charles de Gaulle and his Free French Forces, as well as the FTP (Francs-Tireurs et Partisans) Communists. All these groups pushed their own political agendas, which sometimes clashed with the overall objectives of the Allied forces. Additionally, their security was often lax, posing a threat to SOE members.

in his absence. Unfortunately, the other French parties also scented change, and political disagreements started to break out, with Jacqueline and Pearl using the utmost tact in trying to pacify them.

London was now anxious to recall both Southgate and Jacqueline, but with victory in sight, neither wanted to miss it. In the end, Southgate remained and Jacqueline returned on 9 April 1944. Three weeks later, in an uncharacteristic move, Pearl, concerned that Maingard appeared very tired now that he had started taking over as Southgate's second-in-command, organised a short break to celebrate May Day with a picnic and a swim with friends in order to reinvigorate him. It was on this day that Southgate, also tired and hurrying, forgot the primary security rule of watching for a danger signal and was captured.

As soon as Pearl's group heard, Maingard informed London, Pearl and Cornioley left for the Les Souches estate, and the others dispersed, many in the woods nearby. Later Pearl and Maingard decided to split STATIONER into two parts with new names. She took the north of the Indre and Cher valley in the Valançay–Issoudun–Châteauroux triangle, calling it WRESTLER, while Maingard took the area south east of hers calling it SHIPWRIGHT.

It became obvious to them all that D-Day was fast approaching. More supplies and agents were dropped on Pearl's grounds. Strangely, she was nearly caught by surprise on the night before the Allied landings, as her only local wireless operator was in hiding (Maingard was now in SHIPWRIGHT), so she missed her normal transmission from London. However, she and Cornioley organised cutting all road, rail and telegraph links in her network, as she, quite rightly, believed this is what SOE would have expected them to do. It worked so well that soon 'Wanted' posters went up, offering 1 million francs for her capture.

On 11 June the Germans attacked Les Souches, assuming mistakenly that a large Maquis group was hiding in the woods of La Taille de Ruine nearby. In reality Pearl had only a small number of Maquis, but three German garrisons were sent to attack them. Picking up her things she cycled to the outhouses where their weapons were stored, until warned of the fast advancing Germans. Dropping everything, she took refuge in a cornfield, (where the corn was about 3 feet (1 metre) in height), while around her everywhere exploded into fire. She was pinned down in the field slowly crawling forward when the wind rippled the corn, exposing her in the open under the blazing sun until nightfall, with the Germans taking pot shots at her from time to time. Then she had to run and find shelter in another farm. The worst thing was that her wireless and all her weapons and stores were gone.

Left: Virginia Hall (1941–1942), (codename: Marie), a remarkable American. She single-handedly established the HECKLER network in Lyon and others, despite her handicap of a wooden leg. (Courtesy of the Special Forces Club)

Right: Yvonne Rudellat (1942–April 1945), (codename: Suzanne). Leaving the safety of her job as a hotel receptionist, she joined SOE and arrived in France by felucca (specially adapted fishing vessel). Her success in recruiting so many members to the ADOPLHE network, led by her and Pierre Culioli, encouraged SOE to send more women agents to France. (Courtesy of the Imperial War Museum HU98857)

Left: Andrée Borrell (1940*–July 1944), (codename: Denise). She and Lise de Baissac were the first woman agents parachuted into France. Andrée became courier to the agent Francis Suttill (codename: Prosper) and his ill-fated network PHYSICIAN. To the outside world she pretended to be his sister, in reality she was his right-hand 'man', recruiting new members to the network. (Courtesy of the National Archives)

Right: Lise de Baissac (1940–August 1944), (codenames: 1. Odile, 2. Marguerite) she initially worked alone as courier and organiser of the ARTIST network, which was very successful and she went on to help her brother, Claude, with the important SCIENTIST II network, which aided the Allied armies in the run-up to, and aftermath of, the D-Day landings. (Courtesy of Rita Kramer)

---

* N.B. All dates of 1940 are because the individual was involved in the resistance before she came to Britain and joined SOE. Otherwise her SOE life starts with her landing in France, 1942 onwards.

Left: Mary Herbert (1942–September 1944), (codename: Claudine), born in Ireland. She was sent by felucca to be courier to Claude de Baissac of the SCIENTIST network, based in Bordeaux. She often travelled between Bordeaux and Paris. (Courtesy of Mrs C. Pappe)

Right: Odette Sansom (1942–April 1945), (codename: Lise). She left her three young daughters to join SOE and become courier to the charismatic Peter Churchill in Cannes for the SPINDLE network. Later she claimed to be married to Peter and that he was Prime Minister Winston Churchill's nephew. (Courtesy of Geoffrey Hallowes)

Left: Sonia Olschanezky (1942–July 1944), (codename: Tania). Sonia was Jewish and born in Chemnitz, East Germany. She wanted to become a dancer, but after the German invasion of France, to where she had moved with her family, she joined the Jewish resistance. When she was released from prison she became a full-time courier for Jean Worms of the JUGGLER network, although she was never officially recognised as an SOE agent. (Courtesy of Rita Kramer)

Right: Jacqueline Nearne (1942–April 1944), (codename: Jacqueline). She parachuted into France with her organiser, Henry Southgate of the STATIONER network. Her work as a courier kept her extremely busy and she travelled widely through the Auvergne and into the Hautes Pyrénées. (Courtesy of the Special Forces Club)

Left: Julienne Aisner (1940–April 1994), (codename: Andrée). Julienne was a film impresario, who worked in her office overlooking the Champs Élysées, Paris. She helped Henri Déricourt of the FARRIER network arrange drops and pick-ups for SOE. (Courtesy of Louis Lauler)

Right: Francine Agazarian (1943), (codename: Marguerite). She was supposed to join her husband, Jack, as his courier, however she was seconded to Francis Suttill of the PHYSICIAN network, as she proved to be very good at changing papers at the town halls. She suffered greatly from the stress of her role and lost weight towards the end of her time. (Courtesy of Liane Jones)

Left: Vera Leigh (1942–July 1944), (codename: Simone). Vera, a dress designer from Paris, became involved with the 'Pat' escape line and went on to be trained by SOE. She was landed back in France by Henri Déricourt's Lysander and became courier for the INVENTOR network of Sidney Jones, working with the DONKEYMAN network and agent Suttill in Paris. (Courtesy of Rita Kramer)

Right: Noor Inayat Khan (1943–September 1944), (codename: Madeleine). She was born in Russia, but her unusual ancestry meant that she was an Indian princess, daughter of the founder of the Sufi branch of Islam. She was gentle and quiet. She worked as the wireless operator of the CINEMA network of Henri Garry and used clever evasion tactics. (Courtesy of *This England*)

Left: Cécile Lefort (1943–February 1945), (codename: Alice). She loaned the bay below her villa to SOE for the Brittany 'Var' escape line, and worked as a courier for the JOCKEY network of Francis Cammaerts on the left bank of the Rhone. (Courtesy of the National Archives)

Right: Diana Rowden (1943–July 1944), (codename: Paulette). She arrived on one of Henri Déricourt's Lysander landings to be courier in the Jura mountains for the ACROBAT network, led by John Starr. (Courtesy of the National Archives)

further news of arrested persons except that BERNARD & GABY were
known to be in prison for some time at another Gestapo H.Q.
Extract from censorship letter addressed to miss martine DUSSANTEY, french Convent,
Hitchin, Herts: from 15th June 44 until 6th Sept 44. I was in prison at KARLSRUHE
French, born of British parents. *& I saw 8 English women amongst whom*
Married. *6.12.17 in Marseilles   was Elaine Plewman.*

Description:
Height: 1m 55
Hair: dark brown
Eyes: blue
Round face.

Volunteer, F.A.N.Y.

Husband:
224,250 Lt. T.L. Plewman
53rd Heavy Regt. R.A.
Army Post Office,
England, has been informed.

Elaine Plewman (1944–September 1944), (codename: Gaby). Elaine spoke four languages, making her a promising recruit for SOE. However, she landed badly on her parachute drop and took two months to join the MONK network in Marseille as a courier to Charles Skepper. (Courtesy of the National Archives)

Left: Yvonne Cormeau (1943–September 1944), (codename: Annette). She was born in Shanghai and left her young daughter behind to serve for SOE. She was parachuted in as a wireless operator for the WHEELWRIGHT network, organised by George Starr. (Courtesy of Major Farrow)

Right: Yolande Beekman (1943–September 1944), (codename: Mariette). She hid her heavy B2 wireless transmitter in an attic near St Quentin, during her work with the MUSICIAN network of Gustav Bieler. (Courtesy of the National Archives)

Left: Pearl Witherington (1943–October 1944), (codename: Pauline). Pearl proved to be an outstanding courier to the huge STATIONER network. After its organiser, Henry Southgate was captured she took half of the network in the north of the Indre and Cher valleys, renaming it WRESTLER. She soon amassed a large and devoted following of Maquis, numbering up to 3,500 men. (Courtesy of the National Archives)

Right: Madeleine Damerment (1941–September 1944), (codename: Solange). Like so many other SOE agents her involvement began with helping in the 'Pat' escape line. She went on to act as courier for the BRICKLAYER network of France Antelme, south of Paris. (Courtesy of Rita Kramer)

Left: Anne-Marie Walters (1943–August 1944), (codename: Colette). She became a courier in George Starr's WHEEL-WRIGHT network in the south of France. She guided escaped prisoners from Eysses Prison to safety, as well as helping in the battle of Castelnau. (Courtesy of Cécile Walters)

Top Left: Eileen Nearne (1943–June 1945), (codename: Rose). Unfortunately, soon after landing with William Savy of WIZARD, he left to tell London of his discovery of VI rocket sites, and she moved to Réne Dumont-Guillemet of SPIRITUALIST, near Paris. (Courtesy of Mary Evans Picture Library)

Top Right: Denise Bloch (1942–January 1945), (codename: Ambroise). She was Jewish and worked as an unofficial courier for SOE networks. Then trained as a wireless operator, she worked for Robert Benoist of the CLERGYMAN network, near Nantes. (Courtesy of Rosemary Rigby/J.P. Barrault)

Below Right: Yvonne Baseden (1943–April 1945), (codename: Odette). She was parachuted into France with her organiser, the Baron Gonzagues de St Geniès to form the network SCHOLAR in the Jura. Her wireless transmissions set up the first-ever daylight drop by the USAAF for the Maquis. (Courtesy of Yvonne Burney)

Left: Maureen O'Sullivan (1944–October 1944), (codename: Josette). Due to an urgent demand for wireless operators, Maureen was only partially trained before being parachuted into France to the Mayer brothers in FIREMAN. Despite suffering from a chronic chest complaint, she cheerfully mastered her skills on transceiver and cycle. (Courtesy of the National Archives)

Right: Lilian Rolfe (1943–January 1945), (codename: Nadine). Lilian proudly sported Brazilian flashes on her WAAF uniform. She was hardworking and put her A Mark III transceiver to good use for the HISTORIAN network of George Wilkinson. (Courtesy of Professor Rolfe)

Right: Violette Szabo (1943–January 1945), (codenames: 1. Louise, 2. Corinne). Leaving behind a young daughter, Violette entered France twice. The first time by Lysander to investigate a failed network. The second time by parachute to resurrect and be courier for Philippe Liewer of the SALESMEN network. (Courtesy of Rosemary Rigby Museum)

Left: Muriel Byck (1943–May 1944), (codename: Violette). She was personally chosen by Philippe de Vomécourt to become his wireless operator for the VENTRILOQUIST network. She was cheerful and hardworking, with many friends. (Courtesy of Martin Sugarman AJEX)

Right: Nancy Wake (1943–September 1944), (codename: Hélène). Nancy Wake was a rumbustious New Zealander/Australian, who became an avid hater of the Nazis during her time as a journalist, when she witnessed their treatment of the Jews. She was known as the White Mouse, her 'nickname' during her time with the 'Pat' escape line. She went on to lead the Maquis in the Auvergne and Allier, under John Farmer of FREELANCE. (Courtesy of the Special Forces Club)

Christine Granville (1939–April 1945), (codename: Pauline). Christine was born in Warsaw and was a fierce Polish patriot. She helped with the escape line for POWs into Yugoslavia, then escaped herself through Asia Minor to Cairo, before parachuting from Algiers into France to the JOCKEY network of Francis Cammaerts with the express purpose of converting Poles in the German forces to the Allied cause. (Courtesy of the Special Forces Club)

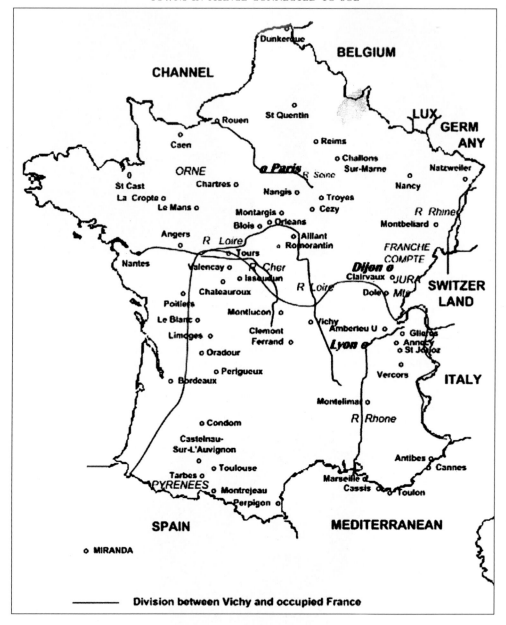

Map of all the main towns covered in the text. Many agents would travel several hundred miles in a day just to criss-cross their own network or meet with members from allied networks. (Courtesy of John Leary)

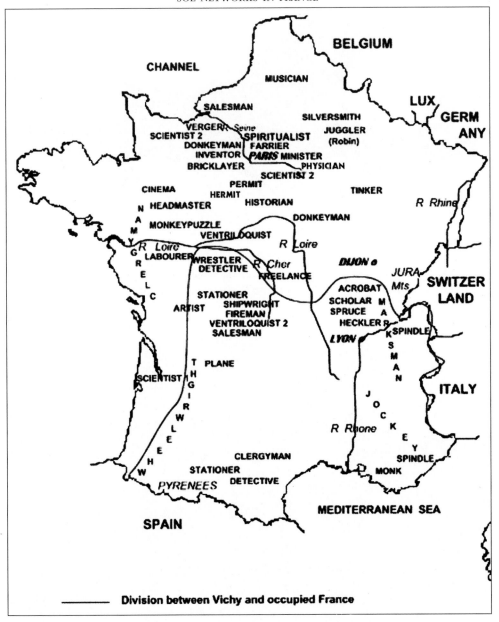

Map of the aproximate locations of all the major networks mentioned in the text. This gives some idea of the staggering size of the SOE web across France, except that they cover the period 1942–44, when many networks fell and others took their place. (Courtesy of John Leary)

One of the more daunting aspects of SOE training for the female agents was the parachute drop. Often agents experienced difficulties with the landing and injured themselves, slowing them down in the field. Here, an agent-in-training is seen jumping from a Whitley bomber. (Courtesy of Group Captain Griffiths)

There was some conflict between the SIS and SOE over the use of planes for drops, pick-ups and landings. A number of RAF officers viewed it as a waste of precious resources needed for the '1,000 Bomber Raids' and the continued war in the skies. However, the agents that they dropped behind enemy lines were effective in the run-up to, and the aftermath of, the D-Day landings. This photograph is of a Lysander aircraft picking up an agent among the Maquis in the mountains. (Courtesy of Group Captain Griffiths)

Top Left: The sturdy B Mark II (B2) suitcase transceiver used in 1943–45, it was capable of sending and receiving messages over long distances. In four compartments with its accessories it had a strong 30 watt output, but at about 32 lbs (14.8 kg) it was bulky and heavy for a woman to carry. (Courtesy of John Brown)

Top Right: The A Mark III transceiver came into use in 1944 and was the smallest issued before miniaturisation by transistors. In two containers, the working parts weighed approximately 9 lbs (4 kg), making it much lighter and strong enough to cover 500 miles. Here it is shown with its spares. (Courtesy of Keith Melton)

Above: Morse Key, used to tap out messages at not less than twenty-two words a minute.

Right: Several kinds of small plug-in crystals and adpator sockets, used for controlling the stability of the wavelength.

(Both, Courtesy of Ronald Irving and photographs by Robert Ibottson)

Marshal Pétain meets the Führer Adolf Hitler at Montoire-sur-le-Loire on 24 October 1940 to confirm the Armistice between France and Germany. (Imperial War Museum HU57383)

REMEMBER THE ENEMY IS LISTENING

A Listening Station in Britain picking up agents' transmissions – often staffed by members of FANY. Eventually there were four such stations at Grendon, Poundon, Bicester and Dunbar. (Imperial War Museum HU47912)

The results of agents' messages: thirty-six American Flying Fortresses made their first daylight drop of 400 containers to the Maquis at Vercors in June 1944. (Imperial War Museum EA34185)

Above: The tall outer walls of a concentration camp topped by broken glass, with ditches and sharp spikes. German guards are nearby. (Imperial War Museum B11679)

Right: A solitary confinement cell, with hand and leg shackles attached to the wall, no windows or daylight, a toilet bowl and letterbox for food. The reality would be far worse than this sanitised view. (Imperial War Museum B10081)

A crematorium with two beds. Sadly a number of SOE's agents ended their brave careers in this way. (Courtesy of Terry Trimmer)

It was with difficulty much later that she managed to contact London and arrange more supplies, wearing a hole in her only skirt with all her cycling. On a positive note, the drops caused a flow of volunteers for her Maquis, beginning with twenty and ending with 1,500 (some later accounts stating, 3,500) untrained men and boys. As the numbers grew she divided them into four groups responsible for a certain area, who were to harass any Germans crossing their section before melting away, and she put a suitable man in charge. When her new wireless operator with his equipment arrived, Pearl was able to summon more supplies, and in all about sixty planes delivered about 150 tons (50,802 kg) of goods and money, although she kept careful control of the numbers of weapons, only requesting what was necessary. Finally, after many requests, she was sent a French military commander, with whom she managed very well. As she protested, 'It was not my official mission to command guerilla fighters, but events were beyond me and I had to make the most of my modest capabilities'. Modest she might be, but her capabilities were not. She ran her four groups well, even acting as instructor to those unfamiliar with the new weapons, and sometimes going with the Maquis and showing them how to lay charges on the railway sleepers and the bridges. She was soon seen to be so competent that her local standing grew, and her men, laughing, called her Lieutenant Pauline or their mother, crowding around her bike when she appeared at their camp. She was an excellent, clear-headed organiser with such a personality, leadership and skill that she could manage most situations to her advantage. She could also rely on the support of Cornioley and the new military commander.

Towards the end of August, her Maquis was ordered to move to the Gâtines Forest, near Valençay. Everyone was angry, including Pearl, as she knew that the men, effective in guerilla warfare in their local home area, were handicapped in unfamiliar terrain. But they had to go, and as she predicted they achieved virtually nothing. In September, a Jedburgh party, which had been parachuted into the WRESTLER network, took part in the surrender of the Elster column of 18,000 Germans to the Americans at Orléans. The Germans dared not surrender to the Maquis, whose constant harassment had brought this about, being afraid of them. Pearl was 'proud to have given her small contribution towards it'.

Shortly afterwards Pearl and Henri Cornioley returned to London, and with her full financial accounts and any left over money, made her report. Then on 26 October she and Henri were married.

Her advice to the youth of today is 'Life isn't easy, but never lose hope and never give in.'

22

ELIZABETH REYNOLDS

She had guts and imagination!

Richard Heslop,
organiser of the MARKSMAN network

As with so many SOE agents, Elizabeth Reynolds had both a colourful character and history, even down to her name.

She was christened Elizabeth Devereux Rochester when she was born in New York on 20 December 1917, to an English mother. Her father was a soldier in the First World War. Her parent's marriage broke up after his return, and some time later her mother married Myron Reynolds, a rich American businessman, who tacked his own surname onto that of his wife's two daughters. Under a series of governesses, she was for the most part in Europe, but at eleven was sent to an English public school, where she spent much time playing sports – sailing, tennis, golf, riding and hunting. At seventeen she travelled to Europe again, once accompanying her step-father, who admired the Germans, on a business trip to Berlin, which opened her eyes to what the Nazis were doing and turned her violently against them.

Caught in France when the Second World War broke out, in 1940 she joined the American Hospital Ambulance Corps as a driver. She returned to

Paris after the Armistice to work at the American Hospital, becoming involved in vaguely anti-German activities, including taking food to imprisoned prisoners of war. This was made easier for her as her step-father was friendly with the Germans. He and her family were now living in Paris, and she, who spoke the language, though poorly, was living with them. In late 1942, she just missed being interned at Vittel with her mother (her step-father had left just in time) and other American residents.* Burying her American passport but keeping her French identity card, she fled, in the company of some Jews, into the unoccupied zone. However, when, in November 1942, the Germans moved into the zone she tried to escape to Britain, and then, because it was nearer, Switzerland. Criss-crossing France she finally reached the barbed wire at the Swiss frontier with some more refugees.

There then occurred an adventurous and confusing period when the Swiss Secret Service, the American Consulate and the British Consulate, recognising her successful evasion tactics, considered using her as a courier to help on escape lines. Directed by one or the other, she made several forays in and out of France during early 1943, usually with refugees and sometimes by accident with other escapees, until the Maquis finally took her over and, on her promise of passing on to Britain their weaponless plight, helped her cross the Pyrénées – 'the most awful experience of my life,' she afterwards said. After some time in Spain, where she had fallen ill, she eventually was sent to London. There she discovered that the Americans disapproved of her because she was too easily recognised, and that for a large part of her time she had been under the wing of the British Secret Service, with their interest in escape lines and future agents.

In the summer of 1943, having been cleared in London by the Patriotic School, the US Embassy and the War Office, she was approved for training by SOE. Her training record was mixed, excellent in all activities such as shooting, rock climbing, skiing and sabotage, but terrified of parachuting. She might have been even more terrified had she known beforehand that even the sturdy little Hudson in preparing to land in France, was going to be shaken very badly when it clipped the church belfry on its descent. It was, in any case, flying very low and executing a dangerous manoeuvre at the foot of the Jura mountains, in order to find the field near Lons-le-Saunier where it was to land her with her fellow agents, in

---

* America was now officially at war with Germany, so any American nationals still in France were interned.

the moonlit early morning of 18 October 1943. She was being sent as a courier, codenamed Elizabeth, to Richard Heslop (codenamed Xavier), as the British part of an Anglo–French mission called CANTINIER, to work with J.P. Rosenthal of the de Gaulle organisation and Denis Johnson, an American, as his wireless operator. Previously, Heslop, on his third mission, had spent three weeks with Rosenthal examining the viability in the Jura and the Haute Savoie, of a Maquis-based network called MARKSMAN, and found it perfect for the purpose.

In any case, a small Maquis already existed but grew after Heslop arrived and it became known that he had the means of summoning more weapons and explosives, though such supplies in the early days were few and Heslop did not encourage wastage. Their network bordered on Switzerland in an area Elizabeth had come to know well. It was a land of high mountains and deep valleys, pine forests and lakes, of bitter cold and snow in winter, busy industrial centres, isolated farms and alpine hamlets. Elizabeth tackled her tasks with the energy needed in such a mountainous region and was constantly on the move, carrying messages and precious supplies, while still helping refugees and escapees. She was efficient and conscientious, unconcerned with her personal safety, though it worried Heslop that her tall, perfectly tailored English appearance made her stand out like a sore thumb, despite her fluency in French and German. However, as long as she was successful in evading the Germans, all would be well. She also had a phenomenal memory, carrying most messages verbatim, rarely needing to hide slips of paper under her feet, which was done if necessary.

The increased size and activity of the Maquis and other groups, such as the FTP Communists, inevitably drew more German attention. Not far away at Amberieu was a German airfield, and German troops guarded vulnerable railway installations and factories, such as the steel plant at Ugine and an aluminium plant at St Michel de Maurienne – some of the resistants' favoured targets. It was unfortunate that this attention usually resulted in heavy German reprisals on the civilian population, but also sent many new revenge-seeking recruits into the Maquis. As a result Rosenthal noted that in the midwinter months – always very hard in the mountains – 500 farmsteads in the Haute Savoie were burned down, making life in that region even harsher than before. In February 1944, the Vichy authorities drafted in 4,500 of the feared and hated Milice and special soldiers to that department. After about two months, they had made about 1,000 arrests, before they were driven out by an enraged and enlarged Maquis. The

German presence caused the majority of a February drop of 220 containers of arms to fall into German hands, but in March a massive daylight drop by eleven USAAF aircraft of about 1,000 containers did reach the Maquis. It was counterbalanced, unfortunately, by a heavy German attack on the plateau of Glières near Annecy, where a small Maquis contingent of about 700 men, emboldened by these supplies, tried to fight it off with great bravery but were no match for the well-trained and heavily armed Germans. So the plateau was cleared. Worse still were the terrible civilian reprisals, and the burning down of nearby farms and sometimes whole villages. This apart, Maquis activity elsewhere increased with success.

In addition to carrying supplies and messages, guiding evaders and other different activities, Elizabeth was never usually involved directly in training men and taking part in sabotage, but on one occasion she was forced to do so, when a leading member of a mission was arrested beforehand. She therefore trained a small group of men, and herself set up the primers, time pencils and plastic explosives for the three railway engines they intended to blow up in the sheds at Annecy. She planned to do this before the curfew at 11 o' clock, a job that could be done in about 12 minutes. By bad luck, it snowed heavily that day and the men did not arrive until late. Nevertheless, she carried on as planned, handing out the sten guns and carrying the charges herself. It was done, though not without further delays and incidents, but they got away with it, with no-one killed.

She continued to play a crucial role in the escape lines, leaving a lasting impression on a young escaped prisoner of war, whom she picked up in early spring 1944 at a poor mountain farm, to guide him on his way onto an escape route. He found her nickname '*la Grande*' suited perfectly her light-hearted but imperious manner, her red-gold hair, her exquisite but mannish tweed costume with a divided skirt, and her dressing case fitted with gold-topped objects, worth about 1.5 million francs at the time. He could have added to these attributes her athletic build and unusual height.

Heslop was now becoming seriously concerned about Elizabeth's safety, and by implication the risk she might be to his network. He felt that she looked too English. Regretfully he decided, though he fully appreciated her work and that she tackled all she was asked to do fearlessly and successfully, that she must return to a London, which fully agreed with his decision. So he made arrangements with SOE for her to be picked up at Poitiers in late March.

He did not, however, allow for her own initiative, which included taking in a visit to Paris on her way across to the pick-up site. Arriving on a blustery March weekend Elizabeth went to stay at a safe house owned by one of her many friends from the Ambulance Service. This lady was Swiss and therefore a neutral. Elizabeth may have indicated to others previously her intention to stay there.

On the night of 20 March 1944, three men called at the house. They were two Germans and a member of the Milice, and they came to arrest not only Elizabeth but her friend also. She was finally caught.

Her treatment, however, was different from that meted out to other SOE women. She and her friend were taken straight to Frèsnes Prison and left over night in a cell together – a marvellous opportunity to concoct a story to explain Elizabeth's presence. They decided to say that she had left France for Switzerland to avoid internment as an American citizen but, homesick for Paris, had returned to stay quietly, selling most of her jewellery to do so. Unusually, she was not able to tell her fabricated story until her first major interrogations some time later at the Rue de Saussaies. By now she was in solitary confinement at Frèsnes and at least once attempted to escape. She also received two food parcels from friends while she was there. After further interrogations it seemed as if the Germans were inclined to believe her; curiously they never once linked her to her work with SOE or her London involvement.

In June came the D-Day landings and shortly afterwards Elizabeth was tried before a judge attached to the German Army. The accusation was that she was in possession of a false French identity card (in fact, it was the only real one she had kept). At the end of the case, the judge confirmed the name of the person who had betrayed her, whom she already suspected, being another in her circle of Ambulance Service friends. She also learned to her relief that her Swiss friend, arrested with her, had been released. Now accepting that she really was an American citizen, she was sent off to internment at Vittel to be freed only a short time later by the advancing Allied troops. After reporting back to London, she returned to live in liberated France.

23

ANNE-MARIE WALTERS

She possessed personal courage and never hesitated to go on any mission.
George Starr, organiser of the WHEELWRIGHT network.

Anne-Marie Walters was born in Geneva on 16 March 1923. Her mother was French and her father, an Oxford don, had become the Deputy Secretary General of the League of Nations. She was educated at the International Boarding School in Geneva, her first language being French, with only her second being English. She usually spent her long summer holidays with her parents and young sister Cici in the south of France. War changed things, and in June 1940 they moved to London. In 1941, she joined the WAAF as an airwoman clerk, where her fluency in French was remarked and took her into SOE. After training she was ready to parachute into France.

She had an inauspicious start in December 1943. The first Halifax bomber carrying her crashed in a fog, killing and injuring some passengers, except for two, Anne-Marie and Claude Arnault, who were only slightly hurt. Before the winter weather closed in, they tried to land again on 4 January 1944, when they floated down safely into a marshy field, just missing a canal, on the edge of a wooded area of the Landes.

She and Arnault were being sent to George Starr, codenamed Hilaire, to work with him and Yvonne Cormeau in the extensive network in south-west France known as WHEELWRIGHT. Since Yvonne for half a year had gallantly shouldered both being wireless operator and courier, Starr had been asking for another courier to spread the load in what he knew would be a momentous and busy year. He had thus been assigned one – Anne-Marie (codenamed Colette) as well as Claude Arnault, to be their explosives expert.

There was a lot of work to be done. As the Allied landings on French soil had not yet taken place, Starr was trying to collect arms and explosives ready for that day, in addition to sabotaging useful targets on rail and communications, as well as giving such help as he could to a small Maquis being formed under a French officer. Anne-Marie was meant to link these activities with the widespread members of the resistance that Starr did not have time to reach. She was also to assist on the escape lines taking downed pilots and escapees hoping to cross the Pyrénées to the relative safety of Spain – a distinctly risky enterprise in the deep snow and ice of the winter months.

On the day after her arrival, she was driven by truck the 55.9 miles (90 km) into Condom, where everyone seemed to know that she had just arrived from Britain, and she was offered innumerable celebratory drinks of wine, which she could not in politeness refuse. It was thus a rather wobbly courier who met her organiser, George Starr, or '*Le Patron*' as he was known locally. Afterwards she was taken to her first 'safe house' by the first of the reckless drivers that it was her fate to use. Their transport was usually a '*gazo*', a name the French mockingly gave any power source on their vehicles, ranging from farm or animal ordure to charcoal, since only the Germans had petrol for their black swift Citroëns. In fact she soon became proficient in driving these unusual vehicles or using her black-market bicycle, or taking trains and local buses, if she could not go by foot. The local bus driver in Condom, whom she got to know, may have guessed what she did and usually let her off before the bus stop where the Germans often inspected papers, and he kept her a seat beside him to avoid the crush, giving her a hot rear end from the engine and a cold nose from the broken window. In the farmhouse where she lodged, she was passed off as a Parisian student called Alice Davoust recovering from pneumonia, since her accent was different from that of the local area. As if to prove her story, some time afterwards she contracted a hacking cough and fever, so that the doctor was called. The family nursed her devotedly and she soon recovered.

Her messages and occasional transporting of various packages or secret suitcases often took her some distances. She described it as:

When I'm not in Agen, I may be in Condom, in Auch, in Toulouse, in Tarbes or Montréjeau. One day I am sent to Auch to collect blank and stamped travel permits, then next I go to Tarbes to take some money to a man who works there. The third I cycle to take a message to the wireless operator or someone else. Then I'm off for three days to Tarbes and Montréjeau where I have to wait for a reply from Arnault or someone else.

Once she had to go to Paris – a very risky enterprise for an agent – on what turned out to be an abortive errand. She was very aware that at any minute she could be stopped and searched, and kept in mind the fate of a seventeen year old boy in Agen, who, during her first week in France, had been arrested by the Gestapo and died the same day of torture.

One of her first missions was with Arnault to arrange, and then partly accompany, a group of escapees, who had been part of the mass breakout, that had taken place the day before she landed, from the Eysses Prison, to Tarbes 100 miles (170 km) away. There were many difficulties. One was that a large group of SS had arrived to eliminate the resistants who had killed some German soldiers at Agen.* In addition the guides at Tarbes were already escorting a large party of Americans over the Pyrénées, so that the Eysses group would have to be found safe houses around Fourcés, while they waited their turn. To cap it all the escapees '*gazo*' truck had its limits, especially on hills, of which there were several. Anne-Marie often travelled ahead on her bike to check the way and to see if there were any road blocks or controls on their route. It was quite an adventurous journey but it ended successfully. There were also other escape missions but with smaller numbers.

At another time she assisted an agent in making up explosives near Montréjeau, and then, with a French police inspector, took four heavy suitcases to Toulouse. It was intended that the resistants there would see them planted in the Ampalot powder factory – the third biggest in France. All went well until the three of them came to the railway station exit, when a policeman stopped the one who was carrying two suitcases. The other two companions, with a suitcase each, went on and waited nearby, soon

---

* Communists working to their own agenda, often ignored the inevitable reprisals on the innocent population.

joined, to their relief, by the police inspector who had been dismissed after showing his inspector's card. After she returned, she heard that the demolition had taken place.

On 16 March 1944, Anne-Marie held her twenty-first birthday party, in a house not far from the Pyrénées, to which, among the other guests, Yvonne Cormeau was invited. Food was heavily rationed of course, but the people with whom Anne-Marie was staying prided themselves in putting a good meal on the table. The memorable masterpiece was a beautifully decorated cake with twenty-one lighted candles – almost impossible to obtain in occupied France. Unexpectedly, it quickly emptied the room, as the lovely candles were pieces of detonating fuse, helpfully painted pink by their explosives expert!

There were other adventures, narrow escapes and a variety of tasks. One was helping to train resistants in the use of arms with which they were unfamiliar, though the men disliked taking instruction from a girl. At other times she was found helping at moonlit receptions for parachute drops. Then, in June, came the 'A' and 'B' notices, warning of the imminent D-Day landings, to take to leading members of the WHEELWRIGHT network. There was a panic when one leader was arrested with his A notice on him. As a result London issued changes, which again had to be hurriedly distributed, and German arrests intensified. In addition, police in Condom started asking questions about a young, blue-eyed, fair-haired girl living nearby, and Anne-Marie was warned to stay out of sight at her host's farm.

After the D-Day landings, she was recalled to Starr's headquarters on the hill-top village of Castelnau-sous-l'Auvignon, where he was Deputy Mayor. He, additionally, had a small Maquis, and Yvonne Cormeau had joined him with a further wireless operator. Both operators were very busy, but Anne-Marie, who thrived on excitement, found it very dull and disliked being engaged on such mundane work as typing reports. This quickly came to an end when a German spotter plane reported Maquis activity in and around Castelnau, and the Germans mounted an attack on the village. She then acquitted herself bravely, unpacking and distributing grenades, but the hand to hand fighting came nearer, and everyone was ordered to evacuate the plateau, leaving only a small band of Maquis to hold it. Starr entrusted the records of the resistants and Maquis to her to hide or destroy, as they would incriminate most of their members in the region. Casting around she found a cave beneath the village church, where she buried them, delaying her escape. She did manage to rescue some of the SOE money from the

Mayor's house, although she was unable to retrieve her identity cards, as the houses around her were being blown to pieces while she ran. As she followed the retreating Maquis she heard the village arsenal being blown up by the rearguard to prevent it falling into enemy hands. Much later, as the sounds of battle faded in the distance, she got a lift into Condom where she caught up with the others, who were cheerful despite their losses.

She stayed with what was to become the Armagnac Battalion, receiving further parachute supplies and several commandos. However, Starr began to feel that she was too volatile, taking too many risks, forming unsuitable friendships and becoming difficult to control, endangering herself and them. So on 1 August 1944 he sent her, under the escort of a New Zealand pilot, back across the Pyrénées, a route on which she had sent so many others before. With her went five other prisoner-of-war escapees. Their journey was not without misadventures, but at length they reached Spain and eventually Britain. Thus ended a short and eventful few months.

24

MADELEINE DAMERMENT

The whole Lille Post Office family was solidly behind the resistance, though
nothing could be proved against them.

Madeleine, named after her mother, was born in Torte Fontain, Pas de Calais
on 11 November 1917, and was one of three sisters. Her father became Head
Postmaster of Lille, near the Belgian border. She did well at school and then
worked in the telephone service in Lille. After the German occupation,
her whole family was drawn into the resistance, initially helping with food
parcels for prisoners of war, which led to her taking part in SOE's DF 'Pat'
escape line as a courier, and also helping SOE's FARMER network, run by
Michael Trotobas. In addition she was credited with the escape of seventy-
five British and American pilots.

Madeleine was described as having a cloud of dark curling hair, dark eyes,
round cheeks and a generous mouth. She was intelligent, vivacious, gentle
and had many friends.

In May 1941, the Germans arrested and then released her parents, driving
Madeleine underground. It may have been at this time that she met Andrée
Borrel of PHYSICIAN in Paris, as the Lille escape line was having to rely

on Paris for communicating with London. She may also at this period have encountered Antelme of BRICKLAYER. Later, in 1942, she was sent away on the same escape line as her pilots. She was captured, and was ultimately released from the Spanish prison just in time by the efforts of the British consul, as she had become very ill. Then she was sent to Britain. After hospital, being treated for a glandular complaint, she recuperated at the Convent of the Sacred Heart in Hertfordshire.

Being completely French, and having had such useful experience in the 'Pat' line (as did Andrée Borrel and Nancy Wake) when recovered she joined SOE's F service. In October 1943, she began her training as an agent, which was shorter than usual, perhaps due to her previous resistance experience. Held up by the bad January weather, she did not parachute into France until 28 February 1944, when she landed near Sainville, 19 miles (31 km) from Chartres. Given the codename of Solange, she was to be the courier for the revived network of BRICKLAYER, sited south of Paris. She jumped with Lionel Lee, their wireless operator, and France Antelme, her organiser, already an experienced agent.

Waiting for them, on the ground below, were Kieffer, Ernest Vogt and other SS men. Realising this, Antelme flew into a great rage. 'I have been betrayed', he shouted. He had been taken in by the messages being played by the Germans on Noor Inayat Khan's wireless. He had been sure it had been sent by her. His mistake had doomed the three of them.

Madeleine was interrogated but not tortured: the Germans rather laughed at her when she refused to say anything. After a brief spell, she was consigned to Frèsnes. She was not there for long. On 13 May 1944, she was taken to the Avenue Foch to meet seven other women, including Andrée Borrel whom she had formerly known. On the same day they were despatched to the German prison of Karlsruhe. She was wearing the same grey skirt and pullover in which she had been captured. Food was not so bad at Karlsruhe, since most of the prisoners were German women, but she could be heard crying at night and sometimes would sing or pray with her rosary. She also became stouter, possibly due to the return of her old glandular complaint. One day she discovered that she could communicate with the girl in the cell next door – one of the women she had met in the Paris gathering. It was Elaine Plewman.

On 12 September 1944, Yolande Beekman, Elaine Plewman, Madeleine, and a late-arriving Noor Inayat Khan, were taken in the early morning to a second-class compartment of a train. There they had an enjoyable day, chatting in the sunshine and admiring the Swabian mountains. Madeleine, who was the only one who spoke German, won some small privileges from their guards. Around midnight they reached a station not far from Munich and walked uphill to the concentration camp of Dachau.

By now Madeleine's clothes were tattered and when she was consigned for the rest of the night to an isolation cell, she was half-naked. There she was cruelly beaten. On the next morning, Madeleine, with two of the others, was taken out and made to kneel in front of a wall, and there she was neatly shot through the back of her neck, her body, shortly afterwards taken and cremated.

It was 12 September 1944 and Madeleine was twenty-six years old.

25

DENISE BLOCH

An experienced woman with knowledge of the world

Training Report

Denise Madeleine Bloch was born in Paris on 21 January 1916. Her parents were French Jews with four children, of whom she was the only girl. She appears to have been educated at Louveciennes, where she learned English as a second language. She was tall, broad-shouldered and sturdy with dark eyes, longish, black, curling hair and a strong face. As she grew up she was considered beautiful. Although sturdy she was not good at sport, and therefore had rather a physical inferiority complex. When she came to SOE after a year's experience in the French resistance, she was capable of handling most situations with complete self assurance and had plenty of courage, determination and a fixed hatred of the Germans.

In 1940, Denise and her family were living in Lyon, where she was employed in the Citroën organisation as a secretary to Jean Maxime Aron. She had also become engaged to M. Mendelsohn, although she later declared that it was only an engagement of convenience to help her in her work. Soon the German crackdown on Jews in Paris caused Jewish resistance movements to grow and spread, many working alongside SOE networks.

In July 1942, Denise was drawn into the resistance by Réne Piércy, who was impressed by her knowledge of English. Her fiancé soon followed her. On 27 August 1942, SOE parachuted in Henri Sevenet (codenamed Rodolphe), a friend of the de Vomécourts, to recall Philippe de Vomécourt (codenamed Gauthier). De Vomécourt's position as Inspector of Railways had enabled him to run the VENTRILOQUIST network successfully since 1941, and Denise's employer Aron (codenamed Joseph) had become his assistant. De Vomécourt indignantly refused Sevenet's message to return to Britain.

Sevenet then turned to revitalise the little DETECTIVE network subordinate to de Vomécourt, which was watching the Tours–Poitiers railway line, and he took Denise to become his courier. He shared the wireless operator Brian Stonehouse (codenamed Celestin) with de Vomécourt, and took over Blanche Charlet as a new courier for Stonehouse, one of whose tasks was finding him new safe houses for his transmissions. Denise was also intended to look after Stonehouse, whose French was not too good, and to carry his sketchbook, from which, despite her warnings, he would not be parted. She felt he was homesick and too young for his job.

One day in 1942, while working as a courier with the resistance, Denise, carrying a bulky wireless in its suitcase, and waiting to go onto a bus, saw the Gestapo doing an inspection of the travellers' papers. She immediately got into conversation with one of the Germans in the queue, her fractured German making him laugh. Having established friendly relations, she took her opportunity to ask him to watch her case while she went to buy a newspaper. On returning she showed her papers to a civilian inspector, retrieved her case, coolly got onto the bus... and got away with it.

All went well until October then everything seemed to happen at once. On 14 October Denise saw Stonehouse, obviously under arrest, being escorted to a Lyon Police Station. He was shortly followed by Blanche Charlet and, on the 30th, Mendelsohn was arrested. Denise's father, by bribery, attempted to release them*.

On 26 October 1942, Denise, realising the danger she was in, left for Marseille, where she received some information about landing grounds. Aware of the risk of returning to Lyon again, and after cabling her mother there, she volunteered to go alone to pass this information on, but Sevenet

---

* In April 1944, Mendelsohn did effect his own escape to Britain.

and Aron insisted on accompanying her. This gentlemanly action cost them dearly. As they were leaving Lyon station Aron was arrested, just missing Sevenet and Denise. So, again, Denise had escaped, and she went to ground first near Lyon and then at Villafranche-sur-Mer until January 1943, only leaving it once, to have her dark hair dyed fair in Nice. At this point Sevenet, believing her safer out of France, enlisted the help of Yvan Dupont (codenamed Abelard) of DIPLOMAT to send her across the Pyrénées. But winter and the German patrols prevented it. On returning to Toulouse they met George Starr of WHEELWRIGHT, who took Denise to work as a courier at Agen with de Vomécourt again. In April, Starr, having just lost his wireless operator as well as another agent, who was about to meet Denise for lunch, felt it time to send her with Dupont back over the Pyrénées again to make for London, now that it was spring and they could take an easy flat route – which turned out to be neither flat nor easy.

After this whirlwind overview of so many networks, Denise, in Britain, after clearance and debriefing, and being enrolled in the FANY as Danielle Williams, in June began a ten-month training with SOE (where she proved quite argumentative) to prepare her to return to France as a wireless operator.

One thing she would be particularly warned about during training was the continuous watch kept both day and night at the Gestapo Headquarters in the Avenue Foch, Paris, for the signals from wireless operators. Relays of about thirty or so German clerks gazing at their cathode ray tubes on every available frequency, searched for any new blip to appear on their tube. They would then telephone the Direction Finders at Brest, Augsberg and Nuremberg, giving the reading of the new frequency, and ask for cross bearings. These found, the Detection Finding vans, full of the most sensitive equipment, would take up the hunt, forming a triangle within a triangle, until they were probably within a mile or so of their quarry, and moving slowly along the lanes or streets. Finally, men on foot in long raincoats, their earphones hidden by their high turned-up collars and hats, read off the distances by miniature meters, on what looked like large wrist watches. In this way they could pin-point the very house from which the signal came.

This was the situation when Denise (codenamed Ambroise), with a new identity and papers for Micheline Claude de Rabatel, landed by Lysander on 3 March 1944, with her new organiser Robert Benoist (codenamed Lionel) at Soucelles, some distance from Nantes. Benoist, a dashing racing driver, was part of a wealthy family involved in the resistance and owning several chateaux used as safe houses and to store weapons on their estates.

He hoped to revive the CLERGYMAN network which he had started and abandoned the year before, because he found that the countryside around Nantes was unsuitable for arms drops, and he had lost his wireless operator. This time working with a very small team, and an experienced courier-cum-wireless operator, he hoped for more success.

Denise contacted London very early and worked hard. Her objectives were similar to those of Benoist. She was to assist in destroying the high pylons over the river Loire at the Île Heron. These carried electricity generated in the Pyrénées to Brittany. She was also to arrange the cutting of all the railway and telephone lines leading to Nantes, in order to disrupt German communications before D-Day. For some of the former operations she could rely on the railwaymen, who were nearly all eager to damage the German invader in any way they could. When these targets had been fully prepared, she accompanied Benoist to his estate at the Villa Cécile, south-west of Paris, near Rambouillet, with forests to the north-west and south-east, where he boasted that he could raise 2,000 men for the FFI. Around the chateau he thought he would find some arms dumps and leaders sheltering after the collapse of his earlier network. Here Denise found friends among the wives of several of the leaders, who had acted as unofficial couriers for them.

With June came D-Day, and all appeared to be going as planned, when suddenly Benoist was summoned to his dying mother in Paris. Then the blow fell. On 18 June he was arrested in the street outside her apartment. The news had hardly reached the Villa Cécile, when on the next day, the Germans again pounced, this time on the villa, where they found Jean-Pierre Wimille and his wife having lunch with Denise. Wimille escaped, but the two women and others were captured.

Denise was held for interrogation at the Avenue Foch. She had sent thirty-one messages and received fifty-two during her three months of freedom, but, true to form, the Germans learned nothing from her, though she might have known more than most. After questioning she was consigned to Frèsnes Prison, but not for long. The Allied armies were advancing, and the Germans needed to remove their last thirty-seven SOE prisoners out of reach of rescue. On 8 August, Denise, with others, including Violette Szabo and Lilian Rolfe, all chained in pairs by the ankles, were sent third class in a crowded train to Germany. A journey that should have taken two days took much longer during a very hot August, partly owing, somewhat ironically, to being bombed by the RAF, and the railway lines damaged by the resistants. They sometimes had to change transport and routes, stopping at several places overnight, including the concentration camp of Neue-Bremm Saarbrücken. In late August they reached the women's concentration camp of Ravensbrück, known to the French as '*l'Enfer des Femmes*' – Women's Hell.

It was built near a Lakeland beauty spot, 50 miles (80.5 km) north of Berlin, on marshy ground – a breeding place for disease. Several smaller enclaves existed outside for working parties doing factory or heavy agricultural work in the community, as well as a Jugendlager for those too ill or weak to work. The wooden huts with bunks, where they slept in tiers of three, were meant to house a third of the numbers which usually filled them.

It was unspeakably insanitary, disease and pest-ridden. Nevertheless the three women, who by now knew one another very well, tried to stay together and managed to share the top one-bed bunk in one of the huts. Two weeks later, on 4 September, Denise and her two companions were sent on a working group to Torgau, where food and conditions were slightly better, so they became more cheerful and planned an escape, foiled at the last minute. Possibly under suspicion, they were sent back to Ravensbrück, beaten and put in the prison block, called the Bunker, underground. On 19 October, Denise and the two others in their light summer clothes were trucked out to Königsberg, to do heavy building and tree felling for a new airfield, in the harshest winter weather and terrible work conditions, until they were recalled to Ravensbrück. By now they were all filthy, in rags, starving and no longer cheerful. A day or two later Denise and the other two disappeared and it was assumed that they had died.

In a large crowded camp, of which Ravensbrück was one of the largest, little went on without someone seeing or hearing about it. Rumour was also rife. Thus one of the women working in the so-called infirmary, knew that the normal method of execution was hanging. A woman in the clothes store later said that the clothing of the three women was returned to her unsoiled, and that this meant that they had been put to death this way. Another woman denied that the clothes had ever been returned. What do we believe?

It is in direct contradiction to the sworn testimony later extracted by the indefatigable Vera Atkins* from a German officer of Ravensbrück, who was then a prisoner awaiting trial:

---

* Vera had spent a year after the war, examining records and interviewing German officers to find out what had happened to missing SOE agents.

I declare that I remember that I had delivered to me towards the end of January 1945 an order from the German Secret Police, countersigned by the Camp Commandant Suhren, instructing me to ascertain the location of the following persons: Lilian Rolfe, Danielle Williams [alias Denise Bloch] and Violette Szabo. These were at that time in the dependant camp of Königsberg on the Oder and were recalled by me. [All of them were in a pitiful state and Lilian too weak to walk.] When they returned to the camp they were placed in the punishment block and moved from there into the block of cells.

One evening they were called out and taken to the courtyard by the Crematorium. Camp Commandant Suhren made these arrangements. He read out the order for their shooting in the presence of [various names of camp officials, including the doctor.] I was myself present. The shooting was done only by Schult, with a small calibre gun through the back of the neck. They were brought forward singly by Cpl. Schenk. Death was certified by Dr Trommer. The corpses were removed singly by internees who were employed in the Crematorium and burnt. The clothes were burnt on the bodies…

All three were very brave and I was deeply moved. Suhren was also impressed by the bearing of these women. He was annoyed that the Gestapo did not themselves carry out these shootings…

Signed: Johann Schwarzhuber,
Obersturmfuhrer of the SS, camp overseer at Ravensbrück.

So the accounts are at variance. Hanging at Ravensbrück was public, slow and did not soil clothes, whereas shooting was secret and did. Were the three to die in order to hide the evidence of German actions inside SOE – its radio game, its agents and infiltrators? Hanging was too public to hide. On the other hand, the officers officiating at the shooting might now be hoping to show that they were only doing this according to orders from a superior. Can we believe this account?

It was, of course, in obedience to the *'Nacht und Nebel Erlass'* ('night and fog' decree) from Hitler. On balance, it seems possible that their deaths were as given by this officer at their execution.

Thus, on or around the 27 January 1945, long after the liberation of France had been achieved, for which Denise had been prepared to sacrifice herself, she died. A sad end after such an eventful, brilliant and brave life. Denise was twenty-nine years old.

26

EILEEN NEARNE

The Germans considered her a silly little French girl who had wasted the Gestapo time.

Eileen Mary Nearne, nicknamed Didi by friends and family, born in London on 16 March 1921, was the youngest of four children (three were to be involved in SOE), of an English father and a Spanish mother. In 1923, they all moved to France where the two girls were educated at convents, speaking both English and French. Caught in 1940 with her family in Nice, Eileen and her sister Jacqueline, using their own money, escaped to Britain. In London they registered for War Service and in 1942 both joined the FANY, Eileen rather later than her sister. In 1943, Eileen was trained as a FANY wireless operator, while, unbeknown to her, Jacqueline was already an SOE agent in France (see Chapter 11). Eileen was sent to one of the SOE Listening Stations in Britain, where she soon realised what was going on, and applied to work as an agent in France. Because of her youth – she was only just over twenty – and the many risks, Jacqueline opposed her sister's wishes. But Eileen's determination won through. Jacqueline later withdrew her opposition and Eileen began training as an SOE wireless operator, with Yvonne Baseden, a fellow trainee.

Like her sister, this small, dark, quiet girl did not make a very good impression on her SOE trainers, who thought her a loner, being both secretive and independent. They did not also realise that her childish, rather fragile appearance masked a strong will and an unexpected talent of being a believable liar.

After two failed flights, Eileen (codenamed Rose) with her organiser, the lawyer and master chef William Savy (of the WIZARD network), was landed by Lysander near Châteauroux on the night of 3 March 1944. They were to form a new network in Paris, which by now was a lethal city for an agent and packed with Germans. Her new cover name was Mademoiselle Jacqueline du Tertre. Next morning she took a train to Orléans and afterwards to Paris where, in the driving snow, she sought a place in which to live and a safe house for her wireless set. Meanwhile Savy had begun hunting for his friend Antelme, who had been on the same parachute landing as Madeleine Damerment. While Savy was seeing Eileen for her regular 'skeds' and building up his new WIZARD network, he began to suspect that Antelme had been captured, and while investigating this he accidentally discovered that the Germans were hiding a large number of V1 rockets, intended for Britain, in a stone quarry near Creil. This information was so sensitive that he felt he must take it personally to London.

Therefore, within a month of her arrival, Eileen had to make hurried arrangements for Savy's return to Britain. Savy also introduced her to René Dumont-Guillemet (codenamed Armand), the organiser of the SPIRITUALIST network, forming very satisfactorily on the outskirts of Paris. He also arranged for a second wireless operator, G. Maury (codenamed Arnaud) to be parachuted in to help Eileen as D-Day approached. By a strange twist of fate, the same Lysander that picked up Savy on 9 April also took back another passenger – Jacqueline – though Eileen probably did not know this.

Dumont-Guillemet, SPIRITUALIST's organiser, was now concentrating on increasing the drops of arms and ammunition, making Eileen's transmissions ever more vital. Fortunately, she was now able to vary the times of her 'skeds', since both before and after the D-Day landings, she was taking messages for other networks short of an operator, and mixed in with these transmissions were scraps on German military dispositions.

In July 1944, having used the house at Bourg-la-Reine for her transmissions for over four months, Eileen felt it was time to move to a different location. When one was found, Maury began using it and Eileen decided to move there herself on 25 July, but on that same day came a most urgent message, so that for just one last time she used Bourg-la-Reine. Thus it was there that she was captured, with scant time to burn her codes and hide her set.

In her light blue summer dress and in chains, she was taken in a Gestapo car to their Paris headquarters at the Rue de Saussaies. There began her interrogation, but the more they pressed, the more she opposed them, and she lied so easily that they began to believe her. She told them that she had been sending commercial messages for a businessman because she was unemployed and needed the money. Further questions were followed by the dreaded 'baignoire', where in a cold bath her head was submerged several times until she nearly drowned, but her story didn't vary, although she now admitted to the next meeting with her boss in a café. So they took her there, dripping wet, to wait for him. A lucky air raid saved her and her cover story was still intact. Also several times she tried to escape, but failed. Eventually she was sent to Frèsnes Prison, placed in a cell with others and dismissed as a silly little girl who had wasted Gestapo time.

Then, on 8 August, she was sent to the women's concentration camp at Ravensbrück, on the way trying to escape again. There, from her hut of French women, Eileen bumped into Denise Bloch and another with her, and heard about another girl from the English huts.

In October 1944, all four, with other women, were sent to Torgau for two months, digging vegetables in the fields. One day Eileen heard from the active one of her fellow SOE prisoners about her plan to escape by obtaining a key to the door in the surrounding camp wall. Eileen, suspicious, advised caution. Later Eileen was told that they had got the key, but someone had found out and they had been forced to lose it quickly. By then Eileen was moved to Abterode and did not see her friends again. There she was to work in an aircraft factory. Refusing to work at this job she was hauled off to have her head shaved and told she would be shot if she wasn't working in 20 minutes. Thereafter she did so, but slowly and clumsily. Back in Ravensbrück on 1 December, she was next sent to Markleberg, making up roads for 12 hours a day in the frost and snow, on less food and in a much harsher regime. Dysentery swept the camp, but Eileen stubbornly refused to give in.

On about 9 April 1945, the women were told they were leaving for another camp 50 miles (80 km) away. It was dark, cold and snowing by the time they marched off – there was no transport. Armed guards swept their torches along the line to check that none fell out. Darkness and confusion offered Eileen her last chance to escape. At about 11pm, passing through a forest, Eileen slipped out of line to hide behind the nearest tree. Then she crept deeper into the forest. No-one saw her go.

The long march continued into the distance. Later, she met two Frenchwomen who had done the same. For two freezing days they slept in a bombed out house, but eventually hunger drove them towards the town of Markleberg, where, turning a corner, they walked into an SS patrol. They were asked for their papers, and one woman who spoke German said they were French volunteers for work in Germany, making their way to meet their new group. Miraculously the patrol let them pass. They went back to the forest to rest and then started walking. Now nearly dropping from starvation and fatigue they realised they could go no further. Approaching Leipzig, they walked into a church and begged help of the priest. A good man, he hid them in the belfry, bringing them food and a doctor for Eileen, who had collapsed in delirium. On the third day, from the tower, they saw white flags everywhere and the first Americans arriving. It was about 15 April 1945. Rejoicing they rushed out to greet their liberators. Then followed a strange time for Eileen.

First she was interrogated by the Captain of the American camp in the presence of several SS officers, who naturally denied all knowledge of her. Next the Americans asked her for her service number, but she had none. Then they wanted to see her papers, and she explained that they had been taken away by the Gestapo. The irony was that when she told the Germans lies, they had believed her, now she told the Americans the truth, they didn't believe her. Then, to add insult to injury, after much more questioning, they sent her to be accommodated with the Nazi women, treating her as one of them. She was told that she would have to pass through many more camps and more interrogations before she could be sent to the British authorities. They said that as there were so many German agents around, they needed to be careful. At her last interrogation in her last camp, she was asked about her landing in France. They expressed incredulity at a plane being able to find a tiny landing place in the dark in such a large country. They thought she was making it up. She was handicapped throughout by refusing to give the details of SOE to them. Who needed enemies when you had such friends?

At last they did contact someone in the British authorities, and she was introduced to a British Major who came to fetch her, listened to her story, and took her to Weimar. Next day she was flown to Brussels to meet a British Captain, who arranged for her to be flown to Britain.

On her return in June 1945, it was hardly surprising that she could barely walk, and after hospitalisation suffered a long physical and emotional breakdown, tended devotedly by her sister Jacqueline.

27

YVONNE BASEDEN

I suppose I thought I would be one of the lucky ones who would get away with it. It's somebody else who is run over by a tram… But I said my quiet prayers all the same.

Yvonne Baseden from *Moon Squadron* by J. Tickell

Yvonne Jeanne Vibraye Baseden was a slim, dark-haired, attractive girl possessed of a natural grace and dignity. The only child of an engineer in the Royal Flying Corps and the daughter of a French château owner, she was born on 20 January 1922 in Paris. In 1937, her parents moved to England, where she attended a convent school.

In 1940, aged eighteen she joined the WAAF, but being bi-lingual, she was asked to help the Free French Squadrons with their technical English. In 1941, she was commissioned and later as a Flight Officer posted to Air Ministry. Here she met Pearl Witherington, already accepted for SOE, who recommended her for it. Thus, under cover of the FANY, she joined SOE in May 1943 as a wireless operator. Her training was rigorous, and so she spent a Spartan Christmas at Beaulieu in 1943, with twenty other agents-in-waiting.

In January 1944, she was introduced to her future organiser, the Baron Gonzagues de St Geniès (codenamed Lucien). Yvonne's codename was

Odette, but her cover name was Mademoiselle Marie Bernier. It was 19 March 1944, on their second attempt, when they parachuted down from a large Lancaster, near Marmande in the south-west of France to a reception organised by George Starr of the WHEELWRIGHT network. Yvonne briefly met Anne-Marie Walters and Yvonne Cormeau. The two new agents made their way separately by train for four days to set up a network called SCHOLAR in the Jura mountains, next to Switzerland and Richard Heslop's MARKSMAN network.

Their main task was to look for suitable dropping zones and provide a new base for air drops to supply the local Maquis. For this Yvonne had three wireless sets, which she hid in such constantly changing places as attics, barns, fields, hayricks and hedges. St Geniès was also to investigate the loss of contact with one of two overlapping networks, and finding its organiser had been captured, he had to take over. Yvonne, therefore, found herself carrying messages around the growing network by day and contacting London by night, as well as occasionally joining St Geniès in training new recruits on how to use the guns and explosives dropped to them.

For the D-Day landings on 6 June 1944, every German telephone and telegraph line had to be cut and more supplies were needed. Following D-Day, it was arranged to send a very large scale drop of armaments to this area in broad daylight, and Yvonne's transmissions were busy making arrangements long beforehand. In the last 24 hours, she had to remain in the dropping zone, sending frequent crack signals throughout the preceding night so that her transmissions guided the planes, and in the last stage she was in direct voice communication with the leading plane by S-phone.

So the peace of a quiet Sunday morning on 26 June 1944 was shattered by the roar of thirty-six huge flying Fortresses of the Eighth Army Air Force, which dropped their great load of 400 containers to the hundreds of waiting Maquis below, who efficiently spirited them away to their hideouts. When Yvonne left, she passed her wireless to a student volunteer to cycle with it to her next destination by a different route.

Just outside Dôle was a tall building known as Les Orphelins – a warehouse with a main hall, a cellar and a loft for ripening the Graf cheeses, which were the size of cartwheels. It was empty at this time of year, except for the Swiss cheese-maker and his wife – its caretakers. Here Yvonne, St Geniès and their resistance leaders met to celebrate the success of their operation, not knowing that the teenager with Yvonne's wireless had been arrested and had his destination beaten out of him.

Meanwhile, the party was just finishing when the man keeping watch at the window suddenly cried out, 'Germans!' Immediately the nine table places were swept away and everyone disappeared to pre-arranged hiding places among the empty packaging and pieces of wood, while the caretaker's wife went slowly down the stairs to open the door. Yvonne and a Frenchman hid beneath the same wooden planks, where she could hear and see all that went on. The Germans came up but their search was not particularly thorough and nothing was found. Nevertheless, they left a sentry behind.

As evening drew on, the dropping temperatures of the oncoming storm affected the water pipes, which began to gurgle. The sentry's suspicions were aroused and he called back the Gestapo. Yvonne remembered that St Geniès had said that with all he knew, if caught he would take his cyanide pill (Yvonne had refused hers). Motor cyclists, some horse-drawn wagons and two car loads of German police arrived – about twenty men – and this time they searched the depot thoroughly, and one by one they winkled out the resistants. Yvonne heard a man removing the planks above her head, and he looked down on her in her blue blouse and grey skirt. He yanked her out by her dark hair and when she struggled he hit her across the face and she fell. They also shot into the ceiling and by chance hit St Geniès in the head, as he was hidden in the loft above. His blood seeped down through the ceiling, revealing his hiding place, and when he was thrown down with the other bodies into one of the two horse-drawn wagons, Yvonne saw he was dead. She, herself, handcuffed to her hostess, and with other survivors, was in the second wagon. In the thunderstorm and heavy rain they were taken to the local prison at Dôle.

A day or two later they were transferred to Dijon prison, to be interrogated singly. Fortunately for Yvonne, the Germans never guessed she was the wireless operator. She was sent to a dank, windowless, underground cell, without food or water, for perhaps days. When she was returned for more questioning, she was so weak that she had to crawl up the stairs. During this unproductive session, one officer grew so angry that he stamped on her bare toes, and they had to drag her back to her cell, as she could not walk. Later they threatened to shoot her if she did not help them. She didn't and they did, but they shot to miss. After still more questioning, they left her in a solitary confinement cell on the woman's ground floor of the prison, but she was given food. During a short exercise period, she noticed another British woman prisoner, and discovered she was Mary Lindell, who had worked on an escape line.

As the Allies drew nearer, she and Mary again met when they were sent by rail to Ravensbrück concentration camp, in late August 1944. They tried to escape but failed, and at Neue-Bremm Saarbrücken, their first stop, they met five other SOE women. After a few days, their journey continued until about 22 August 1944, when they arrived at Ravensbrück. There she went through the degrading admission procedure, and received a pleated red skirt and blue sailor top, on the sleeve of which was sewn a red triangle, indicating a political prisoner and a number. They were told that the grim crematorium chimney was the only way to leave the camp.

After three weeks in quarantine, they went into the regular system of huts and work. Yvonne was lucky in being able to share the top bunk in her crowded hut with Mary Lindell, though shortly Mary was sent to nurse in the hospital. But conditions and food on the camp grew worse as the work increased, and punishments were grave for even the most trivial of offences, or sometimes meted out when no offence had even been committed.

The SS guards, both men and women, took the greatest of pleasure in causing pain and suffering on the hapless inmates in the camp. One day Yvonne, unloading pillows from a truck, unfortunately caused a feather to land on the uniform of one of the guards, who immediately raised his weighted whip, and felled her to the ground with a single blow. It could have killed her, save for the help of a fellow prisoner who pushed her slightly out of the way, so that it fell on her thigh and not her head. She was cruelly kicked as a consequence, but survived.

By December 1944, Yvonne was found to have contracted a spot on her lung: tuberculosis. Her name, therefore, went down to be sent to Belsen. Mary discovered this in time and had it removed and Yvonne was instead admitted to one of the hospital blocks as a patient. So it was here that Yvonne spent her twenty-third birthday.

Now the Allies were advancing deep into Germany, and things at the camp grew worse. There was little water, much disease, more deaths and even more brutal treatment, and still more work. Most inmates were starving, women were fighting over crusts of food and rumours were rife. When they found barrels of oil placed against the walls of the huts, they began to fear they would be burned alive.

In April 1945, negotiations between Count Bernadotte* and Himmler resulted in the appearance of three white Swedish buses outside the camp.

---

* Count Bernadotte was a Swedish diplomat, noted for his negotiation of the release of *c.*31,000 prisoners from German concentration camps.

Groups of women were cleared through the gates to enter the buses. One group contained Yvonne and Mary. It was 28 April 1945.

Yvonne was driven north to Denmark and then shipped to Malmo in Sweden. Then came the plea, 'We have a woman here who says she is... what shall we do.' Air Ministry swiftly arranged transport and soon Yvonne was back in Britain. She was hospitalised, had an operation and a long recuperation.

She was one of the few SOE F service agents who had been to 'Hell' and come back alive.

MAUREEN O'SULLIVAN

*Due to her patience… hard work and willingness to learn, she improved
rapidly and after a couple of months became a first-class w/t operator.*
Percy Mayer, organiser of the FIREMEN network

Maureen Patricia O'Sullivan was born in Dublin on 3 January 1918. As
she was Irish with gingerish hair and matching temper, she was sometimes
nicknamed 'Paddy', though her family knew her as Maureen. Her father was
the editor of the *Dublin Freeman's Journal*, but her Breton mother died of the
Spanish Flu before she was one. She was educated by her Belgian aunt Alice in
Bruges and later at a variety of schools in Europe, speaking fluent French and
English, a smattering of Flemish and German, and some colourful swearing in
Irish. Maureen was highly intelligent, a happy and chaotic mass of emotions,
strong-willed and a real tomboy, popular with men and women.

After training as a nurse in London, in 1941 she joined the WAAF, and
while at RAF Gosforth became friendly with Sonya Butt. They entered
training with SOE within days of each other in December 1943, since
Maureen had been delayed by pneumonia and the chronic chest trouble
from which she suffered, though she never let it interfere with her work,
which was to be a wireless operator.

Her training reports were rarely good, but such was the urgency for wireless operators that without finishing her training in either wireless or security, she was parachuted to a reception near the cliff-top town of Angoulême on the night of 22 March 1944, in a thick fog. Unfortunately, her parachute cords became so tangled that she made a very bad landing and recovered consciousness being breathed over by a herd of curious cows. She attributed her life to the bundles of French bank notes she was carrying at her back.

Percy and Edmund Mayer, codenamed Barthelemy and Maurice respectively, two Mauritian brothers, were her organisers of a network called FIREMAN in the Angoulême area, with a small sub-network. As they found she could not ride a bicycle, it was among the earliest things that Maureen (codenamed Josette) and cover name Micheline Marcelle Simonet, had to learn. One account tells of some early lessons near a German barracks, where the watching soldiers laughed when she frequently fell off. She cheerfully called them all names (in German), and then told them that if they were gentlemen, they would come and help her, and she shamed them into doing so.

As well as learning how to use their transceivers, operators had to change the words in their messages into code, before they could transmit them by their Morse key to Britain. This kept the constantly listening Germans wasting much time trying to break the code to find out what was said. Different methods of creating a code were used by the agents. There was the Playfair method, a line of a poem – sometimes too well recognised even by the enemy, so that those with a gift, such as Leo Marks, the head of SOE's deciphering section, would compose one specially for an agent. Another usage was double transposition. One of the latest and most effective ways was the use of a silk handkerchief with a substitution grid printed on it. This was used in conjunction with the pages on the One-Time-Pad, giving the correct sequence of random keys in groups of five letters. The group of used keys on this page were then torn off and burned, while the handkerchief was kept for the next messages. Copies of this page were held in London.

Wireless operators found that enciphering messages by this method was a vast improvement over double transposition. It was easier, faster and more secure – advantages in the field, which could make the difference between life and death for an agent, far outweighing the extra burden of the pocket-sized, microfilmed, random keys list on the one-time-pad used with it. There were, of course, two safety checks to assure the decoder that the message was genuine.

Maureen's chief difficulties identified during her earlier work was her erratic handling of messages, many of which had her running after them, when they were being blown away in the open. Eventually, by using four envelopes, the contents of which were carefully destroyed within 24 hours, two for un-coded and coded messages IN, and two for coded and un-coded messages OUT, order was restored.

Argenton was Percy Mayer's main base, but his brother Edmund was often many miles away looking after WARDER in the south Indre. He also had no wireless operator or courier, so relied on Maureen for his messages.

Now that she could cycle (but with many spills, bruises and bandages), she often travelled up to 37 miles (60 km) per day, sometimes in hilly country, taking and delivering her messages, until she had a reliable courier. Fortunately, the network was a small one, covering roughly a triangle, bounded by Limoges, Montluçon and Châteauroux, with a number of large towns between, in an area of woods, lakes, hills and rich fields.

Maureen had made friends with the village schoolmaster and his wife at Fresselines. He was the recognised leader of the secret army of the resistance with no political bias. On their advice she changed her cover story to that of his wife helping her seek for a missing parent. They also passed her along to the farms of a number of friends and relations, who willingly sheltered her, and rarely took more than a nominal rent since the civil population in the Creuse was pro-Allied forces. This also went for the police in this area, whereas in Percy's Argenton this was not so, and the uniformed Milice were even more dangerous than the Germans.

Maureen had acquired seven wireless sets, hidden at many unlikely but convenient places. London found her first message so garbled that it took a fortnight to acknowledge it. Her great achievement was that within two months she had overcome her shortcomings, greatly helped by Percy. She had a few narrow escapes that she brazened out. Once, with her set in its suitcase strapped to the carrier of her bike, she was stopped at an unexpected check point. She then made herself so charming to the soldier there, that he forgot his checks, being so pleased at her assignation for that night, which, of course, she never kept. Yet again when challenged as to what the suitcase contained she answered laughingly, 'Oh! A wireless, of course!', and looking so pretty and childish she got away with it.

In the run-up to D-Day, her work load increased enormously, with sometimes seven 'skeds' a day, and on the actual day she was kept at her set day and night. During her time in France she transmitted over 332 messages, though London often was a bit puzzled with her coding. She explained that working in candlelight made it difficult. She also managed to train two replacement civil operators, in case she fell ill again.

Most of the time she was lodged in farms, often lacking sanitation and running water, the discomforts outbalancing their dangers. Also, she very much realised that her hosts risked their lives in keeping her. Thus the network under the two Mayers continued in its quiet and efficient way.

After D-Day it joined effectively in the harrying of the German troops. This happened to the Das Reich Panzer Division, on its march from Toulouse to Normandy, as it crossed into their sector. Unfortunately, in a little village 25 miles (40 km) west of Limoges, a popular company commander was killed, possibly by one of FIREMAN's own resistants. This was not unusual, with the constant sniping everywhere, but, assaulted on all sides, some soldiers lost control and exacted a terrible revenge. The next day in the village they shot all the men and then burned all the women and children in the church. About 700 souls perished in this massacre, leaving the shame of Oradour forever associated with the Das Reich. Later it turned out that this was the wrong village and they were not even supposed to be there but had got confused, as the names in this area were so alike.

The FIREMAN network played its part with the other networks throughout July 1944 and in mid-August, when it was hindering the withdrawal of German troops eastward towards Germany. Over 100,000 Germans were cornered as a result of guerilla and Maquis action, much of it from FIREMAN, and were forced to surrender near Limoges, not to the French, who had brought this about, but to the Americans, as the Germans feared the French more. Unfortunately, because of disagreements between Communists and Gaullists on the one hand and the Gestapo and garrison commander on the other, the surrender of Limoges itself was held up until 20 August.

Now Mayers and Maureen had virtually completed their task. Clearing and mopping up those stranded was left for the French themselves.

Maureen returned to Britain on 5 October 1944, where it appeared that SOE had further plans to send her to Germany, but that stage of the war ended too soon. As she said, 'Monty beat me to it.'*

Despite her many drawbacks, her organisers never heard a word of complaint from her about her living conditions or her continual ill health, and they highly commended her for her courage and resourcefulness.

---

* 'Monty', Field Marshal Bernard Law Montgomery was one of the outstanding military leaders of the war, and the German forces in north-west Germany, Holland and Denmark surrendered to him on 4 May 1945.

29

YVONNE FONTAINE

*Sending SAS Parties in uniform into areas often closely patrolled by SS troops,
drew attention to their arrival*

Yvonne Fontaine

Yvonne Yvette Fontaine was a French girl, born on 8 August 1913. Her early
years were overshadowed by the First World War, and the Franco-German
Armistice of the Second World War must have come as a humiliation to a
highly patriotic young girl, reinforced by the sight of German soldiers in
the streets of her town of Troyes.

Since her home town was part of a busy industrial area, with good
communications by road, rail, canal and telephone, and was within reach
of Paris, it became a target for Allied air attacks, whose aircrew, if they were
shot down and escaped capture, had to be hidden and put onto an escape
line, which in this area was run mainly by the Gaullists. By helping these
men, Yvonne was gradually drawn into the resistance.

Such underground activity had attracted the attention of SOE to this
area as early as 1941, and on 11 April 1943, Ben Cowburn, an experienced
agent, was sent by parachute south of Blois, to revive the TINKER
network of the Aube region, where he was given the codename Germain.

He was accompanied by Denis Barrett (codenamed Honoré) as his wireless operator.

Arrived in Troyes, Cowburn quickly collected an active circle of resistants, among whom was Yvonne. Another was Pierre Mulsant (codenamed André), a timber merchant with access to his father-in-law's fleet of lorries, already used by the resistance for transporting supply drops from the RAF.

Quick-witted and trustworthy, Yvonne easily slipped into the role of courier to other networks, as well as TINKER. Now known as Nenette she travelled everywhere – Piney, Romilly, Chartres, Tonnere, the forest of Chatillon and even, but rarely, to PHYSICIAN in Paris, carrying not only messages but sometimes sabotage materials.

TINKER received numerous air drops and had many small sabotage successes, such as dusting itching powder on the shirts and singlets of German submarine crews, and on 3/4 July 1943 destroying six railway engines and badly damaging six more in the locomotive roundhouse in Troyes. But there were disasters. Several leading resisters were captured, including one who gave away sensitive information about Cowburn. Also, two rather disorganised Maquis at Chatillon and Lusigny were badly mauled, while a few attacks on important targets had to be given up. Worst was the arrest in July 1943, of Francis Suttill and many members of PHYSICIAN, who increased the danger to TINKER, because PHYSICIAN's agents knew too much about their network. As a consequence, Cowburn flew out in mid-September 1943, leaving Barrett, with Mulsant in charge and Yvonne as courier. Mulsant worked on quietly but with little result, so it was decided to recall all three to London on 15 November 1943.

Neither Mulsant nor Yvonne, though they had been working for SOE for the greater part of 1943, had been trained by it, therefore this was the opportunity to do so, and since Mulsant, Barrett and Yvonne had worked so well together, it was planned to return them to France to form a new network called MINISTER, in the Seine-et-Marne department. It was perhaps dangerously near their former area of the Aube and nearer Paris, but Mulsant's background knowledge could be an advantage. They were therefore sent back in March 1944.

On a moonless night on 25 March, from a boat used mainly by the escape lines, the newly trained Yvonne landed on the North Breton coast. From there she made her way to Paris, where it was arranged for her to be picked-up and briefed by Mulsant, who then escorted her to a safe house in Melun where she was to start her official work as the courier Mimi. After a while, Mulsant felt she could now organise some of his receptions, freeing him to concentrate on other things like sabotage.

This was the time when SOE wanted to increase the supply drops. Yvonne, therefore, was involved in finding suitable fields for receiving the drops and finding suitable parties to take and store them, as well as setting up guards and guiding lights, the latter task she often carried out herself. She also had to keep in close touch with Barrett to transmit her messages and special requests. Sometimes she had to wait several nights for drops that never arrived and occasionally she had to carry and distribute the materials herself, under the very noses of the Germans. With D-Day rapidly approaching, around sixty containers were parachuted down at night in five receptions, during the two months of April and May alone.

In late April, Mulsant had moved to Nangis, to stay in contact with some of the groups there, and Barrett and his wireless were now based in Melun, so Yvonne had to move to Nangis, to shorten her travelling distances. Even so she still continued her journeys by train, lorry, tram, bus and bike, with messages and instructions from Mulsant, around the area from Donnemarie-à-Moutois, Nemors, Bray-sur-Seine, to Paris and other towns and villages. The pace seemed to increase by the arrival on 17 April of a three-man American party and the arrival of a lone American on 10 May.

It was the dropping of a uniformed SAS* party in the forest of Fontainebleu in late July that was the cause of disaster. The party got into difficulties and radioed for help. Mulsant, taking his wireless operator with him, attempted a rescue. The SAS men meanwhile had withdrawn, and their would-be rescuers were captured instead. A further disaster was fortunately avoided when Ben Cowburn, hoping to rescue his two old partners, parachuted into the forest himself on 30 July, just missing the Germans and also his friends.

Nevertheless, the legacy Mulsant left behind was considerable. Nangis had become a busy centre of resistance; sabotage ranged from cutting underground telephone cables and overhead wires, to the spreading of tyre bursters on the roads used by the military. The activity spread to Donnemarie-à-Moutois, where with the aid of the gendarmerie, who were wholeheartedly with the resistance, much useful damage was done. Resistants in the small towns and villages in the area, assisted in receptions for drops and small acts of sabotage. One successful coup was made by the

---

* The Special Air Squadron (SAS) was formed in 1941 as an elite Commando force to carry out daring raids behind enemy lines during the war.

Maquis near Bray-sur-Seine, who by breaking the lock gates caused the canal water to drop 20 inches (50 cm). This created long delays for the heavy canal barges carrying vital military supplies to the Germans, until repairs (badly done) were finished. There were also some French commando units and three FFI groups operating in the region of Jouey-le-Châtel.

The late July arrests of Mulsant and Barrett had left the MINISTER network without a head, which could have stopped it had it not been for Yvonne, who knew very well the work and the leading individuals of the different parts of the network. Her drawback was losing the wireless contact with London. By taking risks she did manage to pass a few messages through other wireless operators, but this was limited. News of the advancing Allies came from clandestine wirelesses, but not in sufficient detail.

Yvonne's journeys became more difficult as the German Army established more road blocks and check-points. A wallet full of papers was needed and much time wasted, severely affecting the number of visits, some very urgent, that she could do in a day. The Germans also increased paid informers, making receptions and sabotage even more hazardous. Supplying food and necessaries to growing number of Maquis and FFI troops also put more strain on a population already badly hit by shortages, especially in the larger towns. Nor were the German troops so well disciplined as before, becoming more nervous as the Allies neared.

August brought renewed hope that the liberation would be soon. The Germans were shooting more hostages, and their reactions grew more unpredictable. This was Yvonne's most difficult time. She had to rein in the hot-head resistants whose actions might provoke heavy reprisals, while she needed to increase sabotage to hamper the Germans and help the Allies. The situation in and around Paris was ready to blow up until the German surrender of 25 August, shortly after the news of the Allied landings in southern France. The last few days of August, therefore, saw skirmishes between the Allies, the Germans, the local FFI units and a swollen Maquis, while the Germans tried to withdraw. It now fell to Yvonne, with the help of several liaison officers, to mark the liberation of the people of Nangis and Melun and her area, to count up the sad costs and to collect information, material and parachutages which might be useful to the Allies. Then, in the atmosphere of euphoria, she had to extract what reports she could from the leading resistants in the MINISTER area. These she took with her when she finally was overrun by the Allied armies in September. She was flown back to London on 16 September 1944, her part in the war being successfully completed.

30

LILIAN ROLFE

Because she was registered by the FANY under her married surname Fauge, she was not recognised by Vera Atkins as SOE, and because she worked for a British network, Yvonne's work for the resistance was not recognised by France either – a great pity for a highly successful and competent agent.

> *Jeune anglaise voluntaire... elle parvint grace à ses solides connaissances*
> *techniques et à son beau sang-froid à transmettre... Après l'arrestation*
> *de son chef, elle n'en continua pas moins courageusement son travail,*
> *au milieu du danger croissant... Reste un vivant symbole de l'amitie*
> *Franco-Britannique.*

> *[A young English volunteer... who thanks to her solid technical knowledge*
> *and her cool nerve succeeded in transmitting... After the arrest of her chief,*
> *she went on with her work no less courageously, in the midst of growing*
> *danger... she remains a living symbol of Franco-British friendship.]*
>
> From citation for her Croix de Guerre 1946

A tall, dark-haired girl, with steady dark eyes, plump face and a mouth made for smiling – this was how Lilian Vera Rolfe was sometimes described by friends. She also loved music and dancing. She and her twin sister Helen were born on 26 April 1914 in Paris, daughters of an English accountant and a Russian mother. They had a happy childhood in France, as their parents adored the twins. Later Lilian spent a summer holiday, possibly in Woking, Surrey, to improve her English, but it was cut short by a serious attack of rheumatic fever. In 1933, when she was nineteen, the family decided to move to Rio de Janeiro, joining a growing British population in Brazil. Lilian found work in the Press Department of the British Embassy.

The outbreak of war made her anxious to do something more useful to help, so she left for Britain in February 1943 and joined the WAAF on 16 May 1943, proudly sporting her Brazil flashes* on her uniform sleeve. Very soon her strong patriotism, her maturity, intelligence and fluency in several languages brought her to the notice of SOE, which she joined officially on 24 November 1943 to work in France as a wireless operator. A training report in the following March commented that she was good at coding and steady with Morse, although not as good in 'handling' wireless equipment, but would improve with practice. Friends training with her at that time commented that she was very unhappy, recovering from a failed love affair, but this did not seem to affect her work.

She was landed on 6 April 1944 by one of the two Lysanders bringing agents to the Touraine area, on a field near Azay-sur-Cher, with her transmitter and receiver strapped to her waist. Lilian was very lucky in being given the newest of the transceivers, the A Mark III for her messages. Its chief beauty in its operator's estimation was its weight, at 9 pounds (4.8 kg) in its suitcase, and 5½ pounds (2.5 kg) without. It was the smallest set available to SOE in France during the war – almost completely miniaturised before the advent of transistors. It easily handled regular transmissions for more than 500 miles (804 km), and its construction is much admired.

She was among the many agents being poured into France by SOE ahead of D-Day, wireless operators being the most essential and vulnerable. Not only that, but she was destined to work in an area, part of which had been covered by the 'burnt out' network of PHYSICIAN and was now thick with Gestapo. Her organiser was George Wilkinson, codenamed Étienne, whose landing had preceded hers. He had been tasked with the setting up of a network called HISTORIAN in beautiful country, based on the cathedral town of Orléans, with other sections at Nangis and Montargis.

---

*   Denoting her Brazilian connections.

He also had to contact nearby networks to promote good relations and set up future plans. To his west, HEADMASTER was recovering and back in action after many difficulties. To his south VENTRILOQUIST was doing the same, while to the east, DONKEYMAN seemed quite secure. Many networks had risen and fallen in this central area, a testament to the high detection rates so near Paris – the hub of German counter-intelligence and wireless monitoring operations. It was thus a very dangerous assignment.

After Lilian (codenamed Nadine) arrived, she discovered that her organiser was already busy, making his contacts and trying to create his new HISTORIAN network. She therefore concentrated on her alibi as Claudie Irene Rodier, familiarising herself with her area, possible landing grounds and dropping zones, safe houses, and making useful contacts of her own, including the leaders of the local Maquis. She was not able to join up with Wilkinson until 2 June, when having got his network organised, he came back to find her.

From then on Lilian's work came thick and fast and, using her codename of Nadine, she had many messages to and from London to handle, as it was then only a few days to the D-Day landings. Among her earliest requests were for the Maquis of the Loiret to receive substantial and desperately needed supplies of arms, but soon after the landings there were demands from all quarters of all kinds, since HISTORIAN, with its increasing numbers of resistants, was now playing its own part in hampering the transfers of enemy troops being sent north to reinforce the Germans facing the Allied beachheads. HISTORIAN's resistants were also supporting the Allies as they tried to advance. Cutting communications, derailing trains and guerilla warfare all required more and more supplies, so Lilian was kept busy at her set. Nevertheless, mindful of her security training she kept on the move from place to place, because she knew detection vans were hot on her heels, trying to track her signals down, as fast as she could send them.

Then came her first blow. In late June, Wilkinson was trapped near Orléans and captured. By now he had been sent several more assistants, and soon a local leader called Pierre Charie took over the command of the network and Lilian continued working for him. She was also active in other ways: once she was involved in an engagement with enemy troops near Olivet.

At the end of July, the Gestapo, preparing to evacuate Montargis, made a final sweep of all known or suspected resistants in their area. In pursuit of one of its leaders, they raided a house at Nangis. The man they sought was not there, but they found a girl lodger whose papers did not satisfy their inspection. She was handcuffed and taken to their Orléans headquarters, only for them to discover to their great surprise, that, by accident, they had picked up a much more important member of the resistance. Searches revealed the wireless set and they realised that she was the elusive wireless operator of HISTORIAN – Lilian Rolfe. In just under four months she had sent sixty-seven messages, noted as being remarkably accurate and clear, despite adverse conditions.

For Lilian, this now meant a rapid transfer to Paris, to the intensive interrogation of the Gestapo. Not then, or at any other time, did she give the Germans any information that would be useful, and they must have quickly realised this, because she was soon sent to Frèsnes Prison. For the Germans too, time was running out, as the Allies started to advance and the Free French forces often took over towns and districts ahead of the liberating armies. In mid-August the Gestapo staff left Paris, the city being freed by its own people a week later. One of the Gestapo's final gestures before they left was, on 8 August, to put their remaining thirty-seven SOE men and women prisoners on a train for Germany.

Thus Lilian found herself chained by the ankles to another SOE agent on the long, hot journey to Ravensbrück. Late in the following, boiling day, the train was held up by an RAF air raid. Their guards jumped from the train to take cover, and in their absence the two girls crawled along the corridor to the men's two compartments, repeatedly carrying water that they had taken from the train lavatory to the parched men. Unfortunately, train and lines were damaged in the raid, prolonging their suffering while they waited for alternative transport that turned out to be cattle trucks, which stopped occasionally at a few places, a stables, a Gestapo headquarters and then Neue-Bremm Saarbrücken concentration camp, where they stayed a few days before continuing their slow journey.

It was about 22 August by the time Lilian arrived at Ravensbrück. In a crowded hut, housing hundreds of women on three tier bunks, she shared a top bunk with Violette Szabo and Denise Bloch. The way they were treated was as harsh as their work, and food was starvation rations. On about 4 September, with Violette and Denise, together with Eileen Nearne from another work group, she was sent on a month's working party in the fields at Torgau. As food and conditions were better, Lilian, with the others, was involved in a foiled escape plan, before the original three (Eileen had been sent elsewhere earlier on) were returned to Ravensbrück. Perhaps they were now under suspicion, because it seems that they were all beaten and sent to the punishment block of the Bunker, existing on scarcely any food. When finally released on 19 October, it was to be sent over 300 miles (482.8 km) to a party working to build a new airfield at Königsberg, in the bitter winter weather. They felled trees, dragged heavy carts of rocks and dug pits up to their waists in freezing water. Disease ran wild through the workforce and, unsurprisingly, Lilian fell ill with a lung complaint. Weak from exhaustion she was sent to the camp hospital.

After Lilian's short respite, on about 21 January 1945, she discovered that all three of them had been again recalled to Ravensbrück by a special order from Berlin. This time they were sent straight to the punishment block where more beatings followed. It seemed as if it was a last attempt by the authorities to break their spirits. One person who saw them when they emerged described them as walking skeletons, in rags with matted hair and blackened faces. Lilian had to be carried, she was in a piteous state. Denise could hardly stand and even Violette was nearly at the end of her strength and only just managed to walk. This was the last that anyone saw of them. They just disappeared, as so often happened on the camp. They probably died on 27 January 1945, whether by hanging or by the ceremonial shooting through the back of the neck as testified by the camp overseer of Ravensbrück (see Chapter 25). Afterwards their bodies were reduced to ashes in the crematorium.

Thus Lilian died, within months of the Allied victory that she had worked for. She was thirty years of age.

31

VIOLETTE SZABO

The life that I have is all that I have
And the life that I have is yours;
The love that I have of the life that I have
Is yours and yours and yours.
A sleep I shall have, a rest I shall have,
Yet death will be but a pause,
For the peace of my years in the long green grass
Will be yours and yours and yours.

Leo Marks (principal codebreaker for F Service),
part of his code poem for Violette

Violette Reine Elizabeth Bushell was born in Paris on 26 June 1921, the only daughter of the five children of an English father and a French mother. The mother was a tailoress and the father moved around from France to Britain, working, among other things, as a taxi-driver and a second-hand car salesman. Violette, wherever her family was, always spent her summer holidays with her aunt in France. In 1932, the family finally settled in Brixton, London, and Violette attended a London school, leaving at fourteen to become a sales girl, and for a few months joined the Land Army.

She was tiny, slim and attractive, with a clear skin, dark hair and eyes and an incandescent beauty, although she always was an incorrigible tomboy, an athlete who loved cycling, sports and shooting, and was always filled with irrepressible gaiety.

In July 1940, in a whirlwind romance, she met at the Bastille Day Parade in Hyde Park, and married, a Hungarian soldier from the French Foreign Legion. In his absence she tried work as a telephonist and then in the ATS as a predictor operator on the anti-aircraft guns, leaving in 1942 before her daughter was born. It was only four months later that she heard of her husband's death in North Africa.

Revenge drove her into the arms of SOE in July 1943, but her trainers were not entirely satisfied with her, feeling her too fatalistic and lacking in initiative and finesse. Her parachute training also delayed her when she sprained her left ankle. Her unsatisfactory reports, however, were overruled, and she was given a very difficult assignment. It appeared that while Philippe Liewer (codenamed Clément) had been recalled to London, the SALESMAN network he had created, centring on Rouen and Le Havre, had been broken up by the Germans and many resistants arrested. Now Liewer was returning to assess whether the network could be revived.

Violette was landed by one of the two Lysanders on 6 April 1944 near Azay-le-Rideau, on her first mission to act as courier to Liewer. In Paris, they discovered that for Liewer to go near Rouen was to court arrest. Instead Violette (codenamed Louise), under the cover name of Corinne Reine Leroy, would have to visit it alone. There she made discreet enquiries, judged the damage to the network and its members, and concluded that it was in too bad a state to restore – indeed was too dangerous for anything. On a quick visit to Le Havre, she also saw evidence of V1 sites along the Normandy coastline, and brought back a 'Wanted' picture of Liewer that she had torn off a wall. Passing through Paris on her way back she bought a few presents and a dress for her daughter. She returned by Lysander on 30 April.

After a short break at home, she again volunteered to work with Liewer on a second mission to resurrect SALESMAN elsewhere. This time they parachuted down from an American Liberator to land near Sussac on 8 June 1944 to a reception by the French Maquis. Violette (now codenamed Corinne) was to be known as Madame Villeret, still a courier to Liewer, who was tasked to restart his network between Limoges and Périgueux in the Haute Vienne, to the south of the new networks formed by Pearl Witherington and Amédée Maingard from the old STATIONER.

Violette spent one-and-a-half days cycling around by road, passing on Liewer's instructions and explosives to his supporters. Liewer (now codenamed Hamlet), however, soon found that his supposedly trained Maquis was badly disorganised, and he needed to contact Jaques Poirer, the promising young leader of an adjacent network renamed DIGGER, at his headquarters at Château-le-Virolle. As this was nearly 31 miles (50 km) away, Liewer decided to send Violette to assess the quality and willingness of Poirer and his Maquis to follow his instructions. She was to be given a lift part of the way in a black Citroën driven by a local Maquis leader called Dufour (codenamed Anastasie). She could then finish the rest of the journey on her bike, which was strapped to the side of the front passenger seat door.

The country roads were normally quiet, but it was 10 June, soon after D-Day and it was their bad luck to meet an unexpected road block near Salon-la-Tour, set up by an advance party of the north-bound Das Reich division.

Liewer's account of what followed came from Dufour a few days later. Waved down by the soldiers, Dufour brought the car to a stop near a farm, some distance from the German platoon. Then throwing themselves out and in the shelter of the car, he and Violette started shooting, she with a sten gun given her by Liewer, and a fierce gun battle commenced. (Many years later, the car was found in a hedge, riddled with bullets). After a while the two of them began retreating through a high wheat field behind the farmhouse, towards a nearby wood, each firing in turn to cover the other's movements. But the Germans, now augmented with armoured vehicles, followed and threatened to cut them off. Just then Violette's weak ankle gave way, and on reaching an apple tree in the middle of the field, she insisted that Dufour leave her, while she kept the Germans at bay. When she ran out of ammunition, she was captured. To be caught with any weapon was an admission of guilt, yet some recent eyewitnesses' evidence indicates that when captured she was unarmed, and there have been doubts about what really happened.

Whatever the situation, the Germans took the scratched and begrimed Violette to their headquarters in Limoges. There, in another building, she was painfully interrogated, which may have involved torture, as she knew the most up-to-date information on her network. She remained silent. A rescue attempt was made but it was too late, since after six days she was sent on 16 June to Paris and the Gestapo of the Avenue Foch, where she endured the cold bath, electric shock treatment and sleep deprivation, along with other forms of torture. As she refused to say anything useful, she was finally consigned to Frèsnes Prison.

On 8 August, still wearing her white blouse and navy skirt, she was put on a train to Ravensbrück with other SOE women, shackled by the feet in pairs. It was scorching hot weather. The next day, while their guards took cover during an air raid, giving up her idea of escaping, Violette and her fellow prisoner, Lilian Rolfe, crawled along the corridor, taking water from the lavatory to the parched men in the two compartments behind theirs. 'My God that girl has guts' commented Yeo Thomas, one of the men. Afterwards, everyone was transferred to trucks. They stopped at Neue-Bremm Saarbrücken concentration camp for a few days, before reaching Ravensbrück in late August 1944. Here, prepared for quarantine, the dress allocated to her sported a red triangle with an E, for an English political prisoner.

On 4 September, Violette, Lilian Rolfe and Denise Bloch were transferred for a month to Torgau to work in the fields, where food and conditions were so much better that she started to plan an escape, with a copy of the key to the outside door of the camp. Eileen Nearne, also working there, was included in this plan. Unfortunately, shortly after Violette managed to get the key someone betrayed them and Violette had to lose it quickly. (Eileen by this time had been transferred elsewhere). On 5 October, Violette, Lilian and Denise returned to Ravensbrück, and Violette seemed to be under suspicion. She was beaten and relegated to the punishment block. Odette Sansom, in a cell next to hers, could hear her taunting her jailer.

On 19 October, Violette and her two companions were sent 300 miles (482.8 km) to the cold north, wearing their same thin clothes, to the hardest camp of all – Königsberg. They were to help clear swamp land for an airfield. Often working up to their knees in freezing water or snow on scarcely any food, disease ran through the camp. It even took its toll on Violette's spirits, but she still struggled to cheer up her companions.

Late in January 1945, they were all recalled to Ravensbrück by a direct order from Berlin, and Violette was sent for a few days to the infection block, since her legs were full of ulcers. Then followed another stay in the punishment block.

In the evening of 27 January 1945, she emerged to join the dying Lilian and fragile Denise to walk barefoot to the execution wall. They were in rags, thin, their faces and hair matted with dirt. After the formal order was read to them they were each shot neatly through the back of the neck, and their bodies afterwards burned.

However, there is doubt as to whether they died of hanging or shooting, despite the sworn testimony of the camp overseer. Was there a cover up by the German High Command to hide the facts with a legality? (See Chapter 25). At least Violette and her companions must have known by then that the France they were giving their lives for was now free, and that the Allies were winning the war.

'Violette was the bravest of all of us' averred Odette Sansom. Violette was still only twenty-three years old.

32

MURIEL BYCK

She was a small, dark, pretty little woman, earnest and serious… Later
we girls thought of her with awe at the enormity of the task she had
taken on… I always shudder when I think of those vast empty fields of
France and how they must have looked to a young woman dropped into
enemy territory.

Audrey Ririe, WAAF

The land of the Loir-et-Cher in the centre of France was rich in smiling
pastures, sleepy ancient towns, ornamental châteaux and thriving industries.
Here SOE sent a flurry of agents to prepare the resistants just before D-Day.
Among these was Muriel Byck. She was born on 4 June 1918 in Ealing,
London. Her parents were Russian Jews, who had lived in France and
finally Britain, where they became naturalised British, as she now was. She
was educated in Germany, France and Britain, ending in the University of
Lille, France. From 1936 she was working in London as a secretary and then
an assistant stage manager at the Gate Theatre until the war. Then she joined
the Red Cross and the ARP (Air Raid Precautions organisation), moving
in 1941, as a National Registration clerk, to Torquay, where her mother,
now divorced and remarried, was living. In December 1942 she joined the

WAAF as an airwoman and worked at the RAF Records Office. Here her fluent French attracted the attention of SOE, where in July 1943 she began training as a wireless operator.

She was reported as intelligent (8/10), quiet, determined and very self-possessed, but lacking in experience, and with little aptitude for the paramilitary element of training. For this contradictory bunch of attributes, she needed time and more training, both lacking in mid-1944. The fact that she was Jewish with an ingrained hatred of Nazism, as well as being a very competent wireless operator, overrode all other considerations.

She was the personal choice of Philippe de Vomécourt (codenamed Antoine or Major St Paul) – who normally couldn't stand SOE-trained agents. He was going to re-establish his now smaller VENTRILOQUIST network in the Orléans-Blois area of the Sologne. Only in one matter did Muriel disagree with him. During her training she had become engaged to another agent working for the American OSS, and he had presented her with a leather-covered powder compact, such as could never be bought in France, but which she insisted on taking with her. De Vomécourt could not allow her to keep it until he had suitably aged it, and rendered it unrecognisable. In fact, owing to a torn leg muscle, he did not catch up with her until his landing on 17 April 1944. She therefore, had to follow the instructions of Christopher Hudson (codenamed Marc/Albin), a fellow escaper with de Vomécourt from Eysses Prison in January, who was now on his way to take over another network. Nevertheless, they were held up by bad weather and did not parachute down until 9 April 1944, near Issoudun. As it was Easter Day, a man in the reception party pressed into Muriel's hand a small gold cross and chain, which, touched by the gesture, she wore to her grave.

By this period, SOE was able to give most organisers several wireless operators, male and female, of whom Muriel was one. She also had not one but four more wireless transmitters of the smaller A Mark III variety, which she hid in various places within a 10-mile (16.1 km) radius of Salbris, now having a less rigid timetable for her skeds. In 1999, one transmitter was discovered in a barn that was being demolished, so cleverly had she hidden it. Of the others, one was in a village attic, and another in a woodland shack. One wireless was kept in a shed, attached to the scrapyard, near the garage run by her present host, Antoine Vincent. He was a leading resistant, in whose house she lived for a few weeks, as Salbris was to become de Vomécourt's headquarters. Muriel (codenamed Violette) was now known as Michèle Bernier.

Despite her frail looks she was always cheerful. With a laugh and a quick wave, she would pedal off on her old bike to deal with her 'telegrams', and on her return, or later that night, she would disappear to code and decode and finally pass on her messages to de Vomécourt, and then transmit any new ones for him. Occasionally also she acted as courier to other local resistance groups or sabotage teams.

She was not without shocks or surprises. Shortly after de Vomécourt arrived, he and Vincent took her out for a good meal in a black market restaurant. Here she found herself surrounded by Germans, but was forced to remain sitting and appear calm. At another time she was in the scrapyard shed, sitting on a box amid the tangled wreckage of old cars, tyres and rusting metal, tapping out her message to London, when suddenly she had a feeling that she was being watched. Still tapping away as if undisturbed, but really giving London her warning sign, she ran her eye quickly around her surroundings. She then became aware that the knot-hole in one of the wooden planks in the shed wall had become alive. An eye was watching her. Then it flickered and was gone. She jumped up and ran towards the spot in time to see a German soldier leaving the yard. Where was the man who was supposed to be guarding her? He must have been called away. She was in terrible danger, and all her friends with her. She recalled all the stories that she had heard about torture and imprisonment. What should she do? Then her training kicked in and although shaking with fear, she began to act coolly. First she must pack away all her equipment. Then, she must wipe out any trace of her presence, moving pieces around, and spreading the plentiful dirt and dust and even cobwebs, so that it looked highly unlikely that anyone could have been sitting there in all that mess. Then shaking like a leaf, she returned with her suitcase to Vincent's house. He was busy with a customer in his office, but catching sight of her through the window realised that something was amiss. At the same time de Vomécourt's car drew up outside. A sixth sense had warned him also that something was wrong. Both men heard from the nearly breathless Muriel what had happened and decided she must be moved. Very quickly, she and her equipment were safely stowed away in the back of the car, and it was on its way.

The Germans did come later to follow up the soldier's story. They hadn't believed him, it sounded too incredible, but they had to investigate. Their searches were half-hearted and apologetic, particularly when they were confronted with an obviously unused scrap dump, so thickly coated with the accumulated grime of years (Muriel had done an excellent job), that it patently had housed no-one, let alone a wireless operator and her equipment. Their informant was a fool and a dreamer. They were sorry to have disturbed the good Monsieur Vincent – such a helpful man – but of course he would understand. No hard feelings. They clicked their heels and shot out their arms in salute; 'Heil Hitler'. Then they departed in a cloud of dust. The poor soldier received ten days' detention.

After this fright Muriel moved to a new lodging, posing as a sick secretary from Paris. De Vomécourt then became her 'uncle', who called frequently to take her for long walks in the 'good country air', while her alarm sometimes woke her at 'unusual' times at night to 'take her medicine'.

In early May, de Vomécourt perfected plans to damage the arsenal that the Germans had created at Michenon, a former French Army depot, now enlarged by the Germans with the aid of forced labour to cover 50 acres. It stored ammunition, shells and bombs for the use of its troops, but the resistance could not attack it because it was so heavily guarded by soldiers, dogs and electrified fences. Now news had come to de Vomécourt that a number of goods trains would arrive to collect a huge consignment of arms and ammunition to supply their troops in the north of France guarding the Atlantic Wall. The trains arrived and were fully loaded when on 7 May, saboteurs blew up the railway lines at both ends to prevent the newly arrived trains from leaving. London was told and on that very afternoon it passed a message through Muriel to say that Allied planes would bomb the camp from the air after dark. News was passed by word of mouth to the local populace with people working on the camp, to take shelter. Around midnight the sirens began to wail followed by the RAF which bombed the site heavily, and it erupted like a volcano. The ground shook up to nearly 20 miles (33 km) away, while the air was filled with flying debris and flames. Afterwards, escape lines were busy rescuing airmen from the seven crashed bombers.

The effect on Muriel was a surprise. She changed and became white and shaky. Concerned, de Vomécourt sent her away to rest, finally to a blacksmith's family at Vernou. One morning when he visited them, he found them in an uproar. After breakfast Muriel had collapsed unconscious, and nothing would wake her. Three doctors were called. They had to be trusted not to report any suspicious patient to the Germans. Two were puzzled, but the last one diagnosed meningitis. Only a hospital could save her, and the Germans kept a careful check on all hospital admissions. But it had to be risked. An ambulance was called and Muriel's 'uncle' accompanied her to Romorantin and a hospital run by nuns. They did what they could. At 10pm they operated, but Muriel died in de Vomécourt's arms at 7am on 23 May 1944, without regaining consciousness.

Many resistants wanted to attend her funeral, for even in so short a time her quiet charm had made many friends, but for safety de Vomécourt warned them to keep away. He also instructed that she be buried in a zinc coffin, in case her body might later be moved. When the Germans came to catch him after the burial, he gave them the slip by jumping over the cemetery wall and escaping in a waiting car.

Later it became known that Muriel had suffered from meningitis as a child, but kept it secret from SOE in case they might refuse her, as there was always a chance that it might recur. For many years after, her grave was tended by the townspeople, and the children left flowers there. Eventually she was re-buried in the Commonwealth War Graves Commission cemetery at Pornic. Her stone is inscribed, 'Here rests in peace, Muriel Tamara Byck, our only child and beloved daughter.'

33

ODETTE WILEN

Odette Wilen had been parachuted to him as a wireless operator, but had only been partly trained for the task.

M.R.D. Foot, *SOE in France* (1966)

Odette's story was not a very long one, not through her own fault.

Odette Victoria Sar, who was to become a very beautiful, feminine woman, was born in London on 25 April 1919. Her mother was French and her father Czech. Around 1931 he became a naturalised British citizen, and his family with him. Later he became an RAF officer.

In early 1944, Odette was in the FANY as Odette Wilen, at the behest of SOE, which, noticing Odette's facility in French, recruited her as a wireless operator. Her motivation may have come from the death of her husband, a volunteer RAF pilot instructor, killed in a flying accident. Her training was unexpectedly cut very short, so that she could be sent with another wireless operator, René Mathieu, to work for Maurice Southgate (codenamed Hector) – an excellent but not very patient organiser – in his successful network in the Auvergne called STATIONER. He had previously complained that his network was too large for one organiser, and after visiting London, he had returned to a slightly more slimmed down network, still carrying the same name. He had also said that his agents were too few for the area. SOE was now trying to build it up and send the French resistance more supplies in preparation for the D–Day landings.

The two wireless operators, Mathieu (codenamed Aimée) and Odette (codenamed Sophie), parachuted down without incident near Dun-le-Poelier on 12 April 1944, and were waiting in a safe house for Southgate to give them his instructions. After some time Southgate arrived. He left Mathieu behind, and knowing that Odette was only partly trained, took her away with him to Châteauroux by car, and then by train to his base at Montluçon. There he introduced her to Maingard (codenamed Samuel), another trusted wireless operator, who having landed and worked with Southgate for over a year, hoped to become his second-in-command, if one of the new operators could take his place. On that very night at Montluçon, before Odette had time to catch her breath, she was set a test, carefully supervised by Maingard. The result was a sad disaster, and Southgate lost patience, later complaining bitterly (and rather unfairly) of her inefficiency. He immediately signalled London and sent for Mathieu, who fortunately turned out to be perfectly competent. Mathieu then took over from Maingard and was installed in his safe house.

Four days later Pearl Witherington and Odette passed Mathieu in the railway station at Montluçon, as they were catching a train to Le Blanc, where Odette was to stay in a safe house found for her by Pearl's fiancé Henri Cornioley, and approved by SOE until she could be sent back to Britain.

In the interval Southgate had evidently contacted Virginia Hall, who had arrived in France for a second tour called SAINT, this time with the American OSS in the Creuse. However, she often needed to visit Paris, where their paths had crossed at least once already. As in the old days with SOE, she was always ready to help any agents in difficulties and arranged to see Odette.

Plans, at this time, were changing very quickly and failed wireless operators could still be couriers, so Odette next learned that she was to join another group in the Indre-et-Loire département, based around Tours. Its organisers were a trio of men, all of whom were great friends. They had parachuted down on 6 April, just before Odette, to create a new network called LABOURER, and they might need a courier. On arriving they had also left a large sum of money urgently wanted by Southgate in a country café – money which Pearl was later nearly killed trying to extract. No doubt this was why Southgate had called on two of them, the organiser and wireless operator, to find out if they had the money, before he picked up Odette.

This trio was Marcel Leccia/Louis (codenamed Baudouin), Elisee Allard/Montaigne (codenamed Henrique) and Pierre Geelen/Garde (codenamed Pierre), their wireless operator, a Belgian, who had also been a great friend of Francis Suttill and his now defunct network in Paris. Moreover, the three had hoped to gain supporters from Leccia's relations and contacts who lived in Paris and Tours. At present their base was in a safe house at La Châtre near where they landed, looked after by a local organiser.

Unfortunately, not only were their Suttill contacts a danger to them, but although none were aware of it, among their friends, and in their own small fraternity, was a Nazi sympathiser.

It was then the unexpected happened, Allard may have met Odette earlier, possibly in training, but her arrival on about 20 April to join the LABOURER team must have revived their former attraction, so that by the time the team left for Paris, she and the organiser were engaged. She, however, must have remained behind, as she was evidently not with them in Paris and was definitely at La Châtre on 1 May.

On 26 April, Virginia Hall, working at Maidons, was visited by Allard and Geelen, to be given the biscuit box* for which she had asked. They also told her that Leccia and his cousins, both doctors, had gone down for the day to Tours, with some wireless equipment. To their horror the town was full of Germans, who had already caught another wireless operator. They had therefore left hurriedly to rejoin the others. Virginia later learned that before the end of April, all three had left La Châtre and arrived in Paris, where a double agent was waiting for them. There they were all arrested with the rest of their equipment and taken straight to the Cherche-Midi Prison.

By May Virginia began to realise what had happened and it was partly confirmed by OSS on 1 May and by others on 4 May, so it was only by good luck that Odette had narrowly avoided being captured with them.

Meanwhile on 1 May, Southgate had been captured and Pearl Witherington had only escaped by being at a picnic with helpers, including Maingard their wireless operator, but before leaving for the estate of Les Souches she had diverted her route to call on Odette at La Châtre, to tell her to stay put in her safe house.

---

* This innocent-looking Huntley and Palmers biscuit tin held a tiny American-made receiver – a late appearance. Complete with parts it included five miniature tubes, a battery lasting about 30 hours and weighed 2 lbs (900 g). It was known as the Biscuit Receiver-MRCI and was the first used by the American Secret Services.

Afterwards, Virginia and Odette planned to rescue the three from LABOURER with the aid of a prison escape expert from Marseille that Virginia happened to know. A message was passed to them in prison, but their answer dismayed him, 'We are not three but eight'. 'Impossible!' shrugged the expert, and the opportunity slipped through their fingers. Soon after, the prisoners were moved to Germany, and in June, Virginia had to leave and go to the Haute-Loire about her OSS business.

Buoyed up with Virginia's advice and her own wish to be still of some use, Odette risked travelling to Tours, hoping that other small surrounding networks might help. She made a few contacts but the Germans had increased their watchfulness, and she needed help from wireless operators in other networks, which had in any case absorbed many of the surviving resistants. Added to this was the unwillingness of French men to take instructions from a woman whatever the source, and SOE had not sent any organiser to take over from her. In July she finally gave up and accepted the advice to leave. In August she was on an escape line over the Pyrénées.

It seems that during this crossing she met and impressed one of the leaders of the Spanish escape line, surnamed 'de Strugo', who, after the war, she married.

Poor Odette; she had done her best in an almost impossible situation. Knowing that Southgate was a busy man with high standards, SOE should never have sent an insufficiently trained operator to him, especially as he had around five working wireless operators already.

34

NANCY WAKE

Ensign Wake's organising ability, endurance, courage and complete disregard for her own safety, earned her the respect and admiration of all with whom she came into contact. The Maquis troops most of them rough and difficult to handle, accepted orders from her and treated her as one of their own male officers. Ensign Wake contributed in a large degree to the success of the groups with which she worked, and it is strongly recommended that she be awarded the George Medal.

Extract from George Medal recommendation given 17.07.45

Her irrepressible, infectious high spirits were a joy to everyone who worked with her.

M.R.D. Foot, *SOE in France* (1966)

Nancy Wake, the sexiest woman it has ever been my privilege and pleasure to know.

Francis Cammaerts (agent)

Nancy Grace Augusta Wake was born in Wellington on 29 August 1912. Though her parents were both New Zealanders, when their little daughter was only two, they left to settle in Sydney, Australia, where she was educated and brought up. Afterwards, she tried her hand as a nurse in a mental hospital and a bit of journalism.

In December 1932, the Australian wanderlust had her sailing to Vancouver, New York and London. There, in between pub crawls and mixing with all types of people from intellectuals, artists, Communists and bonviveurs, she took a college course on journalism followed by a job in Paris as a reporter for the *Chicago Tribune*. During these years she lived very near the breadline.

In 1934, the year after Hitler became Chancellor in Germany, she visited Vienna with friends and was revolted in seeing at first-hand the Nazi treatment of the Jews. Later, with other journalists in Berlin, where she was supposed to be interviewing Hitler for her newspaper, she witnessed the attacks on Jewish shops, the whipping of their owners and the bonfires of their goods – the violence of which gave her a deep loathing for the whole of the Nazi regime.

The outside world, however, was not interested in her warnings, so Nancy, still poor, went back to her rumbustious lifestyle, as often in the south of France as in Paris, a favourite holiday resort being Juan-les-Pins. In these years she began to understand the French psyche, speaking the *argot* (slang) of the slums as easily as the faultless French of the cultured classes, and, like the French, with the civil war in Spain and recurrent domestic scandals in the French Government she became rather cynical. Then she fell in love and in November 1939, shortly after war broke out, she married Henri Fiocca, a rich steel industrialist of Marseille. Now a different life of ease and plenty offered itself, but with inexhaustible energy, abundant health and insatiable lust for life, she was soon rescuing refugees fleeing south, as the erratic driver of a converted ambulance that she had persuaded her husband to fund while he was in the French Army. With the announcement of the Armistice he was demobilised and returned to Marseille.

Here, inevitably, Nancy was drawn into helping some British prisoners of war incarcerated in the nearby prison fortress. This drew her into working for the growing escape network, known later as the 'Pat' line, guiding downed British aircrew, lost soldiers after Dunkirk, Jews and other escapees out of France. In the line, she willingly acted as a courier, often delivering subversive literature, radio transmitters and messages, as well as escorting people, as she moved from one town to another, mainly in Provence, in the south of France, which she knew so well and where she had many friends. Sometimes she accompanied escapees over the Pyrénées herself.

By now the Germans had occupied Marseille, and Henri Fiocca, working at his business there, secretly supported Nancy's activities with his money, allowing her to use his flat in town and his Alpine chalet as 'safe houses'. She was living a double life and thriving on it – by day a sophisticated supportive wife, cultivating Henri's business contacts and important residents, and by night at intervals becoming the 'White Mouse'* for whom the Gestapo were searching. It was a dangerous life, which she relished. At least twice she was captured and questioned before being released as unimportant, and there were times when she had to go into hiding, but eventually the Gestapo got too near, and Henri urged her to leave by her own escape line. It proved a gruelling two-day climb in the teeth of a raging gale, in winter over the mountains to Spain and thence on to Britain. To deflect attention, Henri remained behind, a decision which was to cost him his life. Nancy did not find this out until the end of her war, a tragedy which left her heartbroken.

Back in London, in view of her earlier experience in France, she was accepted by SOE's F service, and began her training, in which she cheerfully laughed and cheated her way through. The men found her exuberant and boisterous character 'good for morale', as she discovered when opening a locked drawer of reports one midnight, using SOE's own methods. Once she so far overstepped the mark that she was dismissed, only to be recalled a few days later. Another exploit of many was when she cleared a trench full of fellow trainees and her instructor with a live grenade just to show she could do it. In the last part of her course at Beaulieu she shared a room with Violette Szabo. They were an interesting combination.

On 30 April 1944, a Liberator dropped two agents in a field near Cosne d'Allier. One was John Farmer (codenamed Hubert) destined to be the next organiser of FREELANCE. It was to be a new network in the mountainous Auvergne region of France, mainly relying on a considerable army of Maquis led by a rather unsavoury and unpredictable character known as Gaspard. Parachuted down with Farmer, and landing in a hedge, was a very air-sick Nancy (codenamed Hélène), to act as a courier, with the cover name Madame Andree Joubert. Unfortunately, their wireless operator, Denis Rake, did not arrive until some time afterwards, which was to put them into grave danger.

---

* She was codenamed the 'white mouse' by the Gestapo, though she was not mouse-like in reality, except in cunning and discretion.

Lacking the information that they were to have been given by Maurice Southgate of STATIONER, at whose request they were there, but who was arrested before they had time to see him, Nancy then bluffed her way to Gaspard's headquarters. She found that not only was he a brigand chief and his men badly disorganised, but that he planned to murder them and steal Nancy's money, when he discovered that they brought no radio or supplies. Nancy's forcible intervention caused him to send them instead to Fournier a local Maquis leader, who proved better organised and more reliable, so that when Rake, their wireless operator, finally arrived, Nancy made sure that Fournier was the first supplied.

Now the vital London link was established, enabling Nancy to arrange the arms drops for which she chose the dropping zones and reception committees; everything was transformed. Moreover, on 17 May, Farmer and the organiser of a nearby Gaullist group agreed to work together to assist Gaspard's Maquis. Later, when two uniformed American officers were parachuted in to teach the new weaponry to the Maquis, but were cut off by the Germans, Nancy bravely confronted the enemy, herself leading a tiny group of Maquis, and in the midst of a fierce gun battle rescued the Americans.

More recruits started flowing in, and Nancy soon found herself virtually the head of many thousands of well-equipped, disciplined men, who became her devoted followers when they saw she could summon the supplies they needed, take care of their security and was willing to accompany them on their guerilla raids. She had also become their paymaster and storemaster.

After D-Day, the Germans, enraged by Maquis guerilla attacks, amassed a 22,000-man force to destroy the Maquis stronghold spread over a wide plateau at Chaudes-Aignes. There was fierce fighting and Nancy, staying on the plateau until the last moment, taking ammunition to the Maquis rearguard, only managed to escape in time, jumping out of her van just before the bombed vehicle exploded in flames. Her foresight, however, minimised their casualties, and allowed the majority to retreat safely into the mountains. Yet they were still badly mauled and short of the supplies needed to enable them further to harass the German convoys being sent to relieve the hard-pressed Normandy troops. Rake, on the other hand, in his flight, lost his wireless and codes – a serious disaster at such a time. In this emergency Nancy then undertook to cycle alone over 300 miles (500 km) almost non-stop in 72 hours, through the mountains and enemy lines to tell London what had happened. Though delayed and searched several times, eventually she found a Free French wireless operator willing to take her message. After which she returned exhausted and needed three days to recover. But her London call was generously rewarded with supplies.

Thus, in July, the Maquis were again active. They attacked enemy convoys, intercepted wagon-loads of food and set up ambushes. They wrecked electrical installations, arms factories and even the Gestapo headquarters at Montluçon. Nancy was often in the midst of these actions and sometimes their leader. With a new car and wireless operator, she visited and supplied dispersed groups of men hiding in the forests, and looked for new fields for more air drops. Another Maquis leader, Tardivat, arranged for her to be provided with a Spanish protection group wherever she went. He said, 'She is the most feminine woman I know until the fighting starts. Then she is like five men.'

August brought the long-awaited Allied landings in the south of France, and the Maquis skirmishes increased after the fast-withdrawing enemy. Shortly she was able to set up her headquarters in an empty château near Monluçon, where she took the salute at a march past of 10,000 men to celebrate her twenty-seventh birthday. Soon came the fall of Vichy and it was after the victory celebrations there that she heard that her husband had been tortured and shot by the Gestapo, which nearly broke her heart. His money too was gone and she was again penniless, but heaped with honours by France, America and Britain for her courage, tenacity and leadership.

On 16 October she returned by air to Britain. Later that month she took part in Buckmaster's Judex tour of the Allier and Auvergne to thank, and if possible compensate, some of those who had helped the Allies.

We just laughed all the way through the war. What else could we do?
Nancy Wake

35

PHYLLIS LATOUR

I escorted her to some distant farm where she was expected on the air...
On the road we were stopped by a German soldier who searched us... He
did not notice that my belt had rather an odd shape... As I got onto my
bicycle a small wireless part fell on the ground, but the man took no notice.
I picked it up and we went off safely. It had been a big fright.

Lise de Baissac (agent)

Phyllis Ada Latour was the daughter of a Frenchman and a British woman, and was born on 8 April 1921 in Durban, South Africa. 'Pippa', as her friends and family called her, joined the WAAF in November 1941, and was one of the earliest trained to become a flight mechanic on airframes. SOE was impressed by her skills, her patriotism and her fluency in French, and recruited her in November 1943 to be trained as a wireless operator. At the end of this, they felt that she needed more time, but with D-Day looming closer, she was another whom they sent sooner than they wanted.

She was to join Claude de Baissac's SCIENTIST II network in the north of France. In late 1942 and early 1943, de Baissac's earlier SCIENTIST, based on Bordeaux, had reached from Paris to the Pyrénées. Its size and interconnections with the doomed PHYSICIAN network were to damage it badly, though on a smaller scale it survived, but Claude de Baissac was recalled to London.

In 1944, there were big gaps in the existing SOE northern networks, partly due to the activities of double agents and the complicated 'radio game'* played by both sides. Nevertheless, there were a few secret armies in the north ready to hinder the Germans in their area or any south-based German troops moving north. SOE, therefore, needed to place some of its best and most experienced men there to recruit and prepare new resistants, before the probable northern Allied landings.

For these reasons Claude de Baissac (codenamed Denis) was sent in February 1944 to the area around Chartres to restart the SCIENTIST II network. With him came his wireless operator, Maurice Larcher (codenamed Vladimir), and later his second-in-command Jean Marie Dandicolle-Renaud (codenamed René), with Lise de Baissac (codenamed Marguerite), his sister, who joined him at the beginning of April as his courier. By May, de Baissac's new network was functioning well and had spread to cover a large part of Normandy, just short of the coast. Nevertheless, as he, together with Larcher, moved around so much ('*en tournée* [on tour]' as he described it), he needed another wireless operator at his base in his absence.

So, Phyllis (codenamed Geneviève) parachuted down on the night of 1 May 1944, into the Mayenne, an area thick with German troops and German patrols. Consequently, she was only dropped after three false action signals, as the reception party had to keep dousing their lights when German patrols came too near. Even so, she landed more than three fields away and it took her nearly an hour to find them in the dark. She was unhappy with her cover story, and instead de Baissac obtained some forged papers to show that she had left Paris to study painting, and she herself, in case of later having to claim refugee status, obtained some real papers from the Caen Mayor's office, saying she was an art student at Caen.

She made her first contact with London, in the house of a doctor, two days after landing, but moved to de Baissac's isolated farmhouse when warned that the doctor's house was being watched.

A week later, de Baissac left to see some firemen resistants in Paris. Phyllis went to the Caen and Vire area with Dandicolle, a very pleasant young

---

*   This 'game' consisted of captured wirelesses being used to send 'fake' messages on both sides of the Channel, confusing the recipients – a complex piece of counter-intelligence that caused the capture of many agents and their supplies.

man, making contacts for his intended stay there. It was in late May when they were returning to de Baissac's headquarters that they heard that there had been a spy (a grocer) at her reception, and the Germans had found her parachute. Fear of German reprisals had kept locals from helping at receptions, except when offered money, which was why de Baissac usually only used a few local policemen, recruited and well paid by the doctor.

Phyllis and Dandicolle hurriedly cleared the farmhouse headquarters and sent a warning to de Baissac and Lise to avoid it. Then they left to set up a new headquarters in an old barn, which they made habitable. Lise, with her bicycle, lodged elsewhere. Phyllis, on her bicycle, also looked around for suitable locations for her many wirelesses, so that in an emergency she could use the set nearest to her. After the Allied landings there was, unfortunately, a fair bit of interference – a knocking – on her wirelesses from nearby military sets, and in the fields her long aerial sometimes could not make good contacts, though her home station was always helpful and clear.

Shortly before D-Day, de Baissac sent Dandicolle and Larcher forward to establish a sub-network called VERGER, working in the Calvados region near the coast and south of where the landings might take place. They were to arm the local Maquis, encourage guerilla attacks and carry out sabotage attacks around Caen. They worked well until July, when, just before they were due to return, they were betrayed and shot. De Baissac was now concentrating on the Départment of Orne behind them.

Phyllis thus became more important to de Baissac as his main contact with London. At the beginning her situation rather overwhelmed her, as she was practically located on the battle-front, but she soon developed more confidence. De Baissac provided her with guards to protect her, particularly when she was sending messages, for which she did most of the coding and decoding herself.

Inevitably she had a number of narrow escapes. Once she was interrupted by two German soldiers looking for food. Pretending that she was packing her suitcase (containing her set) she told them she was preparing to go home as she had scarlet fever *, at which news they left rather hurriedly. At another time when she was 'sending' in the Forêt de Pail, the German Direction Finding van tracing her was destroyed by patriots before it reached her.

---

* The Germans had an in-built fear of any infectious diseases, such as scarlet fever and tuberculosis – once exploited by Christine Granville, when captured in Hungary.

When the long-awaited D-Day landings came, Lise said, 'for security reasons, we usually kept very much apart from one another, meeting only when necessary. But then we shared the same house for a short and hectic period, during which we spent many hours coding and decoding the messages Phyllis sent and received from headquarters.' When the crisis time passed, all three broke up, each to their own tasks.

De Baissac concentrated mainly on Maquis groups and guerilla warfare, attacking communications and transport needed by the German troops beset by other networks doing similar things. Phyllis noticed at that time that the population became more friendly to the resistance. Her messages too sometimes included information on German dispositions. Jack Hayes arrived to help de Baissac and set up the HELMSMAN network in the Cotentin peninsular, though his task was more about gathering intelligence for the American armies, a task usually reserved for SIS.

Phyllis was on the move even more, especially when the Germans came closer. By then she began to feel that she was able to run more risks and get away with them, which must have given de Baissac and Lise many a headache. But all went well.

As both de Baissac and Lise were further north, which was now overrun by the British Army, they felt safe to appear in uniform. Phyllis was a little later and more to the south before she was overrun by the Americans in early August. Nevertheless, they held her prisoner for five hours, since their description of her did not match her appearance, so well had she mixed with the population around her. Luckily, she was recognised by a guide who knew her. Then she was released, to watch the armies sweep down past her village and south on their mission to liberate the whole of France.

In her crowded few months Phyllis had sent 135 messages, and become a fully competent wireless operator, vindicating SOE's hopes of her.

36

MARGUERITE KNIGHT

One gruesome task she had to perform was to open a fresh grave in order to retrieve some important papers buried with the occupant.

Marguerite Diana Frances Knight (called 'Peggy' by friends and family), the daughter of a British Army Captain and a Polish mother, was born in Paris on 19 April 1920 and brought up there. In 1936, she came to Britain and, continuing her education at Canterbury, qualified as a shorthand typist. During the war, filled with patriotism, she joined the WAAF, but was invalided out following a serious bout of pneumonia. Later, she worked as a shorthand typist at a London electric company. There, at an office party, returning a French titled book, she had a short conversation with its owner in French, ending in an invitation to contact him again. This led her to join SOE in April 1944.

Her trainers were pleased with her on the whole, though some opinions did vary. She was tiny, slim, energetic and pleasant, and everyone liked her. She was not particularly noticeable, but in that modest head resided above average intelligence and a large fund of commonsense. Moreover, she was efficient and very steady.

Unfortunately F service was short of time to put her in place before the Allied landings. Therefore in just over a fortnight she was rushed through a brief training course on explosives and security, with only one practice parachute jump before she was in the air, the first SOE agent taken on an American plane, to parachute down near Marcenay in the Côte d'Or on the night of 6 May 1944. Her drop was successful though slightly off course and in brambles, but her fellow passenger, H. Bouchard (codenamed Noel), the wireless operator, was caught up on a tree. Their landing was also unexpected as their reception party was anticipating canisters, not people. They relieved their new arrivals of all they carried, including parachutes and a wireless, at the same time making so much noise that Marguerite, horrified, suggested that they better leave before the Germans found them. They were rescued by Roger Bardet (codenamed Chaillan) and Michel from their equally 'unsafe' house and then lonely shed, to be taken a few days later from the Côte d'Or, to the Yonne and the house of the DONKEYMAN headquarters in Aillant-sur-Tholon. Here Bouchard still found himself separated from his wireless for several weeks and unable to do anything about it, as matters seemed to go from bad to worse.

Marguerite (codenamed Nicole) was now transformed into a secretary called Marguerite Chauvan. As a courier, she was joining the DONKEYMAN network, led by Henri Frager (codenamed Jean-Marie) with Bardet as her chief in the Yonne, and his subordinate group leader, codenamed Michel. Frager was often away working with his small Maquis around Paris, and trying to set up a sub-network in Normandy under J.L. Kieffer, as well as ambitiously casting his eyes on the Riviera. SOE knew the likelihood of the Germans retreating and moving through these areas if the invasions of Operations Overlord and Anvil were successful.

Poor Marguerite. Incompletely trained and conscious of it, dropped among strangers raucously ignoring security, she had become deeply suspicious of most of the leaders of her group. It was to turn out that her suspicions were correct. Bardet and his friend Kieffer were double agents. Bardet had been 'turned' by Bleicher of the Abwehr, who had already trapped the leading members of SPINDLE – Odette and Churchill. Bardet now recommended Bleicher, known as 'Colonel Henri', to the unsuspecting Frager, as a useful source of German intelligence in Paris. Inevitably, in such a large network as DONKEYMAN, there were other traitors, but all Marguerite had to go on were suspicions.

In the following week Marguerite was only given trivial messages and parachute receptions, as she told her organiser Frager, when he came to check how things were. He counselled her to wait and then come to see him in Paris. She also spoke to Bardet and there was a slight improvement. Michel was a growing problem, and, with no-one to turn to, she nearly gave up. However, her honesty and plain speaking may have influenced the actions of at least two of her leaders.

At length, Marguerite said she must see Frager and soon she was summoned to Paris by Frager's courier. As usual, Michel kept throwing snags in her way, so that her train to Paris was a late one, and she did not arrive in time to catch Frager. When they finally did meet, Marguerite complained bitterly about Michel and his companions – no organisation, discipline or security measures, long separation of Bouchard from his wireless, preventing her travelling to Paris, but publicising her presence and harassing her (possibly sexually). Soon afterwards came news that Frager's courier had been 'accidentally' wounded by Michel. However, Frager sent her back to Aillant to bring him several urgent signals from Bouchard, where she was immediately delayed again by Michel.

That seemed to bring matters to a head. Bardet arrived, followed the next day by Frager, for a meeting of the network leaders, from which she was excluded. Later, she learned that Michel and his companion had been shot as traitors and she was nearly sent to Switzerland as Michel's accomplice, until others, especially Bardet, spoke up in her defence. He seemed to have decided to change sides at this point, and she was the catalyst.

While waiting for the Allied landings to consolidate, Marguerite found herself doing many unexpected things, such as peeling potatoes and preparing vegetables for her group.

Over the next few days everything improved. Frager and Bardet stayed in Aillant. On the day before D-Day, a few resistants, including Frager, Bardet and Marguerite, were nearly caught in a farmhouse. They managed to escape, wet and nettle-stung, to a new headquarters at Villiers, ready for the D-Day sabotage messages for the railway lines at Cézy. It was done after another walk of 18.6 miles (30 km) in the dark, and next day, on bike, Marguerite made the same journey there and back twice. Her days were now filled with courier work and action. In the Yonne, Frager decided to form a Maquis, so that German troops would be the constant targets of guerilla attacks and sabotage.

One night in late June, on guard duty with a small group in the woodland, Marguerite heard a shot. They were being surrounded by several hundred Germans. Delaying to hide their arms stores, Marguerite and one other resistant hid in the surrounding forest all day, while battle went on sporadically elsewhere. All escaped, but the Maquis, badly damaged, dispersed quietly and lay low. Later, a small mobile headquarters of Bardet, Marguerite and four others was formed, but Frager went back to Paris, still in contact with Bleicher.

July was spent in re-organisation, some sabotage, arms drops and training scattered groups of Maquis. Marguerite was busy maintaining contact with neighbouring Maquis bodies, while Bardet seemed to do the work of three men.

Despite the efforts of the resistance, the Allies could not break through the German lines around Caen until mid-July, and in the bocage country the Americans met stiff German resistance. The breakthrough came in August 1944.

On 15 August a three-man American Jedburgh team landed to join DONKEYMAN and was delighted to find a well-armed and trained Maquis of about 500 men, whose guerilla attacks and sabotage of communications were hindering the now retreating Germans.

In this region, however, Germans were still entrenched in several of the large towns, the resistants lacking inside information on their positions there. It was here that Marguerite helped. No-one glanced twice at a young girl pedalling her bike through the streets in broad daylight, showing the right papers. Occasionally she drove at night in a car without headlights. She then returned with what information she had gleaned. She volunteered the same help to the American 1st Army in her area, as the enemy lines in half-occupied towns varied hourly. Later she reconnoitred the countryside for damaged bridges and other impediments. She continued this dangerous work to help the Jedburghs and then an SAS group, until the Americans had passed through her sector and it had been cleared of Germans.

On 12 September 1944, saddle-sore and weary, she hitch-hiked to Paris and then flew back to Britain. Not so for Frager. Bleicher betrayed him and he died at Buchenwald concentration camp. However, Roger Bardet became a hero of the resistance.

37

MADELEINE LAVIGNE

Elle a rendu de très grands services par son courage sous le feu enemi et par son tact. Elle fut le bras droit de SILVERSMITH et elle a mérité la plus grande éloge pour le travail qu'elle a effectué avec lui.

[She rendered very great service by her courage under enemy fire and by her tact. She was SILVERSMITH's right arm and deserves the highest praise for the work which she carried out with him.]

SOE Commendation

A great-hearted lady, for whom I have much respect, and liking.

Henri Borosh (agent)

Madeleine Rejeuny was born in Lyon on 6 February 1912. Both her parents were French – her father a fabric designer based in the town. Madeleine had an ordinary education finished by three years at a secondary school. She was fond of music, dressmaking, tennis and boating. Buxom, serious and conscientious, she had married Marcel Lavigne at nineteen, by whom she had two children, Guy, born a year after her marriage and Noel, four years later. Until the war she was a housewife, but her husband was called up into the Army when the war started, and was made a prisoner of war until his release in November 1943. Then the couple were divorced and did not see one another again. To make ends meet, Madeleine became a clerk in the local Mayor's office, and because she was away so much, the boys were sent to live with her parents in another part of Lyon. She hated the Nazi occupiers and loved her country, but with this unexpected freedom at home, did not know how to set about helping France.

At the beginning of 1943, Robert Boiteux arrived to take over the SOE SPRUCE network, where Pierre le Chêne (codenamed Gregoire), the brother-in-law of Marie-Thérèse, had been wireless operator before being captured. Boiteux moved SPRUCE out of Lyon to the safer woods, vineyards and waterways of the countryside, with the mountains beyond. His role was to alter it from a propaganda machine to doing a little sabotage and stockpiling some arms drops. Although he had collected a small but loyal group of resistants around him, he needed identity papers and other types of documents real enough to pass scrutiny and not risk detection when used. This was when he discovered Madeleine, quietly working in the *mairie* (town hall), who was to develop an unexpected talent of producing acceptable papers over the official office stamp and was willing to ignore the alarming punishments threatened for such actions. More than this, he also found that, with her hitherto untapped intelligence, unexceptional appearance and careful following of his instructions, she could be made into a reliable courier, known to the SPRUCE network as Marianne Latour. Once when he was short of money she loaned him some.

This shortly came to the notice of Henri Borosh, who at this time had been working as a wireless operator to Victor Gerson in the Burgundy area, on the 'Vic' escape line for the DF service. Their need for forged papers, usually in quantity but in too much of a hurry to be sent from England, for downed aircrew, prisoners of war and endangered individuals, was often even greater than that of Boiteux. Borosh found Madeleine willing to help him also. On the escape line she passed by the name 'Leveller'.

By the summer of 1943, Boiteux was growing uneasy. Arms drops were few and small, the SPRUCE network was still little as resistants were apt to judge a network by the arms it could produce. Possible recruits were also disappointed that the hoped-for Allied landings to free France had not yet taken place. Dissatisfaction bred carelessness, and Boiteux began to fear that their security, on which their lives depended, was not as it should be. At last he decided that it would be best to wind up the network, and after warning those staying behind to lie low, he, with his staff (including Madame le Chêne, who had done a little courier work while waiting for her flight) and Victor Gerson, left by a Hudson bomber, arranged by Henri Déricourt, from a hilltop near Angers on 19 August 1943.

After their departure Madeleine and Borosh remained quietly in Lyon. Part of the time Madeleine allowed Borosh to hide his wireless equipment in her house – very dangerous for her if it were discovered. With his escape line background Borosh was now intending to change from the DF escape line to the F service, and could see the need for a new network in the future. He and Madeleine travelled to various areas to examine the prospects elsewhere, and with Gerson's return to France in November, Borosh arranged his transfer. However, by January 1944 Madeleine and Borosh must have been warned that the French police were on their tail, and Borosh requested help. On 3 February, using one of Déricourt's favourite fields near Angers, they both left for England on a Hudson carrying eight passengers, including a politician's wife and a woman keeper of a safe house.

Madeleine, as it turned out, was only just ahead of her arrest by the Lyon police as a terrorist! She was tried in her absence and condemned to forced labour for life, though her sentence was to be reviewed annually.

Borosh was evidently the moving spirit in Madeleine's future, as he wanted to take her back to France with him on his next mission. Despite being a French civilian (once wrongly attributed to de Gaulle's RF), she had been already working, unofficially, for at least one British network in France, and now had considerable experience behind her. SOE F was thus anxious to give her revisionary training as quickly as possible to fit her to work as their agent in the field. She was entered with the FANY in February 1944 under her former cover name of Marianne Latour, which she kept until she finished training. It was, however, to be the cause of confusion, which slightly held her up early in her course, and was used on her citation for an award, and even on her gravestone!

Nevertheless, her training was speeded up in view of her previous experience and the present emergency. It proved quite satisfactory. Since training was all in French, it caused her little difficulty, as this was her only language. Later Borosh excused her only other peculiarity, 'if in English eyes her appearance was rather against her', it was quite acceptable in France. She made a cheerful but nervous student, working hard and being keen to do well. She only did two weeks of a wireless course, it not being considered necessary, as she would be working with Borosh, a fully trained operator, who could complete her training as they worked together so that she would be able to act as his wireless operator. Her ground training was good, but weapons rather frightened her, as did parachute jumping. After watching her two descents, her trainer ominously suggested that 'on operations, the dispatcher may have to *assist* her to make an exit.'

Whether this proved necessary or not, on 23 May 1944, Madeleine floated down into the Saône-et-Loire department in Burgundy to act as courier (and wireless operator in training) for Henri Borosh (codenamed Girard) of the SILVERSMITH network that he was going to set up. They were part of the rush to put SOE F agents in important situations before the expected Allied landings on D-Day. SILVERSMITH was to have two main segments; one centred on Reims in the north and the second in the lower Saône valley, which was to run alongside the ACOLYTE network on the Rhône route from Marseille, which many south-based German troops would be likely to take on their way north.

Once Madeleine was established in Reims, she began looking for some suitable houses for Borosh to rent, so that he could operate his wireless. As she got to know her area, she came into contact with Madame Benazet, who with her husband owned a restaurant and several properties. Soon a regular customer, Madeleine got to know them and very tactfully sought their assistance in finding a suitable house to rent. Her manner inspired such confidence in Monsieur and Madame that she was able to get their permission to rent two of their houses, first at Épernay and then (as a reserve) at Ay, into the first of which Borosh was immediately installed, and was able to use as his base during the months of turmoil that followed. Madeleine, under the cover name of Mariette Henriette Delormes, codenamed Isabelle, then started on her long journeys north and south, carrying messages for arms landings, mail, telephone-wire sabotage instructions, and materials to various people and groups for Borosh and his growing network. Occasionally there were necessary contacts to be made with other resistants elsewhere, new recruits to be drawn in, and also the small group in Paris to deliver instructions to. It was mainly due to her energy and tact that the Reims organisation, one of the two main groups of SILVERSMITH, was thus established on so firm a basis.

Once the northern landings had taken place, Madeleine had also to be even more careful of security, as the Germans were everywhere and more alert and dangerous than the French authorities in watching for saboteurs or spies. She did her work unquestionably well and was of the greatest possible assistance to Borosh. Inevitably she was sometimes caught up in engagements with the movements of the German troops, and often had to pass through areas under fire, showing great courage and commonsense.

During June, July and part of August, in the bitter fighting, the Allied armies were held confined mainly in Normandy, with Reims outside the battle area, but on 15 August, the Allies with a French Army contingent invaded the south of France. This was where the Germans were weakest, with so many troops deployed to the north or tied up combating the French Maquis. Now the second part of SILVERSMITH's network came into play with the other networks around, attacking and holding up the, by now, retreating German armies. Then came the liberation of Paris, mainly by its own people, and finally, on 29 August, the Americans reached Reims followed a few days later in the south when the French and American armies took Madeleine's own home town of Lyon. The fighting in France, however, was not completely over and continued sporadically well into September, as one after another the remaining towns were liberated, and the remnants of the German units left behind were mopped up.

In those last confused months of liberation, Madeleine continued her work. Being unable to return to Lyon until the court there repealed her sentence, she went to stay in Paris. Nevertheless, foreseeing this, her heart was still there with her family, as can be seen in a short note written in May 1944, before she left for France. 'In case of accident, the circumstances of my two children be enquired into, with a view to helping them with a pension if necessary.' Her premonition proved wise.

In Paris, she died very suddenly, aged thirty-three, of an embolism (blood clot) on Saturday 24 February 1945, and was buried there. In November 1946, Britain awarded her, with the approval of Paris, the King's Medal for Courage in the Cause of Freedom.

Nous deplorons profondement la mort inopportune d'une Francaise qui a si bien merite de son pays.

[We deeply grieve the untimely death of this French woman, who has deserved so much from her country.]

Maurice Buckmaster

38

SONYA BUTT

*What little I was able to do was motivated by my love for France, and because
I could not imagine not doing my utmost, when my country was at war.*

Sonya Butt

Sonya Esmée Florence Butt was born on 14 May 1924 at Eastchurch, Kent.
Her father, formerly of the Royal Flying Corps, became a senior RAF
officer during the Second World War. Sonya grew up in the south of France
where her mother had moved after the marriage broke down. There Sonya
ran wild with her brother until the war came, when she returned to Britain
and went to school there. When she was old enough to join the WAAF,
she worked in administration, which she detested and 'got into a lot of hot
water'. SOE came into her life when she applied for an interpreter post,
hoping for a change, but she got more than she bargained for. Her love of
France, her fluency in French and her energetic personality impressed her
interviewers, who took her to be trained by SOE F service as a courier in
the field, despite the fact that she was still only nineteen years old.

During training she met a number of other girls, among whom were
Violette Szabo, Nancy Wake and her room-mate for part of the time, Lilian
Rolfe. In the parachute exercises she fell in love with another trainee, Guy

d'Artois, a glamorous older Canadian who decided to marry her when she winked at him before their second descent. She discovered a natural gift in mixing explosives, memorising the ingredients and tricky quantities as though she were baking a cake, and she and Guy decided to specialise on this, hoping to stay together. Their training finished, they were briefed to go together, but when they got married on the day before leaving everything changed. For safety reasons, SOE sent them separately to different networks, Guy first, and a month later, Sonya.

It was on Sunday 28 May 1944 at 10pm that Sonya (codenamed Blanche) wearing a divided skirt (like culottes), parachuted down at La Cropte to work for Sydney Hudson (codenamed Albin) in his HEADMASTER network. Her cover name was to be Suzanne Bonvie. Unfortunately, things went wrong with the jump. She landed badly in a ditch, damaging her spine, which she had already hurt during training and for which later she needed two operations. Also, the container of her clothes was afterwards found by a German convoy, who by this knew that a female agent had landed. Since this would mean that the Germans would be expecting her to lie low and keep quiet, she resolved to do the opposite, and started eating in black-market restaurants, and appealing to the chivalry of the nicer kind of German officer, sharing his table, laughing with him and being friendly.

Hudson was a very experienced organiser. He had been one of the three agents parachuted into the Auvergne in September 1942, originally covering the area west of Lyon around Clermont-Ferrand. He had the bad luck of being captured within two weeks of landing, but finally escaped in the mass breakout of Eysses Prison, helped by George Starr and Anne-Marie Walters, who had accompanied them part of their way. Now he had returned to revive his HEADMASTER network, but in the Sarthe, centring around the cathedral town of Le Mans to the south of Normandy and backing up the SCIENTIST II network of Claude de Baissac. Hudson's network would be well placed for damaging and delaying German forces rushing up from the south to reinforce those that would have to face the Allied landings in Normandy.

It was only nine days before D-Day, so there was much to be done. Supplies to the Maquis had been greatly increased in 1944, but many of the weapons were of recent manufacture, so that often raw recruits had no idea how to handle them. One of the agents who had landed with Sonya was intended to be their weapons trainer, but in a guerilla engagement with the Germans he was shot. This left Sonya, also briefly trained, to take over. As she later said, she filled in wherever there was need.

She combined this task with her official role as courier, distributing messages, money, food, shoes or explosives on her faithful bicycle, often pedalling long distances to the widely scattered groups, whom she often found anxiously awaiting her arrival. When she returned from active duty she was found to have lost about 40 pounds (18.4 kg) in weight. Occasionally she would take a local bus, but these were not very reliable and road blocks were frequent. Later, she described her work as recruiting for the resistance by day and working with sabotage by night.

One day in late June near Bar-sur-Seine, after the landings, the German soldiers, instead of waving her through a road block, escorted her to their headquarters. They were not satisfied by her papers, which she knew were forgeries. In a small room, another man examined her papers very carefully and began questioning her. As an innocent member of the public she protested volubly, and was sent to a small cell. Late that afternoon she was taken down a long corridor into a large office busy with German clerks. At one table she was asked her name. Then to her relief and surprise the man handed back her papers, and told her she could go. She was free.

Sonya was 5 foot 7 inches (173.7 cm) with dark hair and eyes, a gentle mouth but a determined nose and chin. Her youth and good looks might have misled her enemies but not her friends, and she quickly earned the liking and, not easily given, the respect of those with whom she worked. Young as she was, her cool head and knowledge gave her an air of authority – even to the tough Maquis – so that she eventually became in function, if not in name, the second-in-command of the network. However, she took care to sink well into the background, not to draw attention to herself. To avoid capture, she was constantly on the move, by night sleeping in barns, safe houses or even tents or fields, with only streams in which to wash. Once her group was betrayed by a recruit. Fortunately, she grew suspicious of an invitation to a meeting and did not go, but a number of others who did were caught and shot.

The Normandy landings brought great activity to the network, from cutting the lines of communication and taking part in sabotage missions all over the area, where her special skills came to the fore, and later in guerilla attacks and ambushes as the enemy troops passed through HEADMASTER's Sarthe section, where some of the fiercest battles took place. In August, the Americans, after securing Brittany, swept down south towards the river Loire and then east towards Le Mans taking it on 8 August. After Le Mans was liberated, groups of men went around the town rounding up those they thought had been working with the Germans. One group caught Sonya, whom many had seen eating in black-market restaurants and being friendly with the Germans, which they did not know she used as part of her cover. They hauled her roughly off towards the town centre, as a collaborator, and prepared to shave her head and tie her to a lamp-post to shame her, despite her protests and explanations. The lucky arrival of some of her Maquis saved her in the nick of time.

There followed great celebrations among the resistants in Le Mans, but everywhere the war was still fluid, and fighting continued in and around parts of the city, nor was this the end of Sonya's war. The Americans were recruiting French people, active in the resistance who knew the area well. They wanted their help to gather intelligence about the German forces.

So when Hudson and Sonya reported to the Americans, they were asked to help, even though this was not their work. Sonya in particular knew the people and the terrain very well, as she had travelled so extensively in her work. In the south, where she was brought up and had worked earlier, her information could be of great use to the US generals. It was highly dangerous work that only those with the greater knowledge that she and Hudson had, could do, knowing friends and contacts in enemy-occupied areas, for it might often involve going through or behind enemy lines, understanding their dispositions, advantages and drawbacks and then returning quickly.

De Gaulle in taking over Paris was now dismissing all SOE F service agents, with the single word 'Go' – little thanks for what they had lived and died for to help France. He distrusted SOE's motives, and they were told that their place was no longer in France. Hudson and Sonya, on the other hand, now stayed with papers showing them to be working for the Americans. Sometimes indeed, they posed as collaborators fleeing the Allies, which worked both ways and explained their presence to Germans in occupied towns. Once, driving in an American car, flying an American flag, they returned to a town taken by the Americans two days before. Before they realised, they were met by a hail of German bullets, some of which hit the shoulder of Sonya's jacket, fortunately hanging on the back of her seat, and they got away unhurt. The American advance continued and finally their work was over and Buckmaster in Paris recalled them. Sonya returned briefly to a reunion with her husband in Paris, before flying back to Britain in October 1944.

39

GINETTE JULLIAN

Mon operateur de radio m'a toujours fourni un travail excellent meme dans les jours les plus charges. Très courageuse, elle n'a jamais perdu son sang-froid le jour ou les SS sont venus perquisitionner dans la maison ou elle emettait. Grace a Septime d'ailleurs, tout a ete sauve et la perquisition n'a ete que superficielle.*

[My radio operator always gave me excellent work even on the most demanding of days. She was very brave and never lost her nerve even when the SS arrived to search the house from which she was transmitting. Also thanks to Septime, all was saved and the search was only superficial.]

Gérard Dedieu (agent)

Ginette Marie Hélène Jullian was born in Montpellier, France, on 3 December 1917 – both parents being French. She was among the last recruits accepted by the FANY for SOE, and was trained in parachuting, security and the use of SOE's latest wireless equipment – an A Mark III transceiver – the nearest thing to miniaturisation before transistors, and weighting less than 9 pounds (4 kg) in its suitcase.

---

*   Please note accents have been omitted as in the original text.

She was to become one of a two person team with Gérard Dedieu (codenamed Jerome), a schoolmaster and resister since 1942, who had taken part in the mass breakout from Eysses Prison in early 1944. They were unusual in being the one SOE team that spoke only French. They parachuted down on 7 June 1944, near the village of St Viatre, to a reception organised by Hutton (codenamed Antoine).

As this was the day after D-Day, the situation was fluid and dangerous. People were fleeing from the vicinity of the landings to avoid being caught in the fighting. Railways and roads were choked with all kinds of transport. All routes were interrupted by bombardment and sabotage.

Many of the existing networks had been infiltrated by the Germans or burned-out, while several of SOE's networks' wirelesses were under German control. SOE had therefore been concentrating on those it knew were unaffected and thus unknown to the Germans. This new uncontaminated network was to be called PERMIT, and set up in the Somme-area based at Amiens. But the best laid plans don't always work out, especially at such a time.

When they landed, Hutton (who was in charge of their reception and seemed to be involved in a number of networks) and his Maquis removed the wireless equipment of Ginette (codenamed Adèle) explaining that such suitcases in the Paris area might arouse suspicions, but he let her keep her inconspicuous crystals for when she would find another set at Beauvais. After a day at a safe house, she and Dedieu left on a train for Paris. Here their troubles began!

Hutton had given Ginette a list of addresses of resistants to contact in Paris, but she soon found they had all gone without leaving any forwarding addresses. So she and Dedieu decided to continue on to Beauvais, with several lifts on cars up to Beaumont, where they transferred to bicycle. After some days they reached Beauvais where their last contact lived. She had also disappeared, and the town was emptied of civilians and requisitioned by the Germans. As it was dangerous, they left the next day by train for Paris again, and parted. Dedieu went to find his father-in-law at Asnières, who might be able to help him find the leaders of different resistance movements around Paris. However, after a fortnight of delicate negotiations with them, he could see that they appeared to have too many fierce political rivalries to work together.

Ginette, meanwhile, set off to find Hutton, her wirelesses and forged papers for her new area. At the nearest village she shortly learned that his Maquis had been attacked by several hundred Germans and he was gone.

Hunting for any other organiser able to help her find Hutton, someone put her in touch with a Gaullist group. Then a leader of the FFI, in contact with Hutton, suggested she could join a group urgently requiring the help of a wireless operator in the Eure-et-Loir department. Eventually, with great difficulty, she was able to borrow a wireless set from an American group in the Seine-et-Marne department. Thus she was finally able to be in touch with London, which gave her the much-needed new instructions for their mission. They were now not to go to Amiens in the Somme area, but to work in the Eure-et-Loir department, operating also in parts of Orne and the north part of the Loir-et-Cher. There, at the end of June, she joined Dedieu with a wireless and their work could begin. Ginette's wireless and its reception was very good and each signal was clear. Any lost skeds were due to the current being cut off when the Germans, trying to track her down, came too near. Indeed there were some lively alerts.

At last, she and Dedieu were working as intended, in a different place but still in a network called PERMIT. It was now in the south of Normandy, with its headquarters in the cathedral town of Chartres, and filling up the space between a number of SOE networks. To their left was Claude de Baissac's SCIENTIST II, which just before the Allied landings had been drawn off to Orne, close behind the Allied bridgehead. Below SCIENTIST was Sydney Hudson's HEADMASTER, while below PERMIT was George Wilkinson's HISTORIAN and Henquet's HERMIT. They made a formidable group.

Until the end of June the Allies' beachheads could have gone either way, but by the end of July, Caen, Avranches and St Lô had been taken and the beachhead was safe. In a busy July, Ginette transmitted all Dedieu's plans and requests to London. He also won the support of the military delegate of the FFI in his department, and was soon pulling together thirteen groups of resistants, whose backbone was six well-organised Maquis. They also produced good reception grounds, enabling 450 containers to be dropped in a month – sufficient to arm about 2,000 resistants. As a result, German activity was greatly hampered by sabotage attacks on railways, convoys, telecommunications and other installations, the most audacious being the destruction of the Chérisy viaduct on 18 July, which the RAF in twenty raids had failed to bring down.

August marked a slow advance by the Allies on all fronts, assisted on 15 August by the American and French invasion in the south of France. At the same time, the Maquis and other small resistance groups, helped by planes, attacked and ejected the German garrisons in the town of Nogent, Dreux, Châteaudun and Bonneval, and finally Chartres (also on 15 August) which had been fiercely defended by the Germans, but eventually taken with the help of the advancing Americans, whose arrival caught up with Dedieu and Ginette. They were, at this point, officially overrun, except that Dedieu had been taken prisoner on 12 August but soon escaped. Now PERMIT's short part in supporting the Allied landings and the resistance was over. Dedieu however, was offended by the military delegate of the FFI, whom he had helped so much for the past two months, but who now excluded him from the funerals of his men who had fallen in the capture of Chartres, as well as not inviting him to the official visit of de Gaulle. Dedieu, therefore, left for Britain on 20 August.

Ginette's work was not yet over. During the rapid Allied advance, one of the SAS teams had landed nearby, and the American Major Rolf took her under his wing – extra wireless operators were always useful. London's new instructions told her to move forward in September with the Allied Army towards Dijon. There, four special people, including Ginette, were to be divided into two teams. One team was to go out and gather information. The second, with an American Army Air Force Officer and the news from the first team, was to point out targets for air strikes to Ginette, which, as a wireless operator, she was to relay by radiophone direct to the Army. The work must have been intense and dangerous, as they were all on the front line and occasionally ahead of it.

Their mission was cut short by the extremely fast Allied advance, when the Allied forces from Normandy, and the mixed American and French from the south, joined up near Dijon on 11 September. Thus Ginette's war in France was almost finished. The Germans, except in a few pockets, were in retreat towards the Rhine.

On 22 September 1944, she returned to Britain to report. She had come to free France from German occupation and had seen it happen before her very eyes.

40

CHRISTINE GRANVILLE

She was independent, humorous and fiercely anti-pompous... To use the word brave or courage about her would be a wrong use of the word.

Francis Cammaerts (agent)

Her incredible exploits... only came to light, after her death, but for courage and audacity they have no equal.

Dame Irene Ward in *FANY Invicta*

Maria Krystyna Skarbeka was born on 1 May 1915 near Warsaw, Poland, the daughter of Count Skarbek and his Jewish wife. A normal childhood with her elder brother was marred by the knowledge that some of her father's lands were taken over by the Germans, whom she hated. Though educated in a convent, she proved unruly and resistant to discipline.

Radiantly beautiful, she was graceful, deceptively fragile and with brown eyes and a cloud of dark hair. Highly intelligent, she soaked up languages, but was also a fine athlete, particularly in skiing, which later saved many lives in her exploits on the escape lines across the mountains – all her efforts being geared to helping liberate her beloved Poland from the Germans.

After her father's death in the 1930s, virtually penniless, she became a clerk to a motor dealer. She was twice married, but she grew quickly bored of lovers and admirers alike, though always remaining loyal to her friends.

When Poland was invaded by the Germans, she left her travels abroad for London, and from December 1939 she was employed by Section D, the precursor of SOE, which later took her over, by which time she was becoming known as Christine Granville, a name she kept when she was naturalised as a British citizen after the war.

With SOE's blessing she went into Hungary with the codename Madame Marchand. From there she organised a two-way system of sending supplies for the resistance to Poland, and establishing an escape line for removing British prisoners of war and bringing back information from Poland.

She contacted many Polish underground organisations, some of whom distrusted her Polish loyalties because of her connection with Britain. She also tried to send her mother, a great patriot, into hiding. Her mother refused and later was arrested by the Gestapo and disappeared. London found Christine's reports and her idea of a clandestine news-broadcasting station to Poland interesting. Nevertheless she had to rely on others to take her messages to Britain, because Italy, now allied with Germany, had refused her visa and she was trapped in Hungary. She had also been caught at least once by the Slovenes, through whose lands she had to travel during her further attempts to visit Poland, but they had allowed her to escape.

Help sometimes came to her from the British Legation in Hungary, still nominally unoccupied. This was in exchange for Polish news, of which some valuable items came via a Polish courier. It spurred her on to attempt another return to Poland to rescue some British aircrew, but although that mission was not successful, she returned to Hungary with her biggest coup, bringing back microfilm plans of new German U-boats and gases, as well as showing German troops massing on the Russian border, news which Stalin, then allied to Germany, ignored to his cost.

In January 1941, with Andrew Kennedy, her Polish lover and fellow plotter, she was arrested by the Hungarian Police, handed over to the Gestapo, and roughly interrogated. By a ruse she convinced them that she had tuberculosis and was released.

After this, the Minister in the British Legation felt it best to smuggle her out in the boot of an Embassy car into Yugoslavia. From Belgrade, with Kennedy, she continued on to Istanbul, Turkey, Syria and Palestine, sending back interesting reports to SOE. Everywhere she went she seemed to know many of the most important people and made useful friends. At last she reached Cairo in 1942, virtually penniless, where she remained. Then, to occupy her and alleviate her boredom, she was put onto a number of special SOE training courses until 1944, as she was suspected by most sides of being a spy for the others.

Eventually, after several cancelled missions, SOE sent her from Algiers (Massingham) to Southern France – she spoke fluent if rather breathy French – as Jacqueline Armand, a courier (codenamed Pauline) for Francis Cammaerts (codenamed Roger), the organiser of the JOCKEY network. She was to replace Cecily Lefort (codenamed Alice), captured by the Gestapo. Thus, on the night of 7 July 1944, she parachuted down near Vercors, her arrival as tempestuous as her life, when a high wind blew her off course. She landed badly, bruising her hip and shattering the butt of her revolver. Dressed as a peasant girl, she waited until discovered at daylight by a search party of Maquisards.

Unlike most SOE couriers, she had two main objectives. One was assisting Cammaerts and his Maquis, now mostly based on the Vercors plateau. The second was to subvert any Polish units fighting for the Germans. For Cammaerts she was a perfect assistant, needing little direction, full of initiative and becoming cooler the tighter the situation.

Shortly after her arrival, the Germans were furious at a daylight drop on 14 July of 200 containers of supplies for the Vercors Maquis, followed by the daylight bombing of the German aerodrome at Chabeuil. This caused the Germans to take revenge by razing some nearby towns to the ground, as well as delaying the retrieval by the Maquis of the supplies so painfully won. The Germans also started cutting off, on the Vercors, the many small villages, farms and forests there. In vain, Cammaerts begged SOE for heavy artillery, mortars, anti-aircraft guns and anti-tank weapons*, as he could see a German attack in the offing.

Finally, the Germans, faced with increased sabotage (some of which Christine organised), made an all-out attack on the plateau. From his house on the Vercors, Cammaerts sent Christine crossing and re-crossing the area around them, carrying warnings, advice and requests, but on 18 July, up to three divisions of 10,000 Germans with air support began their first full onslaught, occupying the northern part of the plateau. Then, on 21 July,

---

* At this time they were only supplied with light weapons, which were no real match against the German Army's heavy artillery.

they sent in gliders. Some crashed, but 250 crack SS troops survived to mow down the lightly armed Maquis, who fought with more bravery than arms, trying desperately to hold on. On 22 July, the French commander gave the Maquis orders to leave. There then followed terrible acts of German revenge and barbarity on the captured and wounded Maquis and unarmed civilians.

On the same day, Cammaerts, Christine and a leader of the FFI, with a few companions, escaped to continue resistance elsewhere. Having marched for close on 24 hours, they arrived 70 miles (112.6 km) away at their second base in Seynes-les-Alpes, to go back to subversion and making guerilla attacks on the enemy.

Since Italy had officially surrendered to the Allies in 1943, and was now practically occupied by the Germans, many Italian soldiers considered that they too had finished with the war. Some were forcibly kept in place by German troops, making only token resistance when attacked by the Allies, and many deserted to join the Italian partisans. This behaviour was most marked on the Italian border with France, and SOE was anxious to win them over. This was a task near to Christine's heart. Off she set with a light dancing step, despite long difficult journeys, into the hot, dangerous Italian Alps, travelling partly by motor bike and partly by foot, encountering many adventures on the way.

Once, when ordered by a German patrol to put up her hands, she did so, but with a live grenade in each. Her challengers fled! On another night, on her way to win over Russians and Poles in a much-feared Oriental German legion, and hidden under bushes from another German patrol, she was pounced on by one of their Alsatian dogs. It seemed the end. Instead, the animal lay down quietly beside her and, licking her face, immediately changed its loyalties, ignoring its handler's whistles and shouts. From then on it guarded her jealously until on quitting France she left it with a friend. Yet again, after a gruelling climb to a fort, chiefly manned by Poles, and perched high on a mountain peak, turning the loyalty of its garrison seemed easy in comparison with her ascent and descent of the mountain.

At last, on 15 August 1944, the landings by the American and French armies on the south of France took place. It was for this that Cammaerts and Christine had been preparing. However, two days beforehand Cammaerts and two companions were arrested outside Digne. Fortunately unrecognised, they were nevertheless condemned to be shot on 17 August. Christine, off to subvert more Poles serving with the Wehrmacht, rushed back, and by a trick, at great personal risk, after many hours of bargaining inside the prison, promised a bribe of 2 million francs and protection from the vengeful resistance and the rapidly advancing Allies. Though terrified of riding a bicycle, it was the only way to save time, and them, so Christine rode 24.8 miles (40 km) on difficult mountain roads to send a message, and then with the urgently dropped money in its rubber purse, cycled back in time for her to hand it over on 17 August. To her relief, the prisoners appeared at the gate unharmed. Soon after, Christine leaned from the front seat of the car and said 'It worked'. Some hours later they learned that Digne had been captured. She had only just been in time.

Now Cammaerts and Christine offered their help to the advancing Americans. Christine again worked her magic on turning the loyalties of captured Polish prisoners to join the Americans instead of being prisoners of war, and Cammaerts instructed the JOCKEY network to protect the Americans as they advanced. Eventually Christine reported to the Avignon regional headquarters and hitched a lift to London. Here she was officially commissioned into the WAAF and in November was sent to the Polish mission in Bari, Italy. There SOE's further plans were overtaken by events, and in Cairo, May 1945, she was demobilised.

41

IMPRISONMENT

The ways prisons and German camps were run during the war and the conditions affecting their prisoners' lives, have been touched on briefly in earlier chapters, but some of the details can be filled out a little more here. Fortunately, not all the forty mainly British SOE F-trained women encountered the system, but at least a half did – a few for only a short time. Here I am paying special attention only to the prisons and camps in which most of these special women were incarcerated.

Prisons

Avenue Foch

82–86 Avenue Foch was part of the SD (Gestapo) Headquarters in Paris. It was an impressive four-storey building, with attics used at one time as servants' quarters. Number 84 was where most of the activity concerning the SOE F service went on under Josef Kieffer, the subordinate to Boemelburg who controlled the Counter-Intelligence Branch of the Gestapo and worked mainly in Number 82. In 84, on the second floor, was the wireless section run by Dr Josef Goetz, a coding expert. Above him, on the third floor, agents were interrogated and tortured. The fourth floor included a gracious drawing-room, where, once, eight women agents were gathered before continuing by train to other prisons outside Paris, the Gestapo having learned all they could from them. The attics, containing many small rooms, had an office for the useful Ernest Vogt, a civilian who spoke English, German and French, and acted as interpreter for Dr Goetz. On this floor also were: a guardroom, washrooms and bedrooms that had been divided into seven small cells, lit by barred skylights, for prisoners being retained for further questioning and usually not sent to Frèsnes. No torture was applied on this floor and prisoners ate the same food that was served to the guards, which was quite good.

Frèsnes

This prison, only about 12 miles (19.3 km) away from Paris, was a special case.

Starting as a prison for men only, today it is a huge, dark five-storey building. In 1942 it opened a section for women. During the war its tiny cells intended for one person, usually held two and later more. Each contained an iron bed, a sheet and blanket, a chair and a toilet pan – the only source of water. At the top of the wall was a hard-to-reach, small, sealed window of frosted glass, and sometimes a skylight. Prisoners stood outside their cells to be checked every morning and there were limited exercise periods. The rest of the day was work, peeling potatoes, sewing and other tasks. Inmates were mainly civilians from the Paris area, or those who had been brought into Paris for special questioning by the Abwehr or Gestapo, who might need them again later, and for whom it was an outside holding prison.

There were also solitary confinement cells for punishment. They were underground, cold, damp and dark, their inmates subject to interrogation and torture, cut off from the rest of the prison and any privileges.

Food was poor and very frugal. It was brought on a trolley to ordinary and isolation cells – acorn coffee in the morning, later thin meat soup and a little bread, with a sausage and a few extras on a Sunday. It came in tins, pushed into each cell, but only passed into isolation cells through a type of letterbox in the door. In those the contents held even less food and were less frequent. In any case, the food in Frèsnes was considered near starvation point.

The discipline here was also harsher than in prisons elsewhere. The Abwehr was allowed to use a special interview room in the prison, while the Gestapo could remove prisoners, mainly to the Rue des Saussaies or to the Avenue Foch, for more specialised interrogation or torture.

Other Prisons

Most other prisons, whether in Germany or France, were run by and for civilians, such as in Karlsruhe. They all had similar rules and regulations, though the Gestapo could remove prisoners with the appropriate paperwork, or order harsher treatment for certain ones, as in the case of Noor Inayat Khan in Pforzheim, Germany.

In most prisons, cells for men and women were on separate floors; on the ground floor, cells were long and narrow, with a hatch for food and a spy hole in the door, and there were isolation cells for punishment. Most ordinary cells, meant to hold two inmates, usually held more. They had two iron beds, folded up against the wall, with straw mattresses, two blankets, a folding table, two chairs, a cupboard, a toilet pan and clothes hooks. Each cell had one high, small barred window.

Their daily routines were similar. At 6.30am, a waking bell to dress and clean their room, followed by a breakfast, pushed through their hatch, of coffee and bread. At 8.30am prisoners lined up in the corridor for inspection of themselves and their room. Afterwards, exercise was taken, which consisted of running in two circles in the prison yard for 30 minutes. Between 11.30am and 12 noon, a lunch of thin soup with occasionally a salad or vegetables followed by bread and black coffee was served. Morning and afternoon work was allocated – peeling potatoes, grinding coffee or sewing – broken by a 4pm coffee break, after which work continued until a 6pm supper of bread, thin soup, some margarine and occasionally cheese and coffee. Sunday brought stew with noodles and perhaps something special like sausage. This was followed by a relaxing break until 8pm and lights out. Every fourteen days prisoners had a shower. Talking to other prisoners and passing messages was forbidden, but prisoners managed to do so, nevertheless, by tapping walls or scratching food tins. Food quantities were sufficient, sometimes supplemented by food parcels, laundry and letters from outside.

It was often considered that prisoners were better treated and fed in smaller French prisons than in the larger ones. Eight of the captured SOE women who passed through the Avenue Foch and Frèsnes Prison were sent in May 1944 to the prison at Karlsruhe, where they were treated as civil prisoners. It was thought that this was the choice of Kieffer in Avenue Foch, for easy access should he wish to re-question them, but really it was only used as a pretext, so that he might visit his family who lived nearby. Eventually, drawn to their attention, the authorities in Berlin had other ideas and removed the women.

Transport

When SOE women were moved, if it were to a French concentration camp, as in the case of Natzweiler-Struthof in the Vosges mountains, where the distance was much less, they travelled in a closed truck by road, each in a small cell, walled and chained, within the vehicle. Otherwise, if taken to Germany to a civilian prison like Karlsruhe or concentration camps such as Dachau, Bergen-Belsen, Neue-Bremm Saarbrückenen or Ravensbrück, where distances were longer, transport was by train, though later in the war the journeys for even shorter distances took days, since railways were prime targets for sabotage or heavy RAF bombing raids. Then the authorities had to resort to cattle trucks, box cars or wagons, as lines or carriages in trains had been damaged or were insufficient.

There were also work camps, sub-camps to the main ones, such as Markleberg, Torgau and Königsberg, where the Gestapo farmed out groups to work in factories, farms or heavy labour gangs, where their treatment might be better or worse than in the main camp hiring them out. Naturally, the prisoners had no say in the matter and the Gestapo pocketed the profit.

Transit Camps

Drancy

A former sports ground, set up in a hurry by Marshal Henri Pétain's Prime Minister, Pierre Laval, as a small holding centre for French Jews – men, women and children – and minor resistants and 'unwantables'*. It was about 5½ miles (9 km) outside Paris, to the north west, and very convenient to the trains for Le Bourget, which left weekly, taking inmates to the extermination camps further away. It lasted from 1941 to August 1944, and was originally to hold around 4,500 but was then crammed full of those incarcerated, without shelter or warmth in winter and scorching hot in summer, and with no proper sanitation for large numbers. Food, too, was abysmal. The average stay was about three weeks.

Neue-Bremm Saarbrücken

This small concentration camp used by the Gestapo (not the SS) was, though not strictly a transit camp, sometimes employed as such. Its position was near the French border, just inside Germany. In the case of SOE captives it was convenient for the direct railway line from Paris and Frèsnes Prison to take them on their way to prisons like Karlsruhe, with lines to other camps of less savoury reputation, some now known as death or extermination camps.

Though there is some uncertainty, it could have opened in 1940, but was definitely operational in 1943 until late 1944, when its 'regular' inmates were eastern forced labour groups and political opponents to the Nazi regime. Through its gates, however, came and went Jews, members of the

---

* This might include resistants, those with mental problems or disabilities, who the Nazis considered as sub-human.

French and other resistance movements, and a few prisoners of war, who were only stopping on their way to other destinations.

Inmates were badly treated as a norm, many were chained hand and foot, and all half-starved.

Concentration Camps

Abandon hope all ye who enter here.

Dante, *The Inferno*

In General

These types of camps were quite separate from ordinary civil prisons and the western-European prisoner of war camps. They were meant to contain German criminals and political opponents. In 1933, Himmler, head of the SS under Hitler, created one of the earliest at Dachau, which became the prototype for others.

It was intended that internees pay for themselves and produce a profit, and were to be worked to death. Many were used for medical experiments, while the dead contributed hair, tattooed skin, gold teeth-fillings and personal belongings. Inmates were used as slave labour, often hired out to local farms, mines, gravel pits, roadworks, airfields and, as the war continued, increasingly to armament factories of one kind or another.

Special units of the SS, known as the Totenkopf (Death's Head Battalions, from the death's head badge on their caps), were in charge of these camps, equipped with metal-edged whips and pistols. Brutal lower ranks with rifles guarded the work parties and their discipline could kill an unfortunate. Ironically, discipline in the living blocks was usually kept by representatives of the prisoners themselves, who depended on their fear or favour. Most powerful among the prisoners were said to be the cooks.

The Nazi creed looked on all non-Aryans as sub-human vermin. These especially included Jews, and as the war went on, eastern Europeans, and eventually those of any conquered country. The British they hated but feared, constantly trying to humiliate them.

Prisoners were classified on arrival at the concentration camp. Those intended for 'special treatment' were, under the terms of the '*Nacht und Nebel Erlass*' (Night and Fog Decree), to disappear, and their names not listed on the camp records. The rest, in most cases, wore on their clothes a badge which often affected their treatment. Thus a yellow star showed a Jew, a pink triangle a homosexual, red was a 'political' prisoner, purple was a pacifist, green a criminal, black an anti-social, and so forth. Among 'politicals' were numbered Communists, Socialists and Trade Unionists, to which were added others like gypsies, Jehovah's Witnesses, conscientious objectors, and societies involving secrecy, such as Freemasons, some Catholic priests and members of the resistance.

Most concentration camps were surrounded by ditches, often filled with sharpened stakes. They had barbed wire electrified fences and high walls, topped with many guard towers, manned with searchlights and machine guns. The entrance gate was large and heavy, with its own guard building.

Inside, the camp was divided into two areas, one for the SS guards and administration, and the other for the prisoners. This prisoners' part included among other buildings, such as the kitchens, laundry, mortuary, infirmary, bakery, showers, offices and store rooms, as well as the blocks housing the prisoners. As the war continued, blocks housing 50-100 began to contain many hundreds, while larger blocks built to accommodate 500, when overcrowding grew worse, might house 2,000. Basic hygiene was poor as toilets became blocked, and bombing disrupted the water and electricity supply. Even before this, lice, fleas and vermin spread, with so many souls crushed together, bringing in their train typhus, dysentery, cholera and other diseases like tuberculosis and pneumonia, most caused by damp, malnutrition, brutal treatment and overwork.

Every camp contained a concrete 'Bunker' – a prison within a prison, where inmates for any offence, however minor, had a severe beating on the beating block, sometimes over seventy strokes, capable of killing many men. Then they were shackled in a bare, dank, dark underground solitary confinement cell on virtually one 'meal' in three days, given in a tin through a narrow slit in the door. Some cells could have their temperatures raised or lowered as part of the punishment, so that the prisoner should suffer even more. Sometimes, there were other isolation rooms at ground level for less heavy punishment.

In all camps there was a crematorium for the daily toll of death on camp, and in most camps towards the end of the war a gas chamber was installed for extermination. Other methods of extermination, included hanging, strangling with piano wire on meat hooks, or shooting (possibly the most merciful). All were carried out with Nazi efficiency.

Individual Concentration Camps

Natzweiler-Struthof

Based in Alsace, western France, it was the only extermination camp on French soil.

Built by its prisoners in late 1940, and intended for its prisoners to work in nearby quarries and underground munitions factories. It had over fifty sub-camps in its system. Prisoners wore striped uniforms.

It was a male-only camp, which was why the arrival of four women from Karlsruhe on 6 July 1944 created such an impression that one man, a talented artist with a phenomenal memory, in a work party repairing the path outside the camp, was able to draw, two years later, the faces and dress of each woman. This evidence was supported by two other prisoners who recognised two of the women and talked to them later through an open window. The unusual command to draw the blackouts in all huts earlier that evening was also bound to attract suspicion.

Dachau

Situated in Bavaria, 12 miles (19.3 km) north of Munich, it was built about 1933 to house about 2,500 Germans. In 1934, it threw open its doors to the European Press, claiming that it was to train offending Germans to become good citizens. *The Guardian* newspaper was not impressed.

During the war, prisoners came from about thirty other countries and overcrowding began and so did executions. Prisoners were now worked mercilessly to death, particularly on its many subsidiary outside camps making weapons, aircraft and rockets, which became more important as the war continued. If they did not die of exhaustion or disease, prisoners were hanged, shot or poisoned. Three more SOE women were sent there from Karlsruhe and one from Pforzheim to be roughed up overnight and shot next morning on 12 September 1944. It became a murder camp for the SS.

Bergen-Belsen

It was first used as a prisoner of war camp and for holding hostages, near an army training camp in west Germany. Not set up to be a concentration camp, it was not given that status until December 1944.

As the Allies pushed forward across Germany, prisoners of the camps ahead of them were also moved forward, many to Belsen, which became even more overcrowded. Diseases like dysentery and typhus spread among the starved and exhausted prisoners. In January 1945, a typhoid epidemic raged through the camp. The authorities were unable to deal with such a death rate or control it, having only one cremation oven. Conditions were also made worse by the interruption of camp electric, water, food supplies and medicine, from bombing. In April 1945, 10,000 bodies lay unburied by the time the camp was handed over to the British. Yvonne Rudellat from Ravensbrück survived until just over a week afterwards, and was buried unrecognised in one of the mass grave pits on 23 or 24 April 1945.

Ravensbrück

This concentration camp was intended for women. It was in east Germany, about 50 miles (80 km) north of Berlin, and established late in 1938 in a beautiful lakeside area, dotted with holiday villas, but on marshy ground, a breeding place for mosquitoes. Behind it were pine-covered hills, which overlooked the camp. In 1944, the weather varied. In May, the temperature was very hot, dropping to quite cold at night, with a bitterly cold snowy winter, when temperatures could plunge to 20-25 degrees below zero, or lower.

It was here that eight captive SOE F women spent the later part of their imprisonment. They had been sent at different times during 1944, except for Cecily Lefort, who probably arrived at the end of 1943.

After a very long uncomfortable journey with many other women, they reached the railway station of Furstenburg, the nearest station to Ravensbrück. Carrying their cases and bags, the women had a 6-mile (10 km) walk to the camp, which had become known among the French as '*L'Enfer des Femmes*' (Women's Hell). Escorted by female guards, who had taken over at the railway station, they all passed into the camp.

At first light the camp inside looked quite attractive, its wooden huts lined up in rows, with flower beds and patches of grass along well maintained cinder paths and roadways. Only later what was really within become apparent.

In late 1944, when camps were too full they could not always follow strict protocols, but usually part of the admission procedure required stripping and showering. Then the women stood naked awaiting the first of many cursory examinations on different days by a doctor and a dentist. One pointed cheerfully at the tall black chimney belching smoke, seen through the window, and told them that the crematorium was the only way out of the camp. Finally, after delousing, and a painful cutting of all hair close to the skin – head and body – they dressed in different clothes, left behind by those who died before them, and wore the badges advertising their 'crimes'. They were now ready to be despatched to the quarantine hut, for a period of forty days, to ensure that none brought any new diseases into the camp (where many women died every day).

Afterwards, they were released into their proper huts, sometimes billeted by nationality, since prisoners had come from many countries east and west. Among them were young and old, pregnant women and even little children and babies.

In the old camp the huts were smaller than those in the new part, the latter having only recently finished being built by the prisoners, where the huts were at least twice the size of the old. Every hut was called a block and numbered. It was divided notionally down the middle into two parts, either side being the mirror image of the other. The long central room, the dormitory, was lined with three-tier beds in two rows facing each other, with a straw mattress, foul smelling and full of vermin, and, if lucky, a blanket. There was no heating. Pity the lower tiers, when the upper ones dripped all sorts of filth on their heads. At the side of the dormitory was a common room containing tables, stools and cupboards. Beside this room was the washroom with showers and toilets. Washing daily and keeping clean was the only way to avoid diseases. A Stupova (Supervisor), one for each side, managed each half of the block, and in each block the two Stupovas were answerable to the one in overall charge, the Blockova, recognised by a black armband with her hut number embroidered on it, while the Stupovas' armbands were green. Their standards varied greatly, a few good, but most mediocre or even bad.

Many Blockovas and Stupovas showed favouritism and others were bribable, though all were themselves prisoners. As overcrowding grew worse, each bed usually had three occupants, which in winter, with no heat, did actually offer some warmth. The weakest, without a bed, unless someone took care of them, slept on the bare concrete floor, later scrubbed when cupboards and beds were supposedly cleaned.

Sirens ruled the inmates' days. A siren at 3am woke everyone for dressing and toilet, and the five unlucky prisoners on the rota for that day staggered in with the $5\frac{1}{2}$ or 11 gallon (25 or 50 litre) pails of hot acorn coffee and fresh bread. A siren at around 3.45am signalled Appells (roll-call). Then, whatever the weather, freezing or baking, in rain, snow, wind or ice, everyone went outside their block to stand absolutely still and silent in lines of ten and rows of five, hands on the shoulders of the woman in the line in front of them. No-one was excused, the fit with the sick or dying (and some froze or died where they stood). The Blockova checked them and then came a long wait while the officer in charge of all the blocks moved from hut to hut until all were accounted for, a process sometimes taking over two or more hours. One reason was that prisoners were often moved from hut to hut at short notice, or taken away on transports, or added. A siren signalled the end of Appells and the shivering inmates returned to the shelter of the block and further hut duties – toilets to be cleaned etc.

Soon came another siren for labour roll call, lining up in the central camp road, in block order, and collecting equipment to march off to their assigned duties outside. At a variable time between 8am–12 noon, the soup pail and bread was brought, with 30 minutes for consumption. Some prisoners worked inside the camp at such places as the laundry, the bakery, the decorators, the gardens, the kitchens, the much-prized work in the hospital (Rever) and the knitting hut (usually used for the elderly or disabled, if not weeded out to other camps). Others in groups pulled or pushed the handcarts carrying food, coal and collecting dead bodies for the crematorium.

The sturdier were employed on all kinds of work outside the walls, watched mainly by male guards, armed with guns and whips (plentifully wielded) and guard dogs wearing black coats with embroidered swastikas. On occasion they might attack a prisoner unprovoked. Work times there were controlled by whistles.

On camp, a siren at 12 noon signalled work to cease, and often the soup had by then caught up with them, until a 12.30pm siren followed by the usual labour roll call, marched them back to the place of work – not needed for those outside.

In mid-afternoon came a second serving of soup and bread, until the 6pm cease-work siren, which on camp brought another roll call and march back to the blocks, followed by leisure time, ending with a 7.30pm siren signalling lights off and bed. Such was the monotonous and cruelly hard day they endured. The only way to know if it was Sunday was that the afternoon meal sometimes had a few extras.

Up to this point, if what you have just read gives a somewhat sanitised and orderly impression of the concentration camp, you are mistaken. It does not bring out the degradation of the human beings in the system, both prisoners and guards, nor does it display to the full the utter callousness and cruelty with which it was imposed.

Most concentration camps had two main aims. One was to work its prisoners to death. The other was to extract as much profit as possible from their labour. It was part of the system to de-personalise and humiliate the prisoners, to prove that they were worthless and vile, lower than the vermin that infested the camps. Accordingly, they were treated with mindless brutality and violence, sometimes even sadism. What the guards hated most of all was defiance, and they could strike a victim dead for a single look.

Transports were frequently in evidence, bringing more prisoners to Ravensbrück, or taking work parties from it to various sub-camps like Torgau or Markleberg.

There, prisoners were sub-contracted out to local employers for work in factories, farms, road building or airfield construction, where they were fed and hutted on site and often kept for weeks or months.

Inevitably, there was much favouritism and corruption on camp, and those prisoners who lasted longest had learned to play the system to survive. But, regardless, over all inmates, was the fear of punishment – whipping and imprisonment in the Bunker – or death. Executions were usually at dawn, followed by the dark smoke of the crematorium chimney and the smell of burning flesh, which often floated over the camp. However, most women, if sent to places like the Jugendlager (a late appearance for holders of pink cards), believed it to be a place where they could recuperate. In reality it turned out to be a death sentence, since soon afterwards they were either poisoned or gassed, which is what happened to Cecily Lefort in about February 1945. On other camps for the weak or unwanted, such as Bergen-Belsen, prisoners sent there, died of disease, starvation, brutal treatment, wounds, experiments, sheer fatigue or loss of will to live, though towards the end this was happening at Ravensbrück too, as well as shooting and hanging.

Different authorities vary wildly on the size of the population of Ravensbrück at different times, so that figures given here, drawn from various sources, are only a rough guide. When it was set up it was meant to hold perhaps 1,000 to 1,300 women at around 60–100 per block, but already at the beginning of 1940 it contained about 2,300. By 1943, this figure had shot up by probably 300 or so per block, with possibly 15,000–30,000 on camp. The year 1944 was the time of its greatest expansion, especially towards the end of the year, when, with the Allied advance, prisoners from elsewhere were being moved deeper into Germany to camps like this, but at the same time, new larger blocks for possibly 500 inmates were available. Thus, in early 1944, numbers had stabilised, only to rise sharply to 70,000–80,000 late in 1944, in any case too large for its size. By this time the gas chamber was built and in use, to which the over-fifties, the children and the weak or sick were consigned.

The three SOE girls who were shot there on or about 27 January 1945 could well have been hanged, as by 1945 the camp had a gallows. It was believed, as with other wireless operators and couriers who were put to death, that this was to hide the extent of the German infiltration into SOE networks – though by then there was little point in it. It could, instead, have been to hide German treatment of agents.

By 1945, facilities and supplies were short or cut off. Women were reported to be fighting over a crust of bread, and no more prisoners were to be sent to the camp after January 1945. It has been calculated that in total over the years 123,000–133,000 women were sent there and perhaps 50,000–92,000 died there. However, the great difficulty with all the figures, is that there are so many misleading factors, such as the constant coming and going of prisoners to and from the camp through the continuous movement of the transports, and the appearance and disappearance of individual prisoners (some of the reasons for the long Appells), apart from the heavy attrition on the camp itself.

The lucky ones, and there were a surprising number, survived to be liberated by the Russian Army at the end of April 1945.

Most German concentration camps, numbering it was thought to be over 300, some large and some small, were afterwards destroyed, but a few are today turned into memorial sites as a warning of the inhumanity of man to man.

EPILOGUE

Britain's SOE F service laboured under many disadvantages. It was short-lived, amateur, its agents hurriedly trained and insufficiently briefed – not its fault, but it came into existence lacking much useful background information, in the chaos of the Second World War.

Air Chief Marshal Portal disapproved of its type of work and 'Bomber' Harris begrudged the aircraft and highly skilled pilots of the tiny Special Duties Squadrons, which were diverted from his heavy bombing raids to drop agents behind enemy lines. As SOE's work was sabotage, the squadrons had two tasks: to drop to the resistance arms and materials for industrial sabotage; and to land British-trained agents, who were to organise the resistants, so that they could assist the liberation forces when they landed in the north or south of France.

SOE was not the same as the Secret Intelligence Service (SIS) – the spies. The SIS was a long established organisation, also working in France, which demanded and received, until late in the war, the lion's share of radio transceivers and supplies from the few flights. It regarded the F service as an unnecessary nuisance and often a danger to itself, despite their aims being so similar.

Then there were split loyalties among the French. Did they favour Vichy, Giraud, de Gaulle, other politicians, the Communists or just a quiet life – though most would agree that they wanted the Germans out as soon as possible. But how was this to be brought about? Early members of the French resistance may not have realised how difficult it was for them to be given such supplies as they needed – armaments or light weapons, when Britain was fighting in Africa and Asia, as well as protecting her own homeland.

Moreover, there were two overriding considerations – which still apply. Should the planning and deployment of major resources be short or long term? Supposing everything were to be used short term, now, when it seemed to be urgently needed, then this might mean that there would be virtually nothing left for when the long-term objective finally arrived and required maximum effort. It would require balancing the selfish present against a gain in the unpredictable future. This dilemma faces countries, economies, organisations and even charities to this day. And if it is a problem now, how much more was it in the early days of 1940.

The existence of SOE did bring benefits to the French. Its DF section organised escape routes and its F section gave the French a way of venting their anger and damaging the Germans by sabotage. If cleverly done, it would cause no reprisals, and if successful would save the area from further RAF bombing. It also, by sending in agents to help resistance, gave encouragement to a conquered people, that they were not forgotten or deserted by their ally Britain. It helped the morale of a proud people and held out the hope that one day in the future France would be free.

It was this intangible quality added to patriotism, that enabled Guy Moquet (a French Communist militant) to write in the short scribbled note to his mother, just before he was shot as a hostage at Châteaubriant in 1942, 'Of course I would have liked to have lived, but what I want most of all is that my death shall be of some use... At 17½ my life has been so short, but I have no regrets.'

Little of SOE's work would have been possible without the co-operation and sacrifice of the brave people who helped and sheltered them. For every agent in France there were dozens of anonymous civilians who supported them, despite the risks. These could be a period in a French prison, a concentration camp or being shot. Nor did it end there. It might go so far as implicating the family or innocent relatives who might also be punished – the authorities were merciless and often indiscriminate, meting out the same treatment to young or old.

Figures for the losses among French civilians are so large that accuracy is virtually impossible. For the Maquis and those who fought with them, dying in action in assisting the liberation armies, the figures are probably a gross underestimation, but authorities hesitantly guess at 30,000. In France itself, about 24,000 men and women were executed by the Germans, but a far greater number, over 200,000 by some counts, were sent to work and die in concentration camps, from which only about 40,000 eventually returned alive. These poor souls, sick and weak, often with no family or job to return to, were sometimes shockingly neglected by the state if they lacked evidence of membership of a Maquis, a state army or a recognised resistance group, but *not* a British network. Unfeelingly, some sad heroic remnants, usually women, were told, 'What! You've just had two years free bed and board. How can you claim even a tiny state pension for your long vacation?' Even after the war, France still preserved a male military attitude discounting any contribution by its women. In the same way it resembled the reaction of a triumphant de Gaulle to the surviving SOE agents: 'Go Home! Your place is not here!' Much later his attitude mellowed – too late for many.

Most early resistance networks of F section did not last long, but as the survivors became more experienced, their numbers grew, and after the D-Day landings, led by careful and skilful organisers, the French resistants, as intended, helped in the slow advance of the Allies during the tough fighting across France. Their glory came in the south, where they rapidly cleared the way ahead of the French and American Allied invasion forces of Operation Dragoon, and some days later the French reasserted their pride in the liberation of Paris. By September 1944, nearly all of France had been freed.

And to prove they had no intention to take over the country, as the Germans had, the liberating armies of the Allies swept out of France, freeing other captive countries on their way towards the Rhine and the German heartlands.

And what of the cost to the agents who had been behind the French resistance? Compared with the enormous French figures, the losses among SOE F agents seem minuscule, though, again, figures are variable. It seems that over 400–500 men and women were sent to France, of whom around 119 men were caught with seventeen surviving. But, of course, taking just the forty women, their number was small to begin with, and therefore the number to survive would naturally be small. However, from that number in their case, we do know the exact losses. Before the women first entered SOE, they were told that their chances of survival were about 50 per cent (perhaps less if they were wireless operators). In total it turned out that of the forty sent they lost fourteen, not the expected twenty. One of them would have died whether in France or Britain, and one of them died unrecognised a day or so *after* being freed, bringing the true number down to twelve; eight and maybe more may have died or been imprisoned, due to being tangled in the PHYSICIAN web, which spread its fatal tentacles far and wide. And some might have died partly owing to the double agent Henri Déricourt.

Taking the thirteen female operators of the wireless transceivers (the earliest of whom was Noor Inayat Khan) one would have expected that their losses as a group would have been higher, certainly near the 50 per cent mark. However, it is a pleasant surprise to find that only four died in the prison camps. Their losses in this group would therefore be 32 per cent. Could this have been because they were working in a safer part of the country, or were better protected, or that they were themselves more careful of their security?

Most of the forty at some time or other were arrested and questioned, even if they finally walked free, but of the others captured only luck saved them from joining the fatal fourteen. Certainly, the four in French prison cells fared better than those in the German concentration camps.

On 12/13 May 1944, eight women met at the Avenue Foch before being taken to the station, en route for Karlsruhe prison. They should have been joined by Noor Inayat Khan, but she was diverted to Pforzheim. On 6 July, four of them were taken to the men's concentration camp of Natzweiler where they died of a phenol injection. They were Andrée Borrel, Vera Leigh, Diana Rowden and Sonia Olschanezky.

Then, on 18 July, Odette Sansom was sent from Karlsruhe to Ravensbrück Women's Concentration Camp.

Finally, on 12 September, the last three of the group, to whom was added Noor Inayat Khan from Pforzheim, left Karlsruhe to be shot at the concentration camp of Dachau. These three were, Yolande Beekman, Madeleine Damerment and Elaine Plewman.

On 8 August 1944, three women were sent direct from Frèsnes Prison, Paris, to Ravensbrück. There, on or about 27 February 1945, were shot Denise Bloch, Lilian Rolfe and Violette Szabo.

Five other women at different times were sent to Ravensbrück, with different outcomes. Yvonne Rudellat, still suffering from a bullet in her head, was taken there and then transferred later to Belsen, where she died and was buried unrecognised on or about 23/24 April 1945, shortly after the camp was taken by the British Army. Cecily Lefort grew so weak at Ravensbrück that she was sent to the Jugendlager, and either poisoned or gassed there, about February 1945.

Then there were the lucky ones. Yvonne Baseden was released by the intervention of the Swedish Red Cross on 28 April 1945. Eileen Nearne on a work camp made her escape when on a night march to another camp. She finally reached freedom in April 1945. Odette Sansom had the strangest release, when the Ravensbrück Commandant, still believing her to be related by marriage to Winston Churchill, handed her over to the Americans as a hostage for his life, in April 1945.

Four other women held in French prisons won their freedom in different ways. Mary Herbert, mistaken for Lise de Baissac, managed to persuade her interrogators that she was a Frenchwoman from Egypt and was released in Easter 1944. Blanche Charlet escaped with others from Castres prison on 16 September 1943, eventually arriving in Britain after an exciting boat chase on 20 April 1944. Julienne Aisner, soon to become an agent, landed herself in the Paris Cherche-Midi prison for slapping a German's face, and walked free in June 1941. Elizabeth Reynolds was arrested by the Milice in Paris, and explained truthfully that as an American she was trying to escape internment in Vittel, but was sent there nevertheless until released in August 1944.

But there are two sad stories. Muriel Byck, died suddenly of meningitis, in the arms of her organiser at Romorantin on 23 May 1944. Madeleine Lavigne saw victory in her work as a courier, but died suddenly of an embolism in a newly freed Paris on 24 February 1945.

Some, of course, with great care, good judgement and luck came through unsuspected and unscathed to the end of the war in France. They all knew the risks they ran and were prepared to face them whatever the results. Now they were able to see that the strain, the planning and the effort had been worthwhile. At last, what they had come to do was achieved. Their great friend and ally, France, was free again, and they had made their contribution. They could be justly proud of what they had done. Nor would they ever forget the good friends they had lost on the way.

But there were mistakes – terrible mistakes – made by London and by agents, most on security. Wireless operators were trained to have certain security double checks included in their messages – a bluff check and a true check. Nevertheless, in the rush of sending an urgent message, and thus often under pressure, one or the other might be omitted by accident, or indeed with a German sitting at their shoulder, they might be deliberately left out to show London what had happened – only to have London in response scolding them for forgetting to include their security checks, blowing their needed security sky high. So the German radio technician would be aware of the security checks, and would remember to watch for them or include them when trying to copy another agent's message. Added to all this, of course, for the agent, was the difficulty of using a code, so painfully learned in training, and often getting it garbled in transmission.

In addition to the messages, all agents were advised to keep themselves independent, and not to have any contacts with agents in any other networks. This rule was frequently broken by wireless operators, who often, in the early days when operators were few, carried the messages for a number of other networks. Jack Agazarian was said to be doing this for twenty-four networks, at times. This independence was difficult for men and women, as both tended to crave human contact and preferably that of other agents, who best understood the difficulties of their situations. If, like Lise de Baissac, they stayed apart, they often found the isolation difficult to bear. On the other hand, Francis Suttill (Prosper) and his PHYSICIAN group flagrantly ignored this rule, even to the extent of conversing in English sometimes when they met in a café. Flouting such commonsense advice was bound to have consequences. They might get away with it once, or by luck, twice, but not much more, considering that they were in Paris – a city that was a hot-bed of counter-intelligence organisations and their employees. Suttill's loose tongue and those with him, brought down not only his network, but a whole cascade of other networks around him, with far-reaching implications. However, it was to happen to networks further south, who forgot the rules, though not with such disastrous consequences. Seemingly, many women were better as loners, and it paid off.

One of the many good features that appear commoner among the women than the men was what might be called 'careful housekeeping'. Accounts were sometimes kept of the money with which agents were entrusted, both when they first arrived and later on when it was being spent. It was also noted that a few agents never asked for more supplies of arms or explosives than they needed, in case they were used unwisely. Generally this sometimes shows up among women organisers, who had some say in the management of money, but many women couriers later helped their organiser locate stores they had built up from drops and now wanted to hand over to the Allied troops – a far-sighted move to prevent them falling into the hands of the political feuding parties. Pearl Witherington notes that she made a full accounting of all the money she received and paid out, returning the remainder when she came back to London – seemingly surprising the authorities!

But the last and perhaps crowning loss was not that of SOE but of Britain, which did not build on the store of incredible goodwill, still surviving in places and gathered by the SOE networks throughout France, at the end of the war. It was intangible but important.

Afterwards, when the heat of battle had died down, calm heads calculated the losses and gains. They had learned that even a small underestimated body, like the members of SOE, had a much greater impact through the French resistance than could ever have been calculated.

Against the odds, the French resisters working with the networks were estimated to have been worth perhaps ten to fifteen extra divisions of regular troops. General Eisenhower, impressed by the support of the resistance in France, considered that their efforts had shortened the war in Europe by nine months. A later assessment to the combined chiefs of staff on 18 July 1945 concluded that, 'a substantial contribution had been made to the AEF's victory by the resistance, that had in many cases been guided and supported by SOE.'

So it was officially acknowledged that their work had counted, and all those who had died, had not died in vain.

Glossary

Abwehr	German military intelligence service under Canaris.
AEF	Allied Expeditionary Forces.
ATS	Auxiliary Territorial Service.
BCRA	Bureau Central de Renseignements et d'Action – de Gaulle's Secret Service.
DF	SOE escape organisation. Also Radio Detection Finding Service.
EMFFI	de Gaulle's French Forces of Resistance and RF, SOE, SIS, (but not FTP) combined and put under General Koenig in March 1944.
FANY	First Aid Nursing Yeomanry – A civilian, all female, uniformed organisation, (no longer nursing). Some acted as cover for SOE and Special Forces Training and Care etc.
FFI	Free French Forces in France.
FTP	*Francs-tireurs et Partisans* (Military communists).
Jedburghs	Late 1944, groups usually of 1 British, 1 American and 1 French, (2 officers and 1 NCO), sent to organise and arm resistants.
Judex	Buckmaster and British SOE representatives, toured some F networks to thank its members, in November 1944.
Maquis	French guerillas – men of the brush and forests.
OSS	American secret service.
Rafles	Young French civilians, snatched from the street, to be sent to work in Germany.
RF	SOE-trained French agents, answerable to de Gaulle.
S. Phone	Enabled the pilot flying the plane to speak directly to the agent on the ground, before landing.
SAS	Special Air Service Commandos
SD (SS)	*Sicherheitsdienst.* German political security and intelligence service. Under Himmler.
SHAEF	Supreme Headquarters of all Allied Forces in the war against the Axis powers.
SIS	British secret intelligence service, (from MI6).
Special Duties Squadrons	RAF. Used to transport agents and supplies.
SOE	Special Operations Executive. Its agents worked in many parts of the world, starting in F for France.
STO	French forced labour groups sent to work in Germany.
USAAF	The American Army Air Force.
WAAF	Women's Auxiliary Air Force – contributed 15 volunteers to work as agents in SOE F service.
W/op (r/t op)	Wireless/Radio transceiver operators. The most dangerous work for an agent.

Bibliography

Basu, S., *Spy Princess*, Sutton, 2006
Binney, M., *The Women who lived for danger*, Hodder & Stoughton, 2002
Bleicher, H., *Colonel Henri's Story*, Kimber, 1954
Braddon, R., *Nancy Wake*, Cassell & Co., 1956
Buckmaster, M., *They Fought Alone*, Odhams Press, 1958
Cookridge, E.H., *They Came from the Sky*, Heinemann, 1965
Cornioley, P., *Pauline, Vie D'un Agent SOE*, Par Example, 1996
Cowburn, B., *No Cloak, No Dagger*, Jarrolds 1960
Devereux-Rochester, E., *Full Moon to France*, R. Hale, 1978
Dufurnier, D., *Ravensbruck*, G. Allen & Unwin, 1948
Escott, B., *Mission Improbable*, P. Stephens, 1991
Fitzsimons, P., *Nancy Wake*, Harper Collins, 2002
Foot, M.R.D., *SOE in France*, HMSO, 1966
Forward, N., *The White Mouse*, Melbourne (Australia), 1987
Gleeson, J., *They Feared No Evil*, Hale, 1976
Hastings, M., *Das Reich*, Michael Joseph, 1981
Helm, S., *A Life in Secrets*, Little Brown, 2005
Henderson, D.V., *Fashioned into a Bow*, (ch.6), Pentland Press, 1995
Heslop, R., *Xavier*, R. Hart-Davies, 1970
Jenkins, R., *A Pacifist at War*, Hutchinson, 2009
Jones, L., *A Quiet Courage*, Bantam Press, 1990
King, S., *Jacqueline*, Arms & Armour, 1989
Kramer, R., *Flames in the Field*, Michael Joseph, 1995
Legrand, J.M., *Lysander*, Editions Vario, 2000
Lorain, P., *Clandestine Operations*, Macmillan, 1983
Marks, L., *Between Silk and Cyanide*, Touchstone (NY), 2000
Mason, T.J., *Violette Szabo GC*, T.J. Mason, 1995
Masson, M., *Christine*, Hamish Hamilton, 1975
Mccue, P., *Behind Enemy Lines*, Pen & Sword, 2007
McIntosh, E.P., *Sisterhood of Spies (OSS)*, Naval Inst Press, 1998
Millar, G., *Maquis*, Heinemann, 1945
Miller, R., *Behind the Lines*, Seeker & Warburg, 2002
Minney, R.J., *Carve Her Name with Pride*, Newnes, 1956
Nicholas, E., *Death Be Not Proud*, Cresset Press, 1958
Nicholson, D., *Aristide*, Leo Cooper, 1994
Ottaway, S., *Violette Szabo*, Leo Cooper, 2002
Overton-Fuller, J., *Madeleine*, Gollancz, 1952
Popham, H., *FANY 1907–84*, Secker & Warburg, 1984
Rossiter, M., *Women in the Resistance*, Praeger (USA), 1986
Ruby, M., *F Section SOE*, Leo Cooper, 1985
Smith, M., *Station X*, Channel 4 Books, 1998
Starns, P., Odette, *World War II's Darling Spy*, The History Press, 2010
Szabo, T., *Young, Brave and Beautiful,* Channel Islands Pub., 2007
Tickell, J., *Odette*, Chapman Hall, 1949
Tickell, J., *Moon Squadron*, A. Wingate, 1956
Tillion, G., *Ravensbruck*, Anchor Books, 1975

Tomlinson, T., *Violette Szabo*, Violette Museum, 2001
Verity, H., *We Landed by Moonlight*, Air Data Pub., 1995
Vickers, P., *Das Reich*, Leo Cooper, 2000
Vomécourt de, P., *Who Lived to See the Day*, Hutchinson, 1961
Wake, N., *The White Mouse,* Macmillan, 1985
Walters, A.M., *Moondrop to Gascony*, Macmillan, 1946
Ward, I., *FANY Invicta*, Hutchinson, 1955
Webb, A.M. (ed.), *The Natzweiler Trial*, Vol. 5, William Hodge, 1949
Weitz, M., *Sisters in the Resistance*, J. Wiley & Son, 1995
West, N., *The Secret War*, Hodder & Stoughton, 1992
Wynne, B., *No Drums... No Trumpets*, A. Barker Ltd, 1961

Index